KU-050-427

# DORA

# DORA

## Jean Michel

Written in association with
### LOUIS NUCERA

Translated by Jennifer Kidd

Weidenfeld and Nicolson
London

HERTFORDSHIRE
COUNTY LIBRARY

940.547

9034208

/ AUG 1980

The illustrations were taken from the following books:

*Arsenal Grobow* by Adam Cabala, Krakow 1968; pictures 3, 4, 5, 6, 7

*Deportation* published by La Fédération nationale des Deportés et Internes Resistants et Patriotes, Paris 1967; pictures 1, 10, 11, 12, 13, 15

*Geheimprojekt Mittlebau, Die Geschichte der deutschen V-Waffen-Werke*, Munich 1971; pictures 2, 8, 9, 14

Originally published in France under the title *Dora* copyright © 1975, Editions J.-C. Lattès, Paris.

English translation © 1979 George Weidenfeld and Nicolson Ltd.

First published in Great Britain by George Weidenfeld and Nicolson Ltd. 91 Clapham High Street, London SW4 7TA

All rights reserved. No part of this publication may be reproduced, stored in a retrieval system, or transmitted, in any form or by any means, electronic, mechanical, photocopying, recording or otherwise, without the prior permission of the copyright owner.

ISBN 0 297 77651 7

Printed in Great Britain by Butler & Tanner Ltd Frome and London

To Suzanne, my wife.
To Monique, my daughter.
To my grandchildren.
To my comrades
    dead and alive
    who were at Dora.

# CONTENTS

# INTRODUCTION

On 17 August 1943, the Gestapo took me to a place where, if the world has any meaning, that meaning totally escaped me. I stood 5 ft 10 ins high, weighed 11½ stone; my pulse must have been normal. On 15 April 1945, the British Second Army liberated wraiths who had been living beyond the bounds of reason, legions of martyrs who had been ruled by the lackeys of a régime of violence, agony and death. I weighed just over 6 stone, my pulse was 16, my temperature 102 °F. I was in a coma for forty-eight hours.

When, for the first time in so long, I took a bath at home, my wife, seeing the pitiful state of my naked body, rushed out of the room. She hid so that I would not see her tears nor hear her sobbing. Later she confessed: 'For three months you smelt of death.'

Despite all precautions, the transition from near-starvation to a fairly normal diet gave me jaundice. I asked for a mirror. My face was more green than yellow. Lying there exhausted and nauseous, I heard the doctor in the corridor saying to my wife: 'I don't think I can save him.' I sat up and shouted. They ran to my bedside. With all the vehemence I could muster I said: 'I don't want a doctor who has no faith. I want one who has; who'll try everything and then tell me how I'll get better. An optimistic doctor.' Such a doctor was found.

I know all the eternal arguments between optimist and pessimist. They are abstract. They are the stuff of comfortable conversations. I am an optimist and it gives me no pleasure to say that surrounded by privations, baseness, horror and death, the pessimist is disarmed when he comes up against his opposite. At the darkest hour the will to live eludes definition. Have the sceptics or the alarmists ever managed to survive hell? Doubtless they have, but each to his own motivation, and mine is hope. I say to myself 'I will find a way out of this!' That is what I wanted the doctor to say: he should have agreed with what I felt so strongly. 'I will find a way out of this!' I repeated this to myself every time I came close to damnation: at the wall where I was going to be shot; in the death wagon taking us to Buchenwald; in the dark tunnel at Dora; when we discovered that Himmler was going to have the deportees killed in order to destroy all proof of his abominable crimes; during interrogation when any heroism was crushed, and when the torturer producing more and more new weapons knew that the victim had lost all his defences in the first round. He who fails to recognize the irrational in Man will never know the extent of his capacity for evil, nor his capacity for courage.

Today I am over seventy. I have been silent for a long time. Now, suddenly, as if I wanted the past to speak to the future, I feel the need to tell my story (and that of certain others) when horror was a way of life. I want to write about the mysterious way hope challenges the impossible. I want to say that the will to resist begets the will to conquer. For many, many months I felt as if I knew what was to become of us in the kingdom of death; it was as if I were *living* death and its terrors. And yet I never gave up hope. My guiding star still shone through the gloom.

The belief in common decency, which depends on self-respect, is only a fair-weather conviction. It sets its face against tyrannies wherever they emerge, for, in his duplicity or his blindness, the individual sometimes takes part in justifying evil.

Faith in life, faith in mankind because when most oppressed he shows most nobility, and my catchphrase 'I will find a way out of this': these three things were what helped me to survive one of the most violent outbreaks of insanity in history. This is the story of that hope in adversity, a message in a bottle cast into the sea.

My book is not only about deportation. Dora, with its romantic, feminine name, was never a camp like the others. A Nazi war criminal was to call it 'the Hell of all the concentration camps'. That is not the whole story. Auschwitz, Treblinka, Buchenwald, Dachau: any of the men responsible for these infernos who escaped punishment will be damned for eternity. Dora is different.

Men who were intimately involved with the creation and operation of the camp are today respected, venerated and admired. There has been a huge conspiracy to ensure that those two shameful syllables do not stain the cult of these new idols of modern times. They executed the monsters who, whip in hand, made us toil night and day. They hung the Nazi leaders who dared, in the middle of the twentieth century, to turn men into slaves and re-establish hell on earth. But they have drawn a veil over the indisputable and atrocious fact that this slavery, this unspeakable sum of suffering, misery and death, was put, at Dora, to the service of the manufacture of missiles which may not have enabled Hitler to win the war, but which later – after the Russians and the Americans had shamelessly scooped up the scientists of the Reich, a Reich promised for a thousand years – made possible the conquest of space.

The missiles were the pyramids of Hitler's Germany. Just as the tourist in his espadrilles and gaily-coloured shirt gazes in wonder at the Sphinx, so the visitor to NASA (National Aeronautics and Space Administration) can today admire 'set up in a row before the Space Museum like fantastic arrows pointed at the stars a display of 'hardware' developed by von Braun and his team. At the beginning of one row, resurrected out of a junkyard, stands the grandfather of all the big rockets used today, both in the United States and the Soviet Union. It is a V2.'*

---

* James McGovern: *Crossbow and Overcast* (Hutchinson), p. 238.

# Chapter One

# ARREST

‘Dora, the Hell of all the concentration camps’

*From the interrogation of Doctor Edwin Katzenellenbogen, condemned to life imprisonment at the Buchenwald trial*

The door slams shut behind me. The light goes out. The guards leave, taking my comrades with them. I hear cell doors open and slam shut. I hear the shooting of bolts and the heavy clanking of keys. I am in total darkness. I have had to leave my shoes, tie and belt outside. Funny sort of a hotel....

Feeling my way, I lie down on the bunk. My eyes gradually begin to get used to the dark. The cell is very high. Way above me gleams a little light from the skylight. This light from outside renews my link with freedom, and lifts my spirits despite the locked doors and the bars.

I know I am free; I will be free again soon. The confidence I have always had comes back to me. I know that those who give up hope never return. It is in adversity that hope sharpens its edge. The fortunate have no need of it.

The silence is broken only by the footsteps of the sentry patrolling the corridor. There is something mechanical about his toing and froing; a robot adjustable for any terrain.

I sit thinking about the interrogation I have just been put through, trying to work out a plan of defence. The replies I made were more rehearsed than spontaneous. Nothing that could harm me or anyone else. Have the Gestapo known about us longer than we thought?

I long to talk to the others. As soon as the sentry's footsteps move away, I tap on the thick walls. I tap out a message in morse, first gently, then louder. No reply. I call out 'Pierre' in a low voice. Silence. Once, twice, ten times I try with no result.

I can now make out every nook and cranny of the cell. Human powers of adaptation are truly remarkable. I look up again to the skylight which lets in a little light from the night sky. I lie down.

I wonder if my wife, Suzanne, has been spared. I toss and turn. Something runs over my skin. I feel one nip, then others: the bed-bugs have gone into action. I tighten my clothes around me, trying to find the most comfortable position.

Feeling better, I can relax a little and devote my mind to my predicament, but I have failed to appreciate the vivacity and voracity of the bugs. They are all over me, driving me mad. I get up and walk up and down: two steps forward, two back – the length of my domain. I soon get tired, and besides, it is useless. The bugs are not discouraged. They feverishly enjoy every move I make. I sit down again on the bed and scratch until I draw blood.

It was shortly after midnight when we were brought to the Cherche-Midi. I go over every detail of our arrest: that bastard Schnell who had betrayed us, the trap, the Gestapo.

Outside, two black cars were waiting for us. Pierre Roumeguère and I got into one. Two toughs were sitting in the front. A third sat with us in the back. In the other car were Pierre Clervoy and Jean Kopf, similarly flanked by three guardian angels. We set off in the direction of the Rue des Saussaies. It must have been about seven p.m. It was August; August 1943. The weather was beautiful. Then the cell, interrogation, and finally the Cherche-Midi.

Our rendezvous had been organized by Jean Kopf. An Alsatian himself, he had contacted another Alsatian, Schnell, a Gestapo interpreter. After some negotiation, an agreement was made. For a sum of 200,000 francs, Schnell had promised to arrange the escape of a young woman, a member of our circuit. Schnell had known how to gain Kopf's confidence. The fact that they came from the same region had something to do with it. The exchange was to be made at 26 Rue Hamelin, at the guard's house, at six p.m. We had all contributed to raise the money.

Kopf and Clervoy went on ahead. I do not know why – foreboding, doubt – but I was wary. I told Kopf: 'Before coming up to the flat, I'll telephone you from a bistro in Rue Hamelin. As you won't be able to explain anything, I'll know from the tone of your voice if everything is all right. No need for us all to cop it.' Pierre Roumeguère stayed with me. On the telephone, Kopf's voice seemed quite normal. As I hung up I was already delighted with our success.

Hardly had we stepped outside the bistro than two men seized us. The Gestapo! We arrived at the Rue Hamelin under escort. The young woman we were to have saved was there. Schnell asked me for the money. I gave it to him. A man called Schmidt came out of another room. He was the leader. It was all over. We had been caught red-handed.

The bugs are plaguing me less. Am I getting used to them already? ... I think hard of how I am going to get out of this. The light filtering through the skylight begins to change and strengthen. It is almost dawn.

The sound of mess-tins being dragged along the flagstones interrupts my thoughts. It is morning. My stomach cries out for food. Today it is not to be satisfied. I am far from thinking that I am on the brink of a long, long wait, the start of an initiation to horror....

The door opens and I am ordered to get dressed. In the corridor, I buckle on my belt, lace up my shoes and knot my tie. We go down to the office. My friends are there: Jean Kopf and the two Pierres – Roumeguère and Clervoy.

We leave the Cherche-Midi and set off at once for the Rue des Saussaies. The last figure of the dance.

We are each put into a separate compartment in the Black Maria and it is impossible to communicate, but at the Rue des Saussaies we are locked up in the same cell. Fortunately, Pierre Roumeguère, my closest friend, managed to get rid of the English papers before they could be seized and without our captors seeing. Now the only strategy to follow is to agree on a story and stick to it, whatever may happen during interrogation. As we talk one thing emerges: one of us can be cleared – Pierre Roumeguère. His part in the plan was not known. Even Clervoy and Kopf had only seen him for the first time the previous evening at the Rue Hamelin. Schnell had not known he existed.

Roumeguère, the doctor, is one of my wartime friends. We served together in the Navy Quarantine Service in 1939. Since then we have hardly ever been separated, and then only because of circumstances 'beyond our control'.

Today, as I write, he is still a part of my life. When interrogated, I decided to say that he was with me because he was coming home to dinner, as he did every week, and that he knew nothing. That we have secrets from each other. That you can be very close to a man and not know what part he might be playing. It only needed Pierre Clervoy and Jean Kopf to say the same thing and all would be well. I was so concerned about Roumeguère that I forgot the danger I was in myself.

We waited. . . . It was André Méresse who had formed our circuit : the Intelligence Service of the Volunteer Army. The day after the fall of France, he had begun to reassemble his comrades and soldiers from his unit to resist the armies of occupation. He made contact with other groups – Donnay, Heurteaux, Lhôpital, Chanel, Vengeance. Early arrests decimated the groups but did not completely destroy them. It was then that Méresse gathered together the debris of the original groups under the name of the AV – l'Armée des volontaires (Volunteer Army). We were in every town.

Our work, alongside de Gaulle's BCRA and British Intelligence, consisted of providing information, writing pamphlets and posters which we put up in eye-catching places, and, whenever we could, sending radio messages to London. We also sheltered escaped prisoners and helped them on their way, and hid British and American pilots. We had parachute landing-sites like the ones at l'Yonne, thanks to old Mazeau and his son from Saint-Bris; at la Nièvre, under the responsibility of Labaume, a wine merchant from Cosne; at Caen, organized by the lawyer Gilles and the contractor Duchez; at Poitiers, under the lawyer Renard.

Méresse had been arrested some time in the first two weeks of November 1942.

I wonder if I shall ever see Méresse again, whether he has been tortured, what prison he is in, if he might even be somewhere in the Cherche-Midi. How had he, so sure, so sharp, so alive, reacted to interrogation?

Suddenly, I become more conscious of my own situation. Thanks to my position in the circuit I had to know many things, many

names, though false ones. How well would I stand up to the inter-
rogators?

'What are you thinking?' Pierre Roumeguère asks.

'About the Ethiopians and monkeys. Ethiopians believe that
monkeys do not speak in order to avoid life's problems. In other
words, silence is golden. I was thinking that I wish I were a monkey.'

'It all seems a bit unreal to me, like the ant not knowing what's
happening when you pee on his little castle of mud and twigs. . . .
When I saw those bastards turn up I still thought: this only
happens to other people. We looked so sheepish when they put the
handcuffs on us, like children caught in the act. At last it was
dawning on us that this undercover war wasn't a game.'

Pierre Clervoy asks us to keep our voices down. Roumeguère
murmurs: 'Do you know, Jean, these handcuffs strike me as sym-
bolic. My left fist to your right, me marching on your right? . . .'

In a flash it all comes back to me. The first time I met Pierre
Roumeguère had been at Cherbourg in October 1939. I was secretary to the resident doctor, Kervarec, at the naval hospital. I saw
a big fellow arriving, a sturdy chap with dark eyes set amidst sharply-
defined, satanic features, and a mass of brown hair. He looked be-
wildered in his sailor's uniform. I learnt that he had just finished
medical school.

In spite of his forbidding appearance, he attracted me by his re-
markably sensible arguments. He used to discuss the existence of
God with a priest who had also been conscripted into the navy. Perhaps theologians, or even sceptics, could have convinced Pierre
Roumeguère because of their skill, but the priest had only his faith,
and that didn't carry enough weight.

I remember our journeys in the military trains which took us from
Cherbourg to Paris. On the platform at Saint-Lazare he was met
by his mother and sister, I by Suzanne. He worshipped his mother;
her intelligence fascinated him. Life had not been so kind to me.
A mother murdered by a madman, a father who had vanished without trace. Life had made me. It had been sink or swim.

'I watched people all the way from the Rue Hamelin to the Rue
des Saussaies,' says Roumeguère. 'For a moment the car stopped
before crossing the Champs-Elysées. There were people walking,
aimless, with time on their hands. I shall never forget the looks they
gave us; first astonished, then afraid. A Gestapo car with French
civilians inside; to them we were nothing but shit. It was an

extraordinary sensation. I felt like a bastard showing off with his pals in the Gestapo. I actually tried to act the part, to feel a totally new experience. . . .

'When the car stopped before the entrance of the Rue des Saussaies the gates were open. At that moment, the very personification of a respectable Frenchman was coming towards us. A retired colonel type, with greyish hair, slim and distinguished. He was walking along with his two daughters, at least I assume they were. One must have been about nineteen, the other sixteen: two attractive brunettes. They saw us get out of the car, flanked by the two giants, and chained together. They stared, fascinated by the handcuffs. Then, as if hypnotized, they fixed on my face. Perhaps I exaggerate because of the intensity of that moment. . . . Perhaps my imagination ran away with me? But I tell you, Jean, believe me: I felt as if one of the two girls gave me something . . . like a look of love, a transfusion of energy, a burst of tenderness . . . something sublime. She was moved. There were tears in her eyes. I suppose it must have been the first time that she had seen one man chained to another. Perhaps she was thinking: "So that is what it is to be a patriot. Everything I've heard about those who resist and are arrested is true." We didn't look like villains. She looked at me like a woman saying goodbye to a soldier who is going to war, and wondering if he will return. The vibrations lasted one second but I can still feel them now.'

Pierre Roumeguère whispers. We listen. Is he telling his story to stave off our anxiety? How much longer shall we have to stay in this cell? Have they arrested too many people to interrogate us today? I am hungry and thinking of Suzanne. How worried she must be!

'The interrogation yesterday evening wasn't too bad. They didn't even search us thoroughly, only a quick frisk to see if we carried guns. They didn't make us strip. They emptied our pockets, then asked fairly routine questions, knocking us around a bit for good measure. I don't think they managed to trick us into contradicting each other. I had the distinct impression that their chief was most disappointed with our wallets.'

Roumeguère looks at me. I say:

'Our friend will stay in prison. She looked so sad when it was all over. She felt responsible for it all and I wanted to shout out to her that we alone were responsible. Pitiful! It was pitiful!'

My voice echoes curiously in my ears. I must have spoken louder to express my anger. An anger directed mostly against myself.... But how could Kopf have been so badly mistaken? ... If I were to get hold of Schnell he wouldn't be a member of that lot of bastards for much longer. His breath would cease to taint the air. I have never hated a man so much. I was entering the world of the worst perversions, daily pain, sadism. I was soon to realize it....

Silence. Each man is deep in thought. It is a good way to get out of the trap, to loosen the vice.... I imagine I am at the cinema. No longer in the cell, I am being shown a film. It's a sensation I often experience.

'In the Rue Hamelin, when they put on the handcuffs, I was already aware of the seriousness of that moment for us. At the Cherche-Midi it struck me full force. We had been sucked into the whirlpool, yet at the same time I was enjoying life, I was revelling in my senses of sight, of touch, in every breath, with ten times the intensity. That summer's night that Paris gave us was warm, velvety, almost voluptuous. Soft. I remember the journey across Paris in that car like a woman's caress.'

Roumeguère is wonderful. I love listening to him. I know that when we first met he thought of me as a hustler, a commercial traveller who was always showing off, an unrepentant tout, 'a businessman' he would say disparagingly. It was I who made the first overtures to him. 'Your popularity bothered me. You were too pally with the sailors and the little NCOs in Cherbourg,' he admitted to me later. 'You were everybody's counsel and confidant. Your instinct for sorting things out, your sentimental-brutal side irritated me. If it was a matter of changing a guard rota, if there was a problem, if some difficulty cropped up, if someone needed help, they sent for Jean Michel, without fail. The helping hand, the sheepdog! And then I realized that you used your ability to insinuate yourself into every sphere to help those in need. Life had not been easy for you so you made it easy for others. And you had a quality that appealed to me enormously; a way of looking at life, debunking, laughing at your problems instead of letting them get you down.'

Roumeguère's confession. He demolished contention. He abolished it in himself to ensure more loyalty in his relationships with others. He would get involved. He avoided any relationship that was based on reservations.

'Life is complicated enough! Let everything at least be clear-cut between us,' he used to say. 'I'll do my best to make it so.'

Time passes. Each man seems lost in his thoughts, anxieties and emotions. How will our loved ones survive if we are detained for long? Will families suffer reprisals? What had Suzanne done when I hadn't come home? What will happen to the circuit? Is the war going to end? Will the Allies land soon? We are so worried, and yet we are far from imagining the horror of the death camps.

I return to the one sure thing:

'Roumeguère must be freed. He has the most chance. He didn't know about our activities. He is a doctor at the Pasteur hospital, doing research into contagious diseases. The Gestapo have only to check. He can even be indignant, threaten to complain in high places. None of you had ever seen him before. Let's employ that tactic. That alone will permit one of us to continue the struggle and to warn the others.'

I clung to this idea, desperate though it was....

We make the journey between the Cherche-Midi and the Rue des Saussaies several times more. We do not eat for two days. Though they deprive us of food, there is no embargo on beatings, but not one of us strays an inch from the prepared story.

I found out later, much later, that Roumeguère had been released in the Rue des Saussaies with no money or shoelaces. He borrowed a metro ticket from the baker's shop opposite. He hurried to my wife, told her what had happened, jumped into a bath, asked for something to soothe the bites of those accursed fleas, and said:

'It's better I should disappear. The Germans released me thinking I was a fool, but I am afraid they might reconsider.'

This man, who was to become known as 'Doctor Satan', took a more active part in the Resistance from then onwards.

As for us, we were entering a world where time was not of the same duration, not in the same dimension as in everyday life.... A world where we learned to watch others die and face death ourselves....

# Chapter Two

# A CURIOUS DINNER PARTY

What forges a man's destiny? Hitler's occupation of France had pre-
cipitated me into the Resistance, Schnell's treachery had dropped
me into the hands of the Gestapo: when all is said and done, a common experience in those hard but simple times, when patriotism
left no choice of the sort of attitude to adopt towards the enemy.
A resister in the Occupied Zone could not expect to survive more
than six months in that terrible year, 1943.

My destiny was about to take an extraordinary turn, due to the
course of events taking place far from my cell but on the very night
of my arrest.

During that evening of 17 August 1943, as I fought off the fleas
in the cells of the Cherche-Midi, a curious dinner party was being
held at the other end of war-torn Europe. The setting was ideal
for a film: a Baltic peninsula, gloomy and wild, where before the
war ducks and moorhens were hunted, but which was gradually
covered in buildings and imposing installations. This peninsula was
to become better known by the name of Peenemünde. The guests
too seemed to have sprung from some work of fiction. An over-
excited young woman, Hanna Reitsch, was a fanatic Nazi. Her enthusiasm was so great that in order to better serve the fatherland
she had become a test-pilot; later she was the last person to see
Hitler alive. Facing this voluble Valkyrie in her navy blue suit
bestarred with decorations, sat her host, stiff and solemn, a member
of the Wehrmacht. General Walter Dornberger embodied all the
virtues of the German army, that implacable, icy machine conceived
to kill and enslave the world (but what army does not have these
aims?). A volunteer in August 1914, a prisoner in 1917, since the
defeat Dornberger had been a member of that Reichswehr of

100,000 men, tolerated because of the treaty of Versailles, which had secretly prepared for Germany's revenge. Five years at the Berlin University and an engineer's diploma had enabled him to make an incalculable contribution to the secret rearmament of the Reich. As Chief of Ballistics in the Army Weapons Department, he had in 1930 been charged with investigating the possibilities of a programme of military missiles based on scientific theories which at that time still seemed Utopian and vague.

Dornberger's second guest, a tall, heavy civilian with a baby face, was not yet thirty-two years old. Wernher von Braun, passionate researcher and visionary, had worked with Dornberger for six years. The general had discovered him in a small and private research department in Berlin. He had made him his technical assistant. He had put the powerful means of the German army at the disposal of this young scientist, who already dreamt of going to the moon.

The final guest, Doctor Ernst Steinhoff, the director of the programme of guidance and control at Pennemünde, almost passed unnoticed beside these giants: he was one of those anonymous and meticulous technicians who knew how to moderate the visions of von Braun and transform his impetuous premonitions into concrete reality.

While, on that evening of 17 August 1943, the fanatical Nazi, the soldier, the visionary and the technician made up an anthology of the demented romanticism of the Third Reich (there was only a representative of the ss missing – Hans Kammler – but, as we shall see later, he could not for long stay out of the story), two hundred miles away, six hundred bombers of the Royal Air Force were preparing for one of the greatest aerial battles of the Second World War.

Von Braun and Dornberger had had several tense weeks. When the Nazis first came to power, their missile research had benefited from the unconditional support of the Generals Fritsch and von Brauschitsch, chiefs of staff of the Wehrmacht. Alas! In March 1939 they saw the arrival at their test centre of one Adolf Hitler, disgruntled and disillusioned. Confident in his blitzkrieg strategy, fascinated by all weapons as long as they reminded him of his combat in the First World War, the Führer had shown little interest in their missile. After the success of the campaigns in Poland and France he had even refused them absolute priority – that absolute priority which had to be obtained in the wartime Reich if one wanted to bring off such a programme, which while it was revolutionary, was nevertheless still far from problem-free.

Thanks to the clandestine aid of the chiefs of staff and, from the beginning of March 1942, of the new Minister of Armaments, Albert Speer, the research was able to continue. At four p.m. on 3 October 1942, a guided missile, the A4, (Aggregät 4; device number 4) made a majestic flight, breaking the sound barrier for the first time in human history, howling through the air for 115 miles along the Baltic to fall less than 4,000 yards from its target. On 12 December, Speer won from Hitler the longed-for priority.

The defeats of Stalingrad and the check at Koursk, which rang the knell of the blitzkrieg and the end of the triumphant Panzer onslaught, did not, however, seem to have removed the Führer's last doubts about Dornberger's wonder weapon. The warlord even had a dream in which the A4 could not reach London, and this did nothing to accelerate a project already handicapped by Dornberger's disagreements with one Degenkolb, a specialist in locomotives whom Speer had appointed to organize the mass-production of the A4. On the other hand, the intensive bombing of the Ruhr and Hamburg acted on the leader of the Reich like the sting of a wasp. 'You can only smash terror with counter-terror! You have got to counter-attack. Anything else is rubbish!' shouted Hitler in one of his resounding fits of hysterics at a meeting of the general staff on 25 July 1943.

At midday he signed a decree which read: 'The success of the war against England depends on peak A4 missile output being attained as soon as possible. Full support must be given to all measures designed to secure an immediate increase in A4 production.'[1]

Hitler knew how to make them obey him; I shall relate in detail how his orders were carried out. Before it went on to pave the way for the conquest of space, the A4 made its appearance under the formidable name of the V2 – weapon of reprisal number 2.

The Führer insisted that they produce 900 missiles a month. He wanted 5,000 V2s to rain down on London at one time.[2] Would von Braun and Dornberger be able to achieve this? The delay in the A4 programme now prevented the mass-production of the missile their leader so suddenly wanted: the miracle weapon was not yet ready.

And then the A4 had competition. The Luftwaffe, who lorded over West Pennemünde as Dornberger did over East Pennemünde, had perfected their own flying bomb: the Fieseler-103. Scientifically, the FI-103 – the future VI – was of very little interest. It was a small machine without a pilot, propelled by a very primitive jet-engine and launched by a catapult. After suffering many set-backs the flying bomb, precisely because of its minimal scientific interest, proved to be easier to put into operation than the revolutionary A4. Field-Marshal Goering dreamed of 'Hermann's Christmas present to his good friend Churchill'. Was a second-rate invention going to absorb labour and raw materials and thus compromise young professor Wernher von Braun's brilliant invention?

The preoccupations of the Pennemünde chiefs were weighty and important that evening of 17 August 1943. They became literally vital the very night that I lay awake on the bunk in my cell.

A little before ten p.m., eight of Air Vice-Marshal Bernett's Mosquitoes flew over Denmark into Germany, to the west of Pennemünde, and headed for Berlin.

Throughout the afternoon, German wireless operators had been recording unprecedented signs of preparation by the British Bomber Command. The evidence was irrefutable: after the Ruhr and Hamburg, the capital of the Reich was being threatened. Two hundred day and night fighters immediately took off from airfields in Germany, Belgium and Denmark, to try to prevent Berlin in its turn from becoming a sea of ruins. The roar of the engines, the endless firing of the anti-aircraft artillery, the searchlights, tracer bullets, signal flares – 'Over Berlin,' writes the English historian David Irving, 'there was chaos total and complete.'[3] Six hundred bombers of Bomber Command took advantage of that chaos to attack Peenemünde, which the German air defence had so imprudently left unprotected.

Peenemünde, a deserted and unknown peninsula in the Baltic, had become the obsession of the Allied General Staff.[4] Reports from the Polish Resistance (the work-force at Peenemünde came from Poland), from the French Resistance,[5] from agents operating inside Germany, the interrogation of high-ranking prisoners and aerial reconnaissance had all established that Germany was manufacturing long-range missiles there. Winston Churchill's own son-in-law, Mr Duncan Sandys (joint Parliamentary Secretary to the Ministry of Supply, and as such, with the entire scientific personnel of the ministry at his disposal), had, in April 1943, been appointed to collect and analyse all information about this new and mysterious menace. Despite the opposition of certain experts, in particular that of Lord Cherwell, the Paymaster-General, who estimated that the missile was technically impossible, and with the support of others, such as R.V. Jones, chief of the Air Ministry's scientific intelligence branch (who always evaluated perfectly the extent of the threat posed by the v1s and v2s), Duncan Sandys swept aside all objections. He obtained from the War Cabinet the launching of an unprecedented operation of bombardment. Its code name well reflected London's concern: Operation Hydra.

The ruse of the eight Mosquitoes worked.

Group Captain Searby and his two deputy master bombers dropped 1,593 tons of explosives in three waves of attack on Peenemünde. Early in the morning of the first of the 612 nights I was to spend in the hands of the Nazis, Duncan Sandys telephoned Winston Churchill in Quebec. The British Prime Minister's son-in-law pronounced three words in his nonchalant, distinguished voice: 'Operation Hydra successful.'

General Dornberger had seen 'his beautiful Pennemünde' devastated by what he was himself to call 'a night of fire'. Professor Thiel, combustion-chamber expert, and Chief Engineer Walther had been killed, along with 735 scientists and foreign workers. The city of scientists, the model factory for mass-production, the prototype work-rooms and the testing stands had all been either destroyed or damaged. General Jeschonneck, Chief of the Air Staff, was so overcome by the extent of the catastrophe that he killed himself.

As in all bombings with a strategically precise objective, the damage caused at Peenemünde was finally less important than one would have thought on inspecting the ruins of the secret base the following day. Work on the v2 was held up for only about four to six weeks, but Adolf Hitler, who had stayed awake that night until three-fifteen a.m., had such a fright that the projects of Dornberger and Wernher von Braun were from then on to control the lives – and the deaths – of sixty thousand of my comrades.

Man's murderous frenzy surpasses all imagining when plans

excitedly developed for some great ambition must be realized by the efforts of defenceless men.

Please excuse this chapter which is only a long digression. I have tried to show how our individual adventures were going to play a part in a vast united plan and to introduce into the story people who were to lead man from hell to the stars. From time to time, I will thus feel constrained to go from the microcosm to the macrocosm, from the victim to the torturer, from the most compromised torturer to him for whom the suffering of others is abstract because he is too highly placed in the hierarchy to inflict it himself.

Now back to my story.

# Chapter Three

# HELL'S ANTECHAMBER

One morning I hear shouts, noise, running footsteps ... an agitated activity unlike that of the preceding days in the prison. Are we to be ferried back and forth from the Cherche-Midi to the Rue des Saussaies again?

'Come out one by one.'

'Extracted' from my cell and roughly thrown into the corridor by the German guard, I tie my shoes and fasten my belt in record time. I abandon my tie.

'Face the wall! Hands behind your back!' orders the Adjutant at the far end. He speaks French. 'Answer when your name is called.' I am called in my turn. I am pushed into a room. A few men are waiting there, including Clervoy and Kopf. I look for Pierre Roumeguère. I have not heard them call his name. He is not here. Has he been released? I cling to this hope. I study the faces around me; the Resistance has taught me one rule: to mistrust people until experience teaches me otherwise. I carry this principle with me in another, almost instinctive form. I have always enjoyed reading faces, meeting a look, decoding bearing and gestures, and these signs quickly determine my relationship with the person I observe. I know signs can be unreliable, but this perusal has never failed me. Have I therefore avoided men who could have become my friends? I don't know, but I have not been let down by those who have passed the test – a mixture of empirical evidence and a sort of pre-natal memory. They are men who belong (or belonged) to a certain school of thought, who have (or had) a certain way of looking at things in times of crisis. Men who would follow one path, unfailingly, when it was a matter of instinctive reactions or fundamental principles.

There is an eighteen-year-old boy there, Fred. He has a small, smooth, sickly face. Cap in hand, he waits anxiously for his fate to be decided. They call out four names. I think: that is how they call men out to be shot. I hear snatches of conversation. 'Why are you here? What did you do? – I had seven parachutists at my house. You? – I was planting dynamite ...' – 'They sent me to Messerschmitt. I got fed up with it and cleared off. They picked me up as soon as I set foot in my house.' – 'I was a labour conscript for Germany. I stayed there for two months. I am against the war. I refused to work for the war industry. They sent me back to Paris. Then, hey presto, they came to get me. Will they try us on a Sunday? ...' – 'Where is the tribunal? I don't think they got us together in this room to shoot us.' – 'Are we really going to stand trial?' – 'That's more likely. They can't mess us about like this!'

The door opens to let in new arrivals. Now there are fifteen of us. I am not worried. I always have this feeling deep down inside, a feeling that is beyond logical definition. I can never believe that I am going to die. Every time I brush with danger I feel an extraordinary strength which reassures me.

We go one by one into the adjoining office. They give us back our identity cards, rings and money. . . . I notice that my wallet has been emptied of the 37,000 francs I possessed, obviously not counting the 200,000 previously taken by Schmidt and Schnell. I still have 5,000 francs which I had put into a trouser pocket. No one has seen it.

Fred needs comforting so I whisper: 'Relax. They won't shoot us today.' I smile at him. Another man has overheard. 'That doesn't mean a thing. You can expect anything from these bastards.'

Armed soldiers count us. Roumeguère is still missing. We are taken out into the yard. The prison gate is open. It is impossible to escape: on each side of the gate is a solid wall of soldiers, machineguns at the ready. Before us is a luxury coach with red leather seats. We get on board. There are men there already, prisoners too.

At the corner of the Boulevard Raspail, I see several women peering into the yard. It is early. How did they know? Perhaps Suzanne is there? I look for her, but no, how could she have known. Women trying to recognize their men. Do they come here every morning in the hope of catching sight of a loved one; one last glimpse and then solitude ...?

We are quickly loaded into the coach. We set off. It is a short journey. Soon the coach stops: we are outside the police station on the Quai des Gesvres, in front of the Conciergerie. Another group of men come out. There is the same ceremony as for us: the wall of soldiers, machine-guns; our coach fills up with more travellers. Interrogation is written on their faces. A topography of anxiety.

Pierre Clervoy – little Pierre – has not left my side. We talk to a very likeable boy, Max Princet; brilliant looking, with a high forehead and a dazzling smile. He is bald. I don't know why, but this gives him a kindly air. I think he must be my age, thirty-seven, but he is actually younger. He is wearing a light grey, well-cut suit. He speaks with the fluency of a southerner, but his accent betrays him: he comes from eastern France. I sense that I shall have confidence in this man. He talks to us, but does not allow himself to get carried away. He says only what he wants, without boasting or imprudence. He is not intoxicated by words; he controls them.

'Where are you from?'

'From Fresnes,' he replies. He goes on to say: 'The guard in the aisle is a real shit. He usually forbids us to talk. I'm surprised he hasn't laid into us. Is he allowing us a little conversation like the last cigarette or glass of brandy for the man in the condemned cell?'

'Do you know where we are going?'

'No. We're from Fresnes, you're from the Cherche-Midi, and the last lot from the Quai des Gesvres: that's all I know.'

It is a beautiful day. Summer is out of step with the pain of all these men, whether they hide it or wear it on their sleeve. I look at Paris, and then at Max Princet. I could not then know that this man, wounded in 1940 and hospitalized for a year, at this moment so noble, would die so quickly and so atrociously among the outcasts of Dora.

The coach moves off again. It is full. We take the Boulevard Sebastopol and arrive at the Gare du Nord.

'Perhaps we can escape?' says Max.

Once again, it is impossible. We are surrounded by a wall of soldiers, brandishing machine-guns. It is even impossible to communicate with the civilians, but they do not seem to want to anyway.

... I remember these scenes at the Gare du Nord, and I think of the flood of resisters when it was all over and the Nazi monster had been overthrown. That day, in that corner of Paris, it was in vain that we looked entreatingly for some show of sympathy, of support: we saw not one sign of solidarity. And yet it is at times of internal chaos that those signs are so important. They give heart, though they can change nothing.

Someone asks a railwayman: 'Who are all those men?'

'Terrorists or black marketeers.'

I am seized with helpless anger. 'Terrorists! There are plenty of those in France. Pétain, Laval and their accomplices have really stirred up public opinion. Society may forge men, but there are also men who forge society.'

I feel sick. The railwayman continues: 'The Germans are in the right. There is nothing to reproach them with. If it weren't for these terrorists pushing them too far, there wouldn't be any reprisals.'

What shit! I want to spit in his face. Survival is a matter of compromise: that is what those accessories to defeat ought to repeat to themselves all day long, but they don't. They are the faint-hearted. You cannot escape the canker of fear unscathed. Too many men respect only force.

When I catch anyone's eye, he turns away. Is there one man in this craven troop, just one to whom I can call my name, so that he might tell my wife that I am still alive? Where they are not openly hostile, they avoid meeting my gaze....

The Germans now clear a space around us. What do they have to fear from these clods? I am seething with rage. Fury has made me unjust.... We are on the platform. They put us into comfortable coaches, eight to a compartment. It would have been an agreeable journey were it not for the German sentry in each group of eight. We are forbidden to sit by the windows. *Periculoso Sporgesi....* Other soldiers stand guard in the corridor. As the train moves off I manage to throw one of my business cards onto the track, with the words 'Please tell my wife'. It was never delivered.

The train stops. Compiègne. We alight. There are forty of us, fifteen soldiers. We file slowly through the town, where curiosity is doubtless blunted by the repeated arrivals. Only here the attitude is different. People look at us sadly. We see encouragement and compassion in their eyes.

Compiègne was bombed in 1940. On the other side of the Oise stand houses that have been badly hit by grape-shot and shell. After prison, the walk seems to us like a dream. An illusion of liberty, fresh air.... They leave us in a room strewn with straw. It is a room situated at the entrance of the camp, the infamous Royallieu: history's upheavals bring even noble names into disrepute. We lie down.

An hour later they come to fetch us. In a building behind a barred door, each man in turn undergoes a basic interrogation. In the yard a German NCO, seated at a table, demands our papers and money. We are allowed to keep six hundred francs. I do not mention that I have five thousand. This ritual is neither violent nor even very thorough.

We are sent to the storekeeper. He gives us a blanket, a dirty messtin and a spoon. We are taken to building C7. We are able to speak to the other interns: the 'old boys' who usually know what is going on. The same questions are asked over and over again. 'What do you do? What did you do? Where are you from? Are we staying here? Where are we going? ...' We install ourselves in a dormitory. We naturally form a group: Princet, Clervoy, Kopf, Ragot, Leroy and finally Mathieu, who had harboured British paratroopers. He had been at Fresnes for nearly a year. He was one of those men as capable of heroism in the daily round as in the heat of combat. A dependable, solid man who hid behind his sense of humour if he thought too much importance was being attached to his deeds. 'I had seven Englishmen at my place, so what? ... Can't you entertain who you like? ... I wasn't going to ask the Germans' permission!'

Hope surges in my veins. I cannot think of another way to describe the gusts of life that rush to my head and flood through my whole body. 'We will get out of this, we'll escape long before our sentence is up' – this thought runs through my mind.

There is no food, but we can speak freely and rest. Soon any idea of riding off into the sunset beyond the barbed-wire is supplanted by a more down-to-earth occupation: hunting fleas. They are everywhere; in the straw, in the palliasses. Fleas are to number amongst our closest companions for many months.

Royallieu camp was formerly the barracks for Spahis. There was the large camp and the small camp, where the interns were put into quarantine on the point of departure. To the left, separated by a very high iron fence, lay a third camp – for women. In another yard were tents occupied by neutrals and Americans.

Royallieu was encircled by a road bristling with barbed-wire. At sixty-yard intervals stood observation towers with searchlights built within the enclosure of the ring-road. They enabled the ss to keep us under surveillance. They took no rest at night; accompanied by wolf-dogs they patrolled hourly to compensate for any possible failure on the part of their lookouts.

The time at Compiègne was to be the last recreation period in our little story: a privileged moment, a holiday, a patch of blue sky before the Gehenna of Dora, hell's ante-chamber.... But who could have known?

I met Teitgen. He told me about his children, who had joined de Gaulle in London, and about his career as a lawyer. I talked with the younger Clemenceau. I made the acquaintance of the men who were to become my brothers: Claude Lauth, Roger Cinel, Louis Murgia, Pierre Rozan, all younger than I.

Claude Lauth, with the rounded forehead, had not yet had time to live. He was a poet, headstrong, madly in love with his fiancée. He had an artistic temperament, in the true sense of the expression. He had belonged to the NAP and Françoise circuits in Toulouse. He had been arrested on the evidence of an informer. We were to become inseparable.

An Air France steward, Roger Cinel was of average height. He had chestnut brown hair, blue eyes, was cordial, fluent in three languages: French, English and German. His sense of humour and exuberance concealed a tendency to misanthropy. He too had been denounced and incarcerated at Angers, where his parents owned a large café. In prison he had passed through the hands of Vasseur, the head of the Gestapo – a torturer in the Angevin tradition. Vasseur's cruelty encouraged Cinel's mistrust of human beings. 'It's stronger than I am.... I want to avoid generalities, but I know too much of the meaningless pain men can suffer at the hands of others. Beyond the physical pain lies an intense sadness. It happens on the point of interrogation: why? why is the torturer so fierce; he is a man of flesh and blood, of muscles and nerves just like you? Then the sadness becomes disgust, as it always does when faced with one of the clearer manifestations of human absurdity. Then hatred. You hate the torturer, you hate the good people of France out there, so passive that the great men of this world label them good. They are capable only of servility. There it is: I am set on a course of mistrust and I have drunk from the cup of bitterness. Time tries to efface the resentment. It is difficult ...'

Louis Murgia had extraordinarily black eyes, a velvet expression. He was small, foxy, impeccably dressed. His tanned complexion and Sicilian looks gave him the appearance of a character in an American film about the Prohibition. He explained that he had been arrested because of a misunderstanding. He had undertaken successive contracts for the STO, received his money, then disappeared. An alert policeman had put an end to the game. 'But the police, with all their records, must have known that I have never worked in my life. I am anti work. I belong to a rare breed, whatever is said to the contrary. You need a real dedication to freedom, idleness and laziness to enjoy every single day and night. We're an aristocracy! Others grow tired of it. They lack the heritage of centuries, handed down from father to son! They are obsessed with the religion of work. And yet no church pushes them. Some consider work a sort of atonement on earth with a view to some fanciful hereafter; others can only see the revolution as something which transforms the notion of work. In the past there were the slaves and the wage-earners, bemoaning their hours and their pay; tomorrow there will still be the slaves and the wage-earners; but those fools, unlike us, will be happy with their lot. I see no difference in being exploited and miserable or exploited and content; there are plenty of cuckolds who fly into a rage and plenty who are quite satisfied! But I say that those unsuited to idleness should let others live life as they choose. I am working towards this.' We loved to hear Murgia expound his theories. He was a model of good sense and shrewdness.

Pierre Rozan was arrested in Clermont-Ferrand. His distinction and calm were foolproof. He found it intolerable to raise his voice. Any manifestation of vulgarity was alien to him. He was naturally opposed to violence and yet the invasion and German occupation had driven him into the Resistance. Never once did I see him lose control. Reserved, he spoke only when he deemed it necessary. His graciousness and his courage were his fundamental qualities.

There were the most amazing stories of escapes. A prisoner's misery is often eased by superstitions and false stories: men love to believe in the unverifiable. We were scornful, and yet the hopeful gossips sometimes told the truth; their stories, which spread from group to group, from barrack to barrack, soon became part of the folklore of the camps.

There was the story of the man who had escaped in the rubbish cart: of another who had borrowed the laundry van. Five men were said to have bought the silence of an ss guard on an observation tower; they had crossed the ring-road, simply by slipping under the barbed-wire.

The most famous story was that of a group led by an important member of the Communist Party. He had persuaded the Germans that they ought to build a urinal of a size to meet the organic exigencies of a camp as large as Compiègne. Many interns worked steadily on the construction of this edifice, under the approving eye of the Germans.

One morning, twenty Communists were missing at roll-call. A frantic search took place. Then, under the immense urinal, they discovered a timber-propped gallery, lit by electricity, like that in the most modern mine. The gallery ran under the camp and came out beyond the barbed-wire. The affair caused a huge fuss. It was claimed that General von Stulpnagel, in person, had come to witness the achievement.

This story was the first I heard about the conduct of the Communists in the concentration camps. Discipline, courage, organization, unconditional aid to members of the same party – these were the reasons for their strength. And an unshakeable faith in the future. Happiness is coming....

# Chapter Four

## DEPARTURE
## FOR THE UNKNOWN

---

'Get up!'

Uproar, shouts, barking of dogs and men. I wake and jump up from my mattress. I feel as if I have not been asleep for long. Is it day already? No. Blackest night.

'Get up!'

The guards shout, bawl. What a racket! The confusion of an earthquake. A tempest in heads befuddled with sleep.

'What's the matter with these idiots, getting us up at this hour?' Murgia grumbles.

I look at my watch: it is one a.m.; the German NCOs shout orders and strike us, but not too hard.

We dress; it is important not to be the last one outside. Pierre Clervoy and Max Princet follow me into the night.

We are assembled on the parade-ground. The searchlights on the towers are trained on us, blinding us. The rest of the field is in shadow. What is going on? They've done it! The British have landed; the camp is being evacuated before their rapid advance. 'You saw their planes yesterday evening,' Princet whispers. At about five p.m. hundreds of planes had flown over Compiègne. They were British.

I lapse into my old habit of thinking of things in film images. I had watched this scene before. I often imagine that I have lived a certain event before.

Cars are parked on the parade-ground, not far from our group, the engines running. German officers look us over, as they would a herd of cattle. One of them has a particularly awesome face. He is tall, flabby, with madness in his eyes. Another is like the German mercenaries you see in films. He is giving orders to the second fiddle with the loudest voice in our barracks. He dishes out several slaps to satisfy his need for violence. The light from the watchtowers throws the scene into startling relief. I have an idea. I turn to Max: 'You see, they're too close to us, too far from each other. We could easily seize some as hostages, then escape. It's chancy, I know, but I don't think the guards on the watchtowers would dare fire.'

I look around me. Murgia, Lauth, Cinel and Rozan are not with us. To try it with only three – Princet, Clervoy and myself – will be too difficult, and it would be foolish to involve anyone else. There might be Gestapo informers among us. They were always to be found in prisons, and especially in camps, though it amazes me that men can sink so low. I decide my escape plan is too risky to put into operation....

On this morning of 2 September 1943, one thousand prisoners were chosen. They were herded into the enclosure that was known as the little camp. They had no more contact with the other prisoners.

We were to see some of them again, but in places and conditions which passeth all understanding, as the saying goes; an expression doubtless born out of the majority's ignorance of the aptitude for infernal inventiveness of their 'brothers'. These prisoners were part of the convoy 'Twenty Thousand' destined for Buchenwald.[1] Selfishly, we felt relieved. The last major departure had taken place in June; this was September. We hoped for a breathing space of a few weeks. The obsessive dream of escape could still become a reality.

The day following that 2 September, correspondence being suddenly authorized, I write to my wife. I ask her to send me my Swiss knife with the saw attachment. The longed-for knife arrives in the only food parcel which reaches me, on 14 September.

16 September 1943. Afternoon. Roll-call. Quietly, without unnecessary shouting or brutality, in the square where we are gathered.

The most common feelings are anxiety and joy. Joy for some, weary of waiting, happy at the prospect of moving on which might offer some chance to escape. Anxiety for others, irritated by the idiotic camp life, but unwilling to tempt fate. At least here we are alive. What might happen elsewhere? Feeling more strongly than their more frivolous fellows the distress caused by being constantly aware of death's presence, do they have any better idea of the horrors lying in wait for us?

The ss man on duty barks out the names. Claude Lauth, Max
Princet, Pierre Rozan, Roger Cinel, Louis Murgia, Pierre Clervoy
and I are among the thousand called. The search begins: jacket,
trousers, the soles of our feet. Once again it is purely mechanical.
I am calm enough. Murgia has suggested a hiding-place – just where
the belt folds around the buckle. 'Prisoners who want to write when
it's forbidden hide their scrap of pencil there,' he told me. I folded
my five thousand francs and tucked them in there. I thought they
might come in handy!...

An officer advises those with suitcases to send home what they
do not need. Our destination is vaguely described as 'another camp'.
We suppose he means a work camp. He adds that the discipline
will be more rigorous; according to our behaviour, release might
be a possibility. They put us into the little camp. Guards are posted
round about. We are isolated. The weather is magnificent; summer
seems reluctant to give way to autumn. Pierre Clervoy and I seek
out a corner near a window. We discuss the future. 'We must choose
professions that will increase our chances of escape.... I will say
that I am an officer of the health service and an agricultural
engineer....' I was naïve enough to believe that I would be sent
to a hospital or farm, and then could easily escape. Some illusions
take a long time to die.

Two young boys who have not been designated for this convoy
do not want to leave Rozan because they have taken such a liking
to him and because he speaks German. Permission is granted. One
was a taxi driver from Mans; Rozan cannot remember the other
one's name, or his home town, or what he did for a living. The poor
boys have made a bad choice. They are not to reach Buchenwald
alive. They suffocate in a wagon during the journey.

On the morning of 17 September we leave the camp for Compiègne
station – 1,070 prisoners from Royallieu, marching in fives. One
ss man on either side of the column, every six feet, on the lookout,
ready to fire at the least suspicious movement. We march, worried,
but, I repeat, still far from imagining what lay ahead.

The town is silent, oppressed. Behind the closed shutters, the
inhabitants seem to be sharing our adventure. The atmosphere is
tense, heavy, poignant. The streets are deserted. The Germans have
cleared them. At the station are a few of the curious, and also travellers waiting.

We had learnt that of the convoy of June 1943 – the 'Fourteen Thousand' – one prisoner had taken advantage of the crowded platform. As natural as could be, he had taken a woman's arm, and holding her tightly to him, he had managed to escape by disappearing into the crowd. Today it is impossible. The few people there are kept well out of the way. The mother of one boy, Leroy, aged twenty, is there. She is weeping. Leroy sees her. He shouts: 'Don't worry, mother, I'll be all right.' That cry of hope still echoes in my head after so many years.

A goods train is waiting for us on the track. The ss are posted the length of it with their dogs. We are given a Red Cross parcel and some bread. Our personal effects are returned to us. I recover a little money and my watch. They pack us in: forty, fifty men to each wooden truck. We try not to be separated. Clervoy, Murgia, Cinel, Princet and I manage to board together; Lauth and Rozan elsewhere.

The convoy, the 'Twenty-one Thousand' to Buchenwald, is ready to go. We were about to join the cachectics, the tuberculous, the scurvied, the cancerous, the scrofulous; the people of organized famine and terror; the people who would never forget because they had known hell on earth. . . . Hardly more than a month ago – thirty-three days – I was still free. . . .

# Chapter Five

# THE TRAVELLING COFFINS

As soon as we are all inside our rolling prisons, the train starts. I look at my watch. I calculate our speed at about forty miles per hour. Some detainees at Royallieu had claimed that you could escape at the start because the train moved slowly. They insisted that the convoys did not ever maintain a high speed during the journey, and that some prisoners had escaped from the trains. I thought any attempt to escape would be unlikely to succeed in daylight. Better to wait for nightfall.

An ss man surveys us from an observation cabin outside. I carefully take out my Swiss knife. I had slipped it into my underpants. During the summary search, we had not been made to undress completely. Without wasting any more time I begin sawing at the panel which, as luck would have it, is on the opposite side to the guard. At nightfall, when the convoy slows down, we shall be able to break through the cut panel, jump down and escape. I shall not be there to see the dumbfounded faces of the Germans when they discover the empty wagon. I weigh up our chances. We must wait for the right moment. I imagine the fury of our gaolers. I rejoice inside. It gives me courage.

Suddenly, shouts. Has that bastard spotted me from his perch? No. The shouts come from outside. It is afternoon. The train screeches to a halt. Some prisoners have jumped out. The soldiers fire. Through the vents we see our comrades running. We see them desperately trying to reach a small wood. The ss fire, and fire again. One by one the fugitives fall to the ground.

Helplessly, we watch the massacre. Fists clenched. Hearts swelling. Six are killed at that place. We count them. The Germans are going to make sure they are dead. An officer signals, the train sets off again. . . .

The convoy gathers speed after this first attempt to escape. At nightfall we arrive at a station; I forget its name. We are ordered to strip completely. With blows from rifle butts we are driven onto the tracks, quite naked. The ss inspect the trucks, chasing out the stragglers.

It is not so terrible to be naked outside at night at that time of year. It is the humiliation that hurts. Our friendship, that strong friendship between prisoners, was strengthened. The spectacle was indescribable. They wanted to strip us of all dignity. But who really lost their dignity? The giggling ss, mocking our mortification, or we who were at their mercy, in our grotesque nudity?

I had been the last to leave my truck. Before I was naked I had thought we could escape in the dark. I had almost sawed through the panel, there were only a few more cuts to make. It was imperative that everyone follow me. I didn't want any reprisals against those left behind.

As soon as the Germans had begun rushing around and shouting, I had hidden my knife in the bread I had been given that morning and not touched. I was still at the end of the truck, when an ss guard leapt out of the gloom. 'What's that?' he asked, pointing to the damaged panel. I looked dumbfounded, just as Pierre Roumeguère must have, when interrogated at the Rue des Saussaies. I replied: 'It was like that when we left.' My heart beat fit to burst. Cold sweat ran down my back, but my hands were steady. The guard did not insist; he hurried me outside with blows from his cudgel. I found myself standing naked with the others.

Using their rifle butts and clubs right and left, they make us climb into another goods train. It is impossible to stand up to injustice and armed force. No more for us the 'living space' of Royallieu; the Germans are economizing on transport. We are crammed into the wagons, about one hundred and twenty men to each one. The survivors are to remember that journey all their lives: a chorus of groans, oaths and dying gasps over the familiar sound of the wheels on the rails.

The doors and ventilators are closed: the ss have barricaded them with barbed-wire on the outside, so that we cannot escape.

We are suffocating in the dark. Inside the truck is a large cube: a metal container with a plank placed across it. We could see it by the pale station lights which penetrated the truck through the open door, until it vanished in the press of bodies. Then the door was closed again. This cube was for us to use to piss and shit into during the journey. Piss and shit: the torture of excrement! Pain and purgatory, the one thousand ways to mock human dignity have been recounted over and over again. I shall not attempt to measure the horror of that journey or even to chart the depths to which some men will stoop to degrade others. All I shall say is that we were about a hundred and twenty men in a goods truck, naked, gasping for breath, some trying to get away from the putrescent cube, others trying to get to it to answer the call of nature. For, suddenly, the need was desperate. Was it the fear, dysentery from the camp food, the length of the first leg before we changed trains? The stench! The cube was very quickly full. Did the train lurch, take a bend too fast, was there some sudden movement from the cluster of men? The cube spilled over onto those unfortunate enough to be around it. Cries, protests, threats and oaths in the darkness. And retching too. Soon vomit was mixed with the excrement, while the gloom oppressed us with the stench of despair.

Years have passed. Here and there are calls for forgiveness; but memory cannot erase what reason tries to diminish. You cannot devote your life to resentment. At least, it ought to be so. . . .

Darkness, oaths, abuse, pleas, and suddenly panic. Some begin to stagger. The air is growing thin; we are suffocating. Cinel, Murgia, Princet and Clervoy are near me; we have managed to stick together, in spite of the bedlam around us. We must keep calm. Our lives depend on it. Together we shout, 'Save your strength! Save your strength!' It is the only way to survive; to conserve oxygen, as they do in stranded submarines in films. 'Save your strength. Save your breath.' Was it exhaustion or have they heard us? Gradually the panic subsides.

The trucks are made of wood. Where the panels meet, a little air comes through. If we share this, keeping movement to a minimum, we can stay alive. I turn to Clervoy: 'It's not worth dying, let's breathe through the little gaps.' We set up a rota. 'Each man in turn will press against the wall to get a little air. . . . One group after another, that should keep us going. . . . If we don't do it that way the men in the middle will die.' Cinel, Murgia, Clervoy and Princet help me to enforce the plan. Was this initiative the determinative factor, or was our truck endowed with more fissures than the others? The fact is that of our group not one man died. Sometimes, alas, no amount of discipline or ingenuity can prevail. A metal truck followed ours; when we arrived at Buchenwald, I learnt that of the one hundred and twenty occupants of this coffin, eighty had died. Asphyxiated....

We are still naked. The journey continues. From time to time, cries herald that one of us is losing his reason. Suddenly, a scuffle. A man with a beard, aroused by the constant contact with the bare skin of a young man, is trying to sodomize him. 'Disgusting, filthy.' The bearded man is attacked by those nearest and the boy, drunk with fury. Others call for their mothers, their wives. I think only of survival. The Germans may have constrained me outwardly, but inside the fire of life still burns.

In the morning, the train stops. Footsteps, a loud-hailer, the hiss of the engine, snatches of conversation: the characteristic sounds of arrival at a station. Frankfurt-am-Main. The guards remove the barbed-wire from the doors and open them. Women of the German Red Cross distribute mugs of water. Everyone pushes forward. The nearest and the strongest hands reach out. The receptacles are knocked over. I stubbornly try to restore order. Others help me and the pushing stops. The mugs are handed out, more calmly. Everyone drinks; at least, I hope so. I study one of the women's faces. It is indifferent, used to tragedy. We set off again, still ignorant of our destination.

Later the convoy stops again. I hear someone cry: 'Weimar....' Yes, there we are, over a hundred of us, naked in a cattle truck, in the twentieth century, suffering the tortures of crowding, misery and exhaustion; hostages of an ignoble régime, in the town of Goethe and Schiller, the place where the spirit of Germany was born....

The train stands for a long time. Will we be let out? Have we suffered enough for them? We wait. What is going on outside? What worse torture have they conceived for us? Prisoners of terror, we wonder what our sorry future might be.

At last the door of the wagon opens. In German, one of the ss asks how many men are inside. Cinel translates for me. There we stand, naked, crushed together – the ultimate in caricature. Trousers are thrown in to us. You have to grab them as quickly as possible, in spite of the pain caused by each movement – we are so crowded together. We dress with the speed of a Chaplin film. My pair have been cut for a man with an enormous waist. I have to hold them up with one hand to prevent them from falling around my ankles. These are the trousers they made us remove at the station when we changed convoys. Redistribution is at random.

We are ordered to get down onto the tracks, feet and chest bare. They make us run along the tracks, over the sharp ballast stones. Our feet are bleeding. They drive us towards the road, on the other side of the station. Open lorries are waiting for us. This convoy is also made up of cars full of officers and motorcycles with sidecars. They signal to us to climb into the lorries.

We are driven on by rifle butts and oaths. I am out of breath, my feet hurt, but the fact of having acquired a pair of trousers, be they three times too large, has rekindled my spirit. It is horrible to find yourself naked in front of other men. You feel incapable of even imagining defending yourself. You are more than disarmed; you think only of your nakedness. The Germans had employed the surest and simplest means to prevent escapes during the journey.

As I climb into the lorry, an SS officer standing beside me says to me in French: 'Hide your watch. They'll nab it.' I cannot believe my ears! Is it a trap? Will he be present later at the inevitable search? I never knew who he was; I never saw him again. He was a fellow who knew enough French to say that much to me! And in bistro French, street French, without an accent! With the rapidity of a conjuror I unclasp the strap and slip watch, ring and wedding ring into a pocket. Odd for an SS man! He has done me a great service. If I can find others of the same stamp I will be able to escape, and take my friends with me!

When everyone is aboard the convoy moves off. Preceded by the motorcycles and officers' cars, we follow a narrow dirt road, lined with trees. Standing in the lorries the branches whip across our faces. We have to duck quickly, as the lorry drivers are doing their best not to be left behind by the motorcyclists, who are going at some speed. Cinel, Clervoy, Princet and Murgia are with me. We have lost Lauth and Rozan. We grow uneasy. Then I am reassured by the thought that it is difficult to look around in the throng, that it had been necessary to look where one was putting one's feet on the ballast, to dodge blows, run quickly, and for my part, hold up my trousers with one hand.

Now the road is tarred. There are hoardings with drawings of figures. One way is marked RICHTIGWEG, another KARACHOWEG. The drawings show a priest in his hat, a Jew with a star of David and a worker with a hammer and sickle. Later I learnt that the 'Richtigweg' led to the ss barracks and the 'Karachoweg' to the deportees' camp. What kind of world is this? We come to a large gate. Cinel translates the signs for me: *Jedem das seine* (To each his due) *Unrecht oder Recht, das ist mein Vaterland* (Right or wrong, this is my country). Well, do they doubt it?

We drive in. Our first sight is of three men, faces to a wall, hands tied behind their backs. A sack full of stones stops them from falling. We learn that these deportees had tried to escape. They are there as an example. You do not escape from Buchenwald! They were to stay there three days in this agonizing position – their cross a sack of stones. After those three days of calvary they were hanged. Thus we made the acquaintance of Buchenwald.

We are still in trousers, bare-chested. We climb down from the lorries; shouts and blows hurry us along. I follow the advice of the ss officer who told me to hide my watch. I also hide my wedding ring and the ring Suzanne had bought me all those years ago at Bourguignon. It was a ring with two sapphires and a diamond. I thought I could sell it if I should manage to escape. I put the watch and the rings into my mouth. We move on to the identity parade. They make us undress. It is becoming an obsession with them. I do my best to feel inwardly detached, though far from resigned. They ask us our name, profession, address, civilian status. I reply to the questions easily enough. They warn us in French: 'Give up everything you have; above all, hide nothing. You will regret it. Everything will be returned to you when you are released.'

I must seem as innocent as a daughter of Mary, and my lack of fear fortunately does not appear insolent. Just what is needed. The search is without incident. Others underwent a longer interrogation. Perhaps they showed their fear, perhaps I was luckier, who knows? *Chi lo sà* ... Formalities over, jewels and money are put into a bag marked with the owner's name; all will be returned on the way out. Proper accounting, according to the rules.... For what that cost them! ... But we still believed it....

Trousers under our arms, we are directed towards a building. Still naked we enter a violently-lit room, white-walled and mirrored. I catch sight of myself. I am painfully grotesque; one day someone will pay for this humiliation. In the room are stools; we are ordered to stand on them. Then I see men with electric clippers, plugged into the ceiling. I had never seen such clippers. These are the barbers of Buchenwald.

Immediately in front of me is a tall man, very dark and bearded, perched on his stool. In one movement, with alarming speed, the clippers move over his head, beard, chest, genitals and legs. Is this a comic film, or am I dreaming? The funniest custard pie sequence has nothing on this. The man's expression adds to the humour. He cannot get over the loss of his beard and hair and finding himself as naked as the day he was born. He looks at himself in horror. Is it nervousness, a defence mechanism, the unconscious? I am seized with hysterical laughter. I cannot control it. I laugh and laugh. This breaks the ice. The man begins to laugh too.

How extraordinary it was in that room, where we were being 'prepared' for the worst, to see and hear this outburst of gaiety and hilarity. All those unfortunates, naked, ridiculed, the butt of man's inhumanity to man, were united in laughter. Men who were exhausted by the journey, tormented by anxiety and overwhelmed by their 'reception' felt strengthened. Their behaviour defied and mocked their torturers. Avenged by comedy they laughed in the faces of their gaolers.

The ss are dumbfounded. Then, shouting, they regain control. They are like schoolteachers wondering if they are the object of the joke, while the pupils continue to giggle in spite of the severe expression and threats of punishment.

The blows have the effect of a cold shower. I receive a few more than the others, but I am secretly pleased. I have got my own back a little. In the most unexpected way we, the outraged, have outraged our gangsters of guards.

Shaved from head to foot, we are channelled towards another room. The entertainment continues. There is a tub filled with creosote and water. Our heads are plunged completely under water. We shut our eyes. Then our bodies go in. Next, hot and cold showers with additional alternating jets of hot and cold. It is quite refreshing. There is nothing to dry ourselves with. We are sent to the end of the room. A door opens; in a room they throw clothes to us; the Buchenwald gear.

These were not the striped pyjamas we were to wear when we worked in Kommandos. They were normal civilian clothes with labels on the backs of the jackets saying: KL (*Konzentrationslager*). We are also given a number and a red triangle with the letter F in the middle, which we have to sew onto our clothes. They entrust us with needle and thread; and there we sit, naked, shaved, still wet, sewing on to the jacket pocket the accursed number and, beneath it, the triangle. I do not feel cold, but I am very hungry. I feel dizzy. Some of the men cannot sew very well; friends help them. When it is done, we return the needles and thread.

From that moment on, we are merely numbers. It is a matter of quickly learning your number in German, on pain of blows if you do not answer roll-call fast enough. I am number 21138. Cinel, Murgia, Clervoy and Princet have numbers close to mine. We have managed to stick together all the way to Buchenwald. We dress. Our bodies are nearly dry. But the clothes are soaking wet for they have just come out of the steamer.

Princet had been almost bald already, so the shave has not changed his appearance that much. It is not the same for the rest of us. Clervoy, with his young film-star looks, has lost his seductive quality. We tease him.

We are taken to a block: 56, the quarantine block. It is a wooden barracks set out in rows of bunks on four levels. We are each given a blanket. We are to sleep on straw palliasses. The leader of the block is called Christian Beam. He is a German Communist who was arrested ten years ago. Neither German–Soviet pact, nor Molotov's praise of Hitler, had made any difference to his status. No interval in his incarceration. A life of constraints and brutality....

A great joy is in store for us as we inspect our new prison: Pierre Rozan is here! Safe and sound! We embrace. His calm exterior is a little shaken. Now we are only missing Claude Lauth: then the group formed and forged at Compiègne will be reconstituted.

Beam gives us a little warning in German. This time it is not Cinel but Rozan who translates. He is the interpreter for the barracks. Beam 'teaches' us that we are in a concentration camp. He says that he has known this world for ten years, consequently his experience makes him the boss, and he will allow no infraction. 'I am not prepared to suffer for other people. There must be discipline and no scandal, ever. We must behave with deference and salute the officers. There is only one rule: Obey.' He speaks roughly, gutturally, and shows none of the brotherliness of detention. He is not friendly at all – forbidding, rather. But we say to ourselves that this man must have seen too much.... He seemed to dread any offer, however tentative, of kindness. He was on his guard twenty-four hours a day; always fearing a trap. A hard, implacable man in this sinister place.

He has hardly finished speaking when Claude Lauth bursts into the block. Congratulations all round once again. In the midst of our tragedy we are happy. At Beam's request, Rozan repeats the instructions. We settle down on bunks as close to each other as possible. For us only one thing matters: we seven are together again.

# Chapter Six

# BUCHENWALD

---

*Advice to a newcomer.*

Tied hand and foot
What can you hope for?
To live? To wait?
You have only one day
To learn to bend ...

*Anonymous poem*\*

As expert practitioners of the techniques of horror, the ss had the upper hand when it came to the concentration camps. They signed contracts for work with major industrialists. The occupied territories provided them with a vast reservoir of labour. They drew from it by arresting resisters, rounding up their selected racial enemies and giving chase to whoever might be of use to them, including many prisoners of war. They thus gained possession of slaves for whom they had only to provide food and shelter. But what food and what shelter! When men wield absolute power over others, one can only expect the worst, and when those men are insane, evil, without conscience, their victims have little chance of survival.

As long as Germany's lust for conquest was unhindered, as long as victory succeeded victory, there was no shortage of labour. It was as easy to restock with men as it would be with cattle. (Unlike cattle, however, the deportees were not kept in good health. The labour force was used until it collapsed then simply replaced with

---

\* Most of the poems quoted in this book are taken from *Memorial des camps de Dora-Ellrich* (Paris, 1944). The authors are identified solely by their camp registration numbers.

new arrivals culled from the four corners of the occupied territories.)
The advance of the Russians and the landings of June 1944 forced
Hitler to revise his policy. ss gains had to be preserved, and these
were the result of the labours of their captives. The martyrs' efforts
had to be devoted to the German dream of a sweeping victory thanks
to the new wonder weapons. So attempts were made to keep the
slaves fit (in a manner of speaking!).

The internal hierarchy of the concentration camps was defined by
the ss. They left it to some internees – chosen and controlled by them
– to take care of problems of discipline. Head of these was an internee called Head of Camp or *Lagerältester*. According to the importance of the camp he could have a second in command, *Lagerältester
zwei*. Then came the *Lagerschutz* or overseers.

There were other organizations, such as the *Arbeitsstatistik*, the
*Arbeitseinsatz*, the *Arbeitsdienst* or working force, *L'Haftlingseinsatz*,
*Haftling* meaning 'internees' in the ss vocabulary. *L'Haftlings-
kammer* was the clothing distribution centre; the *Haftlingsrevier*
the infirmary and hospital for internees. Other organizations existed,
including the one for the work Kommandos. Each organization, or
Kommando, was led by a *Kapo*, assisted by a *Vorarbeiter*, a sort
of foreman. In the Kommandos there was often also a *Laufer* whose
duties were to liaise with the different services. The *Blockältester*
was the man in charge of the block where the internees were housed.
As you have seen, it was Christian Beam who welcomed us to
Buchenwald. Internees involved in this hierarchy wore an armband
on the left sleeve of their jacket, on which was written their function. The ss had less violent relations with them than with internees
without armbands, since they were responsible for discipline.

In addition to the number which we wore on our jackets, we were
classified by nationality and category. Beneath the number was a
triangle coloured differently for each category, and inside the
triangle a letter indicating our nationality: ss and Kapos, thanks
to these distinctive marks, knew at once the reason for our deportation and our nationality.

The triangles were of different colours:

*Red*      for political deportees ('political' to the Germans meant
           Communists as well as resisters).
*Black*    for the 'social misfits'.

*Green*     for all those convicted under common law.

*Blue*      for the stateless.

*Violet*    for the 'bible pushers', i.e. the conscientious objectors.

*Pink*      for homosexuals. The Germans called them Article 175 (*Hundertfünffundsiebzig*).

*White*     for deserters from the Wehrmacht, with the w of Wehrmacht. (There was also a white triangle with another type of w for the Wifo: *Wirtschaftliche Forschungsgesellschaft*).

Inside the triangle a letter indicated nationality (only the Germans had no letter in their triangles):

A     American
B     Belgian
E     English
F     French
H     Hungarian
I     Italian
J     Yugoslavian
N     Dutch
R     Russian ... and so on.

Finally, the Jews wore a yellow star of David with the word *Jude* in the centre.

Every camp was organized in this way. Sometimes the ss enlisted the services of the common criminals, sometimes those of the political prisoners. At Buchenwald, the camp was controlled by the red German triangles, the Communists; a number of them had been interned since 1935; some even, since the day after Hitler achieved power.

I admit that the preamble to this chapter might seem forbidding to the reader. May he excuse me. I thought it necessary to provide an overall picture of the concentration camp hierarchy, such as I experienced it. The object of this description is to help the reader to understand my story. When pain overwhelms man at the hands of other men, suffering and murder are premeditated and planned. The returns of horror are in direct proportion to the instruments used. Efficiency reaches all areas of human activity ...

Guttural cries. Reveille. Six a.m. We are directed to the wash house on the other side of the path. We go there stripped to the waist. It is only September, but already it is cold. Frozen, we wash in icy water. 'Good for the health,' Clervoy says to me. We then discover an absolutely outrageous structure: the latrines. . . . Over an imposing hole, hollowed out into a ditch (about three yards deep and forty yards long), is placed a large beam dividing it in two. All along the ditch is a plank on either side of this beam. The internees have to sit on the plank, arses over the void; on the other side the identical system; fifty men on one side, fifty on the other, arse to arse. It is an extraordinary sight.

We learn that the ss collect the excrement. There are shit Kommandos, bare-handed, to be avoided at all costs. They caught every illness imaginable. The poor fellows took the shit in buckets to fill huge, heavy, two-handled drums. These they took to the ss gardens. (We called these great oil drums the 'cubes'.) The ss tormented the men continually with their dogs, which attacked and bit as the fancy took their handlers. One wound in that stench, that repulsive filth, and the victim was done for. What a dung-heap to make one flower to grow! How much shit to make soup for the ss! Nature could have avenged us by contaminating the torturers' vegetables, but the typhus, ulcers, gangrene, abscesses, scabies, haemoptysis, pleurisy, anaemia and typhoid were for us alone.

That evening, we hear shrieks. No doubt about it: they are butchering someone. Such cries, it sounds like the end of the world. We cannot recognize what language it is. Christian Beam says we are forbidden to move. The harrowing cries go on and on, far more sinister and anguished than a dog howling for the dead. In the darkness they are intolerable. The prisoners, with the taste of ashes in their mouths, feel closer to each other, instinctively trying to overcome the despair that wrings their hearts. No film could ever recreate such an oppressive atmosphere. When the cries cease we strain our ears for signs from beyond the grave. Silence. Not another sound. . . .

In the morning we learn the cause of those cries. The man begging for mercy was a Russian Kapo from an evacuated camp.[1] On his arrival at Buchenwald he had been deposed from the rank of Kapo. He had reverted to being one internee among the others, subject to the same régime. That was the rule. Having no further need for auxiliaries, the ss, as soon as the evacuation of a camp had been decided, removed the armbands from the men who had served them. These men then had only their number and triangle; they were at the mercy of their former victims, who had only one objective: vengeance. The SS were amused by the fate of their chosen assistants among the internees. In all the camps in the history of the world it has been so; those who collaborate in horror, indeed those who instigate it, should beware changes or reversals of the situation. Yesterday's executioner could tomorrow languish in prison and suffer a thousand deaths at the hands of a torturer; could in his turn have his head on the block.

The man who had cried out and whimpered long into the night had been a killer. He had hung Russians for the SS. Since their arrival at Buchenwald, his compatriots had kept him under observation. They knew they were going to be able to satisfy their vengeance. The ex-Kapo must also have known he would pay for his service to evil. The game of hide and seek had lasted the whole journey from the old to the new camp. The finale took place that evening, at the latrines. From there had come the cries we had heard. The Russians had surrounded the man who had martyred so many of their kind. First they broke his arms, then his legs. They beat him until he was covered in blood. His body broken, they left him to die on one of the planks over the pit, sneering at his agony. When he begged for the pardon which never came, and beseeched them to put him out of his misery, they returned to their block. In atrocious pain, the Kapo had groaned and wept for hours; he had no more strength to call out. In the morning he was still alive. The Russians returned. They beat him with sticks, and when he was dead they pushed him into the shit.

The SS set up an enquiry. It had little chance of success. There was no result. Christian Beam told us, straight-faced, that there had been an accident – a man had slipped and fallen into the latrine. Alone. Indifference for an epitaph. The Russians were not disturbed by this murder.

That was how well the SS took care of their lackeys. We said to ourselves that this Dantesque scene should give food for thought to those whose submission to the SS had led them to spy on and denounce their fellows, even assisting in the places of torture and at the executions. It is said that in the past there were volunteers for the galleys. I think there will always be volunteers for evil, particularly when it offers advantages, however momentary.

We had much to learn. 'What kind of world have we fallen into?' we wondered every day. Small craft tossed on a frightening sea, would we run aground? The apprenticeship of roll-call reintroduced us to the unthinking routine of the barracks, but a routine of a severity and cruelty we had not experienced before. A discipline for robots, but robots of flesh and blood. They taught us to salute with the striped berets called *mutzen*. When the ss shouted : '*Mutzen ab!*', we had, in one movement, to raise and lower our berets. This ritual was to be performed in perfect time. The sound of the berets slapping against our legs was like a crack of the whip. Woe betide the man who broke the rhythm.

The one-step ballet of roll-call would have been absurd were it not for our exhaustion. It would go on for hours. It was a sight to be seen: those thousands of men, deathly still, in absolute and utter silence – the least murmur was justification for reprisals. Because of its slowness, roll-call was a much-dreaded formality. The forced immobility often caused fainting.

This calvary, in the cold, the snow and the rain, is burned deep in our memories. The ss counted the prisoners hut by hut: the number of deportees had to be correct. Then the total number of those in the huts had to correspond to the overall total of men. It was long, long ... interminable. Since the ss in charge were not good at figures, they would count, recount, make mistakes and start again. They were like clumsy, stupid children counting on their fingers and sucking their pencils: 'I put down seven and carry one ...' You wanted to do the addition and multiplication for them. In other circumstances, it would have been funny. So it is with tragedies; you turn aside a little from them, see them from another angle, and they make you laugh....

Two days after arrival we are told to go and pick out the things that we had when we left Compiègne. Out in the open are our clothes like a giant jumble sale. I find my suit, my wallet and papers. We are told to check in our belongings. Wallets are put into an envelope, clothes and shoes thrown into bags. Envelope and bag bear the name of the owner. 'Everything will be returned to you the day of your release.' 'Sure!' adds Rozan, translating. It is just like the search on the first day for jewels and watches. Do the ss themselves believe that our goods will be returned or are they merely keeping up appearances? I ask myself this again as I consider the attitude of our guards; an attitude born of the rules of detention systems – rules not to be broken, rules rendered even more formal and punctilious by the German character. Before putting my clothes into the bag I feel my trouser belt where it is doubled, near the buckle. As soon as I think I am not being watched, I take a quick look. The 5,000-franc note I had folded and hidden is still there. I retrieve it. If the opportunity to escape arises that cash will be precious. After the 'jumble sale', those who have recovered their goods – most of us – return them to the central store. Everything has to be deposited there.

'Identification', 22 September. Interrogation on identity, profession; a full-face photograph – taken by a machine similar to today's automatics – no fingerprints taken. I have decided once and for all to say that I am an officer in the navy welfare service, and an agronomist. I have not yet lost all my illusions. I still think that they will send me to a hospital or to a farm. Then vaccination. The orderly who inoculates us – and against what I do not know – puts the vaccine in a huge syringe.

We stand in single file; the orderly jabs coolly, quickly and with robot-like precision. He does three, four, five prisoners in one go. When the syringe is empty he refills it and carries on, never changing or wiping the needle. It is perfectly absurd. Here is an organization which cares for the health of its slaves enough to vaccinate them and which, at the same time, endeavours to kill them off as quickly as possible – by the risk of infection from this unhygienic vaccination, by malnutrition, by long roll-calls where they are exposed to the cold, and so on. The paradox is striking.

When all the formalities of admission and integration are completed, work begins. We have been here three days.

In the morning, the numbers are called, as usual. But, instead of being sent to the various administrative barracks, the survivors of our convoy form ranks and march towards the outside. I am assigned to the quarry Kommando – *Steinbruch*. We have not been put back into striped uniforms. We pass by the gate where we had seen the three men, face to the wall, suffer slowly before being hung. Deportees in circus attire, lined up on each side, play us circus music. The sight of these musicians is sinister. I try to catch the eye of one of them. We are marching too quickly; I fail.

We arrive at the quarry. It is open to the sky. There we see a long, long line of prisoners carrying rocks, putting them down, or lifting them up. It snakes and stumbles, an unforgettable sight. ss and Kapos spur the prisoners on; the dogs snap at them; blows rain down on their backs. Sometimes even, for fun, a whim, to speed up the work or for vengeance, an ss or a Kapo throws down a prisoner from the top of the quarry. He screams and crashes down several yards below. Dead. 'An accident. He slipped.' – The guards' funeral oration. Every ten yards the ss on guard, armed to the teeth, stake out the perimeter of the quarry.

With our civilian clothes, we mix with some older inmates of Buchenwald, dressed in striped pyjamas. We have only the saluting beret – *mutzen*. We try to exchange a few words with the others. It is difficult. The ss and Kapos are watching to enforce the rule of silence. From snatches of conversation I learn that fitter and mechanic are the best jobs.

We work: an incessant toing and froing. I have no idea why we are gathering stones. I suppose contractors will come to take delivery of them. Is it uneasiness, uncertainty about our fate? My stomach is knotted, and I am not at all hungry. The menu is not sumptuous: coffee made from barley, a roll and margarine. Lunch and supper: soup that is almost clear. A day's ration: nine ounces of bread.

I touch my watch, my 5,000-franc note and my two rings, all buried deep in my pockets. Scenes from films pass through my mind's eye. As we have come outside the camp, it must be possible to escape from this shit-heap. I imagine the various barriers to be crossed once past the cordon of ss, which circles the quarry. I think of the dogs, then of the words of the guards: 'No one escapes from Buchenwald.' As will be seen, I was not to have the time to transform my dreams of escape into reality. There was only one man, as far as I know, who succeeded in escaping from Buchenwald: my friend Pierre Mussetta. It was on 19 June 1944, nine months, almost to the day, from that morning when I was only dreaming of escape . . .

# Chapter Seven

# MUSSETTA'S ESCAPE

Pierre Mussetta was a force of nature. Of medium height, with dark hair and skin, his voice was gravelly. He became a rare legend in his own lifetime.

A career officer in the Foreign Legion, crack-shot, judo champion, familiar with both long-range combat and hand-to-hand fighting, he ran into danger with the ease that others go fishing. Nerves of steel and an exceptional willpower helped him to thwart disasters; he thought before acting. The SS traders in horror and infamy were no match for him.

In January 1944, with Ascher, he attacked the law-courts at Sète. On 14 February he broke into the hospital at Blois, where Yvette was being held – she was the wife of Guy Bernard of the Fer national circuit who was killed, like Jean Moulin, by the Gestapo. He went through the church to reach Yvette's room. Guy Martin and Françoise, a young woman doctor who later became Mrs Seligman, accompanied him on this mission. After freeing their comrade they took her to a safe place near Vendôme; then they left for Montholon where they spent the night. They abandoned the car, which they had stolen in Paris before the raid, in a barn. Denounced by a film producer, they were arrested on their arrival in Tours and imprisoned in the town jail.

The Tours police chief received a reward of five million francs for their arrest. Geneviève, known as the Tigress of Blois, came for Mussetta after he had been captured. She tortured him. (Geneviève was shot at the Liberation. She paid the price for her fascination with evil, her craving to hear cries of pain, her torturer's vocation.) Curiously enough, Pierre Mussetta aroused the pity of a Mme B., though she too was a member of the Gestapo.

Perhaps she was sickened by Geneviève's excesses. Mussetta's lot improved. He was transferred to Orléans: to the barracks of Dunois where, by coincidence, he had been to officer school. Then he was taken to the Santé and to Fresnes. Then Compiègne, whence he departed on 14 May in the direction of Auschwitz. It was the convoy 'Fifty-three Thousand'.

After several days of purgatory, the wretched passengers arrived at Auschwitz. There, it was discovered that the convoy had come to the wrong destination. It should have gone to Buchenwald; German efficiency also had its mistakes; and after all, the human livestock was of little importance in the eyes of the ss.

In the wagon with Pierre Mussetta there were ten dead, and as many driven mad. It was atrocious. Auschwitz was not expecting this convoy and the camp authorities refused it. Then the ss decided that the trainload would be sent to the crematorium: alive or dead. That was the only solution they could think of. Happily, the Americans got wind of the matter. They warned the German authorities: 'If you exterminate these 1,700 deportees, we will shoot 1,700 German prisoners. . . .' For once the ss backed down. The convoy headed for Buchenwald with its load. You can imagine in what a state of physical and emotional disintegration the internees disembarked. . . .

The news of Mussetta's arrival at Buchenwald went round like wildfire. The camp resistance organization took care of him, in spite of his objections. Colonel Manhes stopped him from joining a Kommando with the men who had been part of his convoy. He was sent to Block 57. In spite of advice to be prudent, the relative safety of Block 57 and the advantages that the organization had arranged for him, Pierre wanted a change. It was impossible to reason with him. He was utterly bored. To be cooped up wrecked his chances. If he stayed in the camp he could not attempt to escape. He succeeded in joining a work Kommando and was taken to another block.

On 19 June 1944, Saint Peter's day, one month and five days after his departure from Compiègne, Mussetta was working as usual in the quarry Kommando. It was pouring with rain. The ss had covered their heads with tent cloth; the prisoners were dripping with sweat and rain. 'If I don't make up my mind, I shall go mad or die of pneumonia,' Pierre said to himself. He also thought that malnutrition would sap his strength if he waited too long. He watched the ss sentries who were, as usual, stationed all around the quarry: one every ten yards. He thought that perhaps the ceaseless downpour would put them off their guard – they were too busy trying to shelter from it. The sky was black, visibility almost nil, the rain diluvian. There would never again be an opportunity like this, he was sure of it. He decided to try his luck.

He managed to slip past the sentries without their noticing him. Was he going to achieve the impossible? He cut across a wood, straight ahead, in the direction of ... France.

Soon, his absence was reported; dogs and guards gave chase. Happily the rain erased his tracks. He suddenly sensed that danger was near. He threw himself into a river and stayed hidden under three feet of water, holding his breath until the very last possible minute. When he lifted his head to breathe there was silence. The ss had gone; their dogs had not sniffed him out.

In the evening he arrived in the region of Weimar. He came upon sentries who challenged him in German. He was shot at. He ran headlong into the night until he felt as if his head, lungs and heart would burst and that a clot of blood was lodged in his throat.

Luckily he came to a gardener's shed. He broke down the door and hid inside. He slowly got his breath back; the sensation of blood in his throat and mouth left him. He was not wounded. He decided to travel no more by night, but by day.

The Germans were in the habit of leaving work clothes and tools in their sheds. Pierre undressed, taking dungarees, a hat and a garden fork. In the morning he left. The fork resting on his shoulder, he looked like a farmer on his way to work. He stole corn and carrots from the fields. One day he killed a rabbit, another day a little wild boar, with well-aimed stones. He went into the woods, made a fire, and snared chickens with needle and thread. He had become as good a poacher as if he had been raised as one. The fight to live made him inventive.

In this way Pierre got as far as Solingen without too much trouble. He changed the tool according to the weather: a spade if it rained, a fork if the weather was fine. He stole them from huts....

He hid in a small hut outside Solingen. He was discovered there by German peasants who said to him: 'Don't go away, we'll bring you something to eat.' Pierre trusted them. It wasn't food that arrived, but a policeman. The policeman arrested him. It was eleven-thirty p.m. (Perhaps some found Germans who helped them.

I met only those who were accomplices in horror. They knew the existence of the camps, they saw the deportees emerge from the miserable convoys, and they were hand in glove with the SS. I saw children pretending to shoot us, with imaginary guns, when they should have felt only pity. Their conduct changed when they understood that the war was lost for them. Then they tried to seem sympathetic in the eyes of their future victors.)

Arriving at night in the deserted square at Solingen, Pierre could not accept that his adventure was over. He could not admit defeat. In spite of his exhaustion from lack of food and sleep, he felt his anger renew his strength. The German was walking behind him. Pierre turned and punched him in the stomach; the policeman doubled up with pain and received a kick in the face which knocked him out for the count. Pierre cleared off.

Time passed. Mussetta continued slowly but surely. The hardest stage was ahead – swimming across the Rhine. He had stolen a rabbit; as he was cooking it in the wood, he heard voices. He moved towards them, with the guile of a Sioux. He found a group of French prisoners of war. He introduced himself: 'I come from Stalag IA, Berlin. I escaped. I'm going to swim across the Rhine.' They dissuaded him: 'You're mad! It's too risky. Wait until morning. Take the ferry with us, it won't look suspicious.' They took Pierre into their Kommando. He washed, shaved – his beard had been a perpetual torment to him; it looked suspicious – and ate. The meal was a veritable feast after all those days in the woods, days of forced fasting when he had not been able to hunt. Then the French took him to a dance. Yes – a dance! Young girls and women were there. And he danced. He thought he must be dreaming.... It was the most astonishing night of his life.

In the morning, as promised, he took the ferry with his new friends. A fork resting on his shoulder, he arrived on the other bank of the river. Though he had so feared this crossing, which had seemed so difficult, he had cleared the obstacle effortlessly. He took his leave of those who had helped him, skirted round Cologne, and headed across the fields for Düren. He wanted to avoid Aix-la-Chapelle. He hoped he would not meet anyone. He followed the Siegfried line for over ten miles; the earth was still scattered with cartridges. Skirting Verviers, he reckoned he would arrive at Boissy-Boursus, a place about nine miles from Liège. There he had a 'letter-box' – a contact. The following day he covered sixty miles and reached his goal, and knocked at the door of Dizier, a member of the Belgian White Army.

Dizier couldn't believe that it was Mussetta who stood before him: he only knew him by reputation. The news of his arrest had even spread to Belgium, in Resistance circles. 'Pierrot was deported,' he said, 'You're having me on. You can't be he.' Mussetta gave names, details, explaining how he had escaped, and Dizier's fear and doubt disappeared. He took Mussetta to the priest who harboured him for two days – the time to take photographs, forge identity papers and organize his return to France. He had a warm welcome. Pierre again told the story of his escape in order to prove that one must never despair. He told them how to attack a patrol, how to survive in the woods, how to get food. After what he had been through, he was in paradise.

He left Dizier and his friends for Aussonne, near Charleroi: there the contact was the Van der Randens. They received him coolly. He was left in the kitchen, while the master of the house was served in the dining-room. He expressed his displeasure in no uncertain terms. Then they apologized and he was given a pleasant room. The rudeness was not repeated. The following day Mme Van der Randen took him across the border in a carriage and left him at Avesnes. He set off on foot again and arrived at Laon. Finding that the trains were disorganized, he went into a bistro.

He was asking the patron how he could get to Paris when an ss officer, who had overheard the conversation, offered to drive him there. There was a lorry waiting for him outside. Was this a trap? A twist of fate as he neared the end of his breathtaking journey? He could neither flee nor refuse without arousing the suspicions or annoyance of the officer. He accepted. And there he was climbing into an ss lorry! It was laughable, excessive, absurd!

Outside Meaux, they were stopped by an air-raid. It was terrible. Bombs were exploding all around the lorry. 'Am I going to die here, after that incredible journey across Germany, at the hands of the Allies and surrounded by the ss?' Mussetta asked himself.... Just as they were all about to throw themselves under the lorry, the attack ended. They were unhurt. The Germans invited him to eat with them. They set off again. A little later on, the ss put him down at the Place de la Nation. He shook a few hands and thanked them. He was in Paris on 5 August 1944, forty-seven days after leaving the quarry at Buchenwald! It was fantastic! His accomplishment

was unique: to escape from Buchenwald and return to Paris in an
ss lorry! It was an adventure not without its ironic side....

Mussetta's feat was so inconceivable that everyone was wary. Was
this really he? How could he have been able to escape from a concentration camp? Finally, gradually, Pierre managed to see people and
to convince them. They looked at him as if he was a visitor from
another planet.

Soon, Pierre Mussetta renewed his contacts with his circuit. His
deeds up until the Liberation of Paris are a chapter in the history
of the Resistance. Attacks on tanks, on German officers, sabotage
– Pierre was indefatiguable. A courageous man before his brief
deportation to Buchenwald, he surpassed himself after his return.
One would have said he fought for every man who suffered there,
those wretches whose lives he shared for a few weeks.

When Paris was liberated, his nerves gave way. He paid for the
strain of his escape, and for the ceaseless activity afterwards. He
went away for a rest and returned his old self: a hero who does not
wish to be reminded of his daily feats.

For the man who had escaped from Buchenwald, that particular
war was over. But, under the yoke of the ss, others were still barely
surviving or dying in terror, ignominy and desperate desolation ...

France was freeing herself; but in the camps, the industry of
death still fed its black smoke to the skies...

# Chapter Eight

# LAST IMAGES
# OF PENAL SERVITUDE

'Nobody escapes from here, except those who leave by the chimney.'
An SS officer is speaking. It is the conclusion of a speech that is
like a dog barking. We do not understand the reference to 'the chimney'. We are ignorant of the existence of the crematoria. The veteran
prisoners have said nothing to us on this subject. There are so many
things that we shall learn later. The number of victims of our convoy
for example: out of 1,070, 150 died on the journey. And 140 died
in the convoy of 4 September which left before ours....

It is October 1943, months before Pierre Mussetta's arrival at
Buchenwald, months before his escape. We are assembled on the
parade-ground. It is dawn. There is torrential rain; the clouds are
low, heavy, stagnant, the very atmosphere generating misery. Yesterday evening, we returned exhausted from the quarry. The officer
has explained that this roll-call will be longer than usual. There has
been an escape attempt. Let everyone realize, once and for all, the
impossibility of such an enterprise! Everyone would be punished
when one tried to escape. As for the fool who tried it, he would
die a horrible death. The interpreter translates.

Today, we shall remain standing for six hours. There will be those
who will collapse from exhaustion, unable to stand the cold, the
rain soaking them to the marrow. It is during these interminable
roll-calls that some deportees will succumb to illnesses which will
be fatal. Death's emissaries lay in wait for us at every turn.

We continued to discover the rules and caprices of Buchenwald;
the prison hair-cut, for example. Some of us had their hair shaved
in a line from centre forehead to nape, the rest uncut. This hair-
style was called *à la Strasse*. Others had all hair shaved except for

a crest. This style was called the '*Huron*'. It wasn't the whim of the barber. The leader of the particular block where the deportees were barracked decided. Doubtless it pleased him to make us look ridiculous. You take your pleasure where you can.

I also learnt that the ss called us the *Stücke* ('scraps'). We were already sub-human beings who answered to the calling of a number, who were only numbers, and now we had become 'scraps'.

I found out that the ss kept *Totembücher* – registers of deaths that we called the Death Books. I discovered that historians, much later, were right to doubt the Nazis' arithmetic. It was mostly during the transports that records of deaths were lost. If a convoy was shunted from one camp to another, the camp of departure noted the *Stücke* despatched, and the camp of arrival the *Stücke* still alive after the journey. Those who had died on the way were not mentioned on either register. There was no Death Book on the trains.

Among the German political deportees, there were some Czechs who held administrative positions at Buchenwald. Pierre Rozan, who slept in the bunk below mine, quickly realized that his perfect command of German would enable him to find a place in the system. An administrative post carried privileges and enabled you to help your compatriots – a trump card not to be ignored. Rozan could have won this position, as well as the chance of staying at Buchenwald. But he, usually so in command of himself, made one error. One day when he was working in the quarry, he heard one of the ss guards say to the Kapo in charge of the Kommando: 'Take thirty deportees and go and fetch fifteen bags of cement.' The Kapo picked out fifteen deportees and ordered each man to carry one bag. Before the zeal of this bastard could add to the men's suffering, Rozan turned to him and said in German: 'Whose side are you on? The guard asked for two of us to carry each bag.' The Kapo was furious. He abused Rozan, upheld the order, and reported him. So Rozan was designated for Dora on 13 October 1943 – Dora, 'the Hell of all the camps' ...

Reveille at six a.m., stripped to the waist; hurrying to the barracks and the round sinks where we washed in icy water under the Kapos' eyes; dressing – without drying ourselves – in the dark and the cold; panting at work because of the meagre diet and the effort forced out of us; the grotesque and unbelievable scene in that monument called the latrines; vengeance against deposed Kapos: these are the images of Buchenwald which spring most often to my mind. And, of course, the long lines of men trudging up and down the slopes of the huge quarry....

The settling of old scores increased. The ss and the Kapos in service did not interfere. Sometimes, badly beaten, more dead than alive, the ex-Kapos were transported to the *Revier* (infirmary) to be cared for. There, the hatred of their former victims manifested itself again, without mercy: one jab, and that was the end of the life of this excrescence. One bastard less....

13 October 1943. . . . We have been at Buchenwald for twenty-five days. We are summoned to the parade-ground. Under orders, we have put on the striped uniforms given to us the night before. We know that the worst has happened. We are leaving for Dora. Those who have not been chosen to go – mostly long-term prisoners – watch us with intense pity in their eyes. They try to hide what they know of Dora, know intuitively and from those rumours that always reach prisoners, though no one has ever returned alive from that damnation. To be designated for Dora was equivalent to being condemned to death. The Communists who held Buchenwald try to keep back their own men; as for the others, too bad – when it's a matter of life or death, protect your own kind.

The ss officer reads the list. There are hundreds of numbers. These are the deportees of our convoy: Max Princet, Claude Lauth, Pierre Rozan, Louis Murgia, Pierre Clervoy, Roger Cinel, and myself. That's it! It's official! Fate has summoned us together! I think of my wife, of Monique, my daughter, who will be six on 23 November; I think of Pierre Roumeguère, my friend, who I imagine to be free. Will I ever see them again?

Lorries make up the convoy. Some draw two or three trailers in which we are crammed, standing. I stand beside a man of great physical strength and flexibility, Jacky the sailor. He is to become my friend.

The journey is chaotic. The ss man driving the lorry fancies he is on a race-track. Carried away by his fervour, he takes the bends at top speed. The trailers sway and swerve, and barely escape overturning; particularly those in third position. At every bend the ss roar with laughter. To see the deportees fall about against each other is a great joke. Roger Cinel suddenly finds himself hurled up against the windscreen of the driver's cabin, and it breaks. The lorry stops at once. Thinking that Cinel has attacked him, the driver wants to shoot him; happily, understanding German, Roger is able to explain and excuse himself.

The journey continues. We are still standing in the lorries and trailers, tossed about in every direction. On one bend, sharper than the others, the driver does not slow down at all. It is a miracle we do not overturn. We all fall over. Once again, the convoy stops. 'Sit down!' shrieks the ss man. Rozan replies, 'It's impossible, there's not enough room.' – 'You don't want to sit down? All right, we'll see!' The driver goes to his cabin and returns with a cudgel. He hits out at heads, shoulders, arms, at random. He froths at the mouth and is bathed in sweat. Finally, under the blows, everyone sits down. Of all solid bodies, there is none more easily compressed than the human body....

We are on the floor, sitting on each other's knees, clutching our painful and bloody limbs. The convoy continues on its way. We arrive at Dora sitting down.

# Chapter Nine

# DORA

Dora, Dora
a dog, a cat
name of flower or animal?
Whatever she is,
how happy we shall be
to leave Dora.

*Daniel Primet*

The setting-up of the camp of Dora and its annexes is part of the history of the development of the German secret weapons and the bombing of Peenemünde.

*Reichsführer* Heinrich Himmler had always dreamt of an ss empire. The hazards of the Russian campaign – 'the deplorable Stalingrad affair', according to the ss – forced him reluctantly to postpone the hour when his blond Aryans would colonize the world for a thousand years, in model farms served by castrated sub-humans, the *tchernoziom* Slav. Until this could come about Himmler, as Albert Speer reports, 'wanted to turn the concentration camps into large modern factories – especially for armaments, with the ss continuing to have direct control of them' – a prelude to 'an economic empire extending from raw materials to manufacturing'.[1]

The bombings of the Ruhr had radically modified Adolf Hitler's opinion of the effectiveness of the A4. As early as 28 June 1943, Himmler rushed to Peenemünde. In the officers' mess of the secret base, he berated Dornberger, Wernher von Braun and their scientists until four in the morning with political diatribes: 'The Führer thinks and acts for the benefit of Europe. ... Stalin is a new Genghis

Khan.... The blood of Tartar conquerors flows in the veins of the Russian leaders', and so on.

The following day, 'the great thinker' attended the launchings. The first was a failure: 'All I have left at my command are hand weapons,' Himmler would have said sarcastically. The second missile, on the other hand, took off perfectly in a cloudless sky. 'Caught off balance by the sheer grandeur of the launching and by its brilliant triumph',[2] the *Reichsführer* reacted as good ss leaders should: he began immediately to tie together all the tenuous threads which would lead him to such a fine prize.

'Peenemünde will belong to the German people,' he had proclaimed to Dornberger in April 1943. 'I will protect you against sabotage and treason.'

Dornberger did not show much enthusiasm. Unmoved, loyal to the traditional army, he refused to join the ss with his arms and missiles. They showed their teeth at once. Dornberger's adjutant, Colonel Zanssen, the base's commanding officer, was dismissed and Himmler himself began to bring pressure to bear on Hitler to achieve his obsessive ambition: 'an economic *konzern* dependant on the ss.'

The A4 would be its finest fruit.

In the eyes of the ss, Adolf Hitler had one single fault; he did not always accord the visions of his 'faithful Henri' the interest they deserved, particularly when they were fiercely opposed by another of his disciples, the former architect, Albert Speer. Not that Speer, on the subject of the ss empire, displayed any outdated humanism. As a good technocrat, he hardly appreciated the 'visionary spirit' of the *Reichsführer*. He claimed *urbi et orbi* that: 'We had had certain dismal experiences before the war with such ss projects, which had promised us bricks and granite.'[3] The concentration-camp labour that the *Reichsführer* lent to German industry was not always as lively as Himmler claimed. The factory managers of efficient Germany went as far as to complain 'that the prisoners arrived in a weakened condition and after a few months had to be sent back, exhausted, to the regular camps'.[4]

The bombing of Peenemünde was to silence Speer permanently. It proved beyond doubt that the classic militarists of the Wehrmacht and their associates in private industry were incapable of keeping the weapon which would save the Reich a secret.

'God help us if the enemy finds out!' Hitler had said. 'In this project we can only use Germans.'

Alas! Not only was Peenemünde – where the pilot factory for the v2s was to have been set up – practically razed to the ground, but the private establishments for the mass-production of the missiles were also attacked by the Allied air forces. These were the Zeppelin factories of Freidrichschafen and the Rex factories at Weiner-Neustadt. They also suffered devastating bombing.[5]

The ruins of Peenemünde were still smouldering when, on 22 August 1943 at eleven-thirty a.m., Himmler arrived at Hitler's HQ in the 'Wolf's Lair' in East Prussia. Diplomatically, 'the faithful Henri' was less surly than usual. He came to offer Speer 'his help'.

'He proposed,' the Minister of Armaments relates, 'to guarantee secrecy ... the simplest way. If the entire work force were concentration-camp prisoners, all contact with the outside world would be eliminated. Such prisoners did not even have any mail.... He offered to provide all the necessary technicians from among the prisoners.'[6]

Unable to offer a 'more satisfactory arrangement', Speer, the technocrat, was tempted. Having learnt from unhappy experience, Hitler in his turn renounced his dream of missiles made entirely by Germans and ordered that 'utilizing to the full the manpower which he has available in his concentration camps, every step must be taken to promote both the construction of A4 manufacturing plants, and the resumed production of the A4 rocket itself.'[7]

Thanks to the bombing of Peenemünde, Himmler's grand design began to take shape; the miraculous missiles would be exclusively built by the ss and their slaves.

Though a 'visionary', Himmler was, as Speer himself admits, a 'perfectly objective realist', and the man he chose to effect the construction of the rocket factories was an excellently-qualified representative of his Black Order.

Aged forty-two, born of respectable bourgeois family, with a distinguished academic record, the *Brigadeführer* ss Kammler was the director of the ss construction services and, as such, responsible for those 'architectural marvels' of Auschwitz, Treblinka and Maidanek. He was also responsible for the development of an innovation: the gas chamber. As blond and cold as Reinhardt Heydrick

– they were both physically and intellectually in the same mould – this former officer of the engineers had served in the Air Ministry. He was, according to Speer, 'a cold, ruthless schemer, a fanatic in the pursuit of a goal, and as carefully calculating as he was unscrupulous'; this did not prevent Hitler's Minister of Armaments from admitting that 'at the time ... I rather liked his objective coolness'.

An ss officer of that stamp was not the man to waste time. As early as 26 August, Kammler proposed to Dornberger and Speer (Wernher von Braun does not seem to have been present at this meeting) that they build factories for their missiles at a site as secret as it was romantic – the Harz Massif, in the centre of Germany. In these deserted valleys, near the town of Nordhausen, seventy miles west of Leipzig, an immense network of tunnels and galleries ran through the hill of Kohnstein. For centuries, sodium sulphate had been excavated there. In 1938, Ammoniak, sister company of I. G. Farben, had taken an interest in it. That same year, a government firm, the Wifo (*Wirtschaftliche Forschungsgesellschaft* – Company for Economic Research) was ordered to store motor fuel there in preparation for the war. Kammler suggested that the whole place should be enlarged. He would instal, in the tunnels – a guaranteed shelter from Allied bombs – assembly lines directed by one of Speer's collaborators, Alben Sawatski, Hentschel 'Tiger' tank production expert.

On 10 September, from his 'Wolf's Lair', Adolf Hitler approved the creation of this subterranean complex of factories and decided to give it the name *Mittelwerke* – Central Works.[8]

We, the deportees from France, Belgium, Holland, Italy, Czechoslovakia, Hungary, Yugoslavia, Russia, Poland and Germany, were to know these subterranean prisons by another name, the melodious code name chosen by the Nazi concentration-camp rulers: Dora.

It was barely eleven days since the British had bombed Peenemünde. Hitler had wasted no time in making a decision.

Nothing was ready to receive the deportees; no equipment, however basic. The 'B-tunnel', the only one dug, was nothing but an immense oblong cavern, not bricked at all, too low for the use the Germans now envisaged for it. The secret weapons, the v2s, were to be produced here. The underground factory had to be built very quickly, all intact or repairable machines from Peenemünde had to be transported and new ones installed.

Two administrations were to run Dora. One was the special office

for the production of the v weapons. It brought together the scientists and major technicians. The other was the *Rüstungskontor
GmbH*, placed directly under Speer's control. This second group
had financial responsibility for the project. In November 1943 a new
firm, the *Mittelwerke GmbH*, had the right of inspection of the production of v weapons at Dora. Construction and drilling of tunnels
was directed by ss *Konstruction*, under Hans Kammler.

After 1 November 1944, when Dora ceased to depend on Buchenwald and became an independent camp, it was called Mittelbau KL.
The three principal camps were Dora, Ellrich and Harzungen.
There were, altogether, thirty-two annexed camps. The octopus
spread out its tentacles right in the centre of Germany.

The first 100 deportees arrived at Dora on 23 August 1943, the day
after the meeting between Hitler, Himmler and Speer. From that
day onwards, the steady stream of convoys from Buchenwald unloaded their human cargo, before other camps – because of the with-
drawals of German troops – added theirs. There were no installations in the first tunnel, except for a few scattered tents and a wooden
sentry box for the ss guards. The missile slaves worked ceaselessly
in fear for their lives, terrorized by the sadistic ss and Kapos. In
the beginning, they drilled, expanded and fitted out this tunnel
almost without tools, with their bare hands. They carried rocks and
machines in the most shocking conditions. The weight of the
machines was so great that the men, walking skeletons at the end
of their strength, were often crushed to death beneath their burden.
Amonia dust burnt their lungs. The food was even insufficient for
lesser forms of life. The deportees toiled for eighteen hours a day
– twelve hours of work, six of formalities and controls. They slept
in the tunnel. Cavities were hollowed out: 1,024 prisoners in hollows
on four levels, which stretched for 100 yards.

The deportees only saw daylight once a week at the Sunday roll-
call. The cubicles were permanently occupied, the day team following the night team and then vice versa. Very faint electric bulbs
lit this nightmarish scene. There was no drinkable water. You had
to make do with any water you could find, for example where con-
densation formed. You lapped up liquid and mud as soon as the
ss had their backs turned, for it was forbidden to drink 'undrinkable'
water.

The cold and damp in the tunnel were intense. The water that oozed from the rock caused a disgusting, permanent clamminess. Chilled to the bone, we felt as if our emaciated bodies would go mouldy. Some prisoners went mad, others had their nerves shattered as the installation progressed: the constant din was one of the causes – the noise of machines, of pick-axes, the bell of the locomotive, continual explosions, and all of it echoing mercilessly in the closed world of the tunnel. No heat, no ventilation, not the smallest pail to wash in: death touched us with the cold, the sensation of choking, the filth that impregnated us. As for the latrines, they were barrels cut in half with planks laid across. They stood at each exit from the rows of sleeping cubicles.

Often, when the ss spotted a deportee sitting on the plank, they would stare at him, laugh, go up to him and roughly push him in the barrel. Irresistible! Never had those gentlemen laughed so much. Particularly as all the deportees suffered from dysentery.... Then, covered all over with shit, the poor fellow, more despairing than ever, would crawl back to his hollow; back to infest his friends, to roll in the dust to clean himself, there was no other way. Germany, the cleanest nation in the world, exemplary for its hygiene, provided nothing for its regiments of slaves. Conditions of animal care in its farms are even said to be an example to the world, but to them a deportee was a lesser creature than a cow, a pig, a chicken, a worm feeding on that chicken....

It was at Dora that the deportees began to understand the silence of the old men of Buchenwald, their looks of compassion at those who were leaving. They knew, those old men, that you only return from Dora dead. And you return dead to feed the fires of the crematorium. For in the beginning there was no crematorium at Dora. They transported the corpses, and those that were not yet quite corpses, by lorry to Buchenwald. There were Kommandos for this task who stacked up these things which had once been men, under the orders of ss men with Gummis (electric cables encased in rubber) who hurried along the work.

Whatever the job, it had to be done quickly. That is the rule in countries which use slave-labour. It did not matter that deportees died of ill-treatment and exhaustion in the first months of their detention. Others were there to take their place.

The ss beat the detainees without mercy. Everything must be sacrificed to achieve the goal. The fate of the Third Reich depended on it. They threw themselves zealously into the role of persecutor, surpassing even themselves in barbarity. The number of victims? Not important! What a sight there was each morning when the ranks of those we unkindly called 'the Muslems' would present themselves at the tunnel exit to ask for a medical examination. With the appaling odour of putrefaction emanating from their decaying bodies, they hoped for a help that would not come. They died there in despair, without even the strength to beg for mercy, and the Buchenwald crematorium lorries came to take them away. The corpses were piled up endlessly, the numerous arrivals replacing those who died, before giving up their lives in their turn.

It was not until March 1944 that the barracks were completed. At Dora, the work was as terrible as ever, but we could at least leave the tunnel for the six hours of rest allowed. At Ellrich, however, at the other end of the tunnel, where the work had begun later and was not as far advanced, the deportees suffered the same conditions as in the first months at Dora.

In January 1945, new SS officers and soldiers came who had been evacuated from Auschwitz. The assassins did not interrupt their work. Some surviving Jews were also arriving from Auschwitz, some as early as September 1944. After a few days work in the tunnel, one of them spoke these words to me, words which I can still hear distinctly: 'Compared to Dora, Auschwitz was easy!'[9] Conditions reverted to what they had been at the beginning. As the Russians and the Allies advanced, the Führer's HQ wanted to speed up the work and research, so that the absolute weapon might yet change the course of the war.

Two tunnels, nearly 2 miles long, 14 yards wide, 10 yards high; forty-six parallel tunnels 220 yards long, some dug deeper to cater for the manufacture of the V2s, but mostly 30 yards high and used for the testing and assembly of the immense V2s which weighed over 13 tons and were 16 yards long; railway lines which linked the two tunnels, and rejoined those of normal services on the outside; stores of V1 flying bombs and V2 rockets in most of the parallel tunnels, with the exception of the north section which were used by the Junkers company for the manufacture of aeroplane engines; construction from August 1944 onwards of three other tunnels to the north-east and west of Kohnstein and in the Himmelsberg, near Woffleben, because the Germans required even more space to make liquid oxygen, synthetic petrol, a new unknown rocket baptized 'Typhoon' and referred to as the A3 and A9 (each of these tunnels had five parallel tracks, and eight to ten transverse tunnels completed the construction); and much more that I, a little mole buried in the bowels of the earth, could not have discovered. Eighty per cent of all this was built by starving, suffering, weak and despairing men, from 23 August 1943 to 11 April 1945, the blessed day that the American troops liberated them. In the meantime, they succeeded in sabotaging the Nazi death machines, ensuring that the V1s and V2s stayed on the ground or exploded in the air, well before reaching their targets.

Sixty thousand men were deported to Dora. Thirty thousand did not return.

# Chapter Ten

# THE FIRST DAY'S WORK
# IN HELL

'No matter the number of human
victims, the work must be executed and
finished in the shortest possible time.'

> *Brigadeführer* ss *Kammler*
> *to one of his subordinates who*
> *drew his attention to the*
> *horrible conditions suffered by*
> *the deportees at Dora*

We arrive at Dora during the evening of 13 October 1943. Roll-call is organized immediately. The six hundred and fifty deportees of the convoy are lined up. An ss officer reviews us. He roughly questions one man in four. He asks, in German: 'How old are you? Why were you arrested? What is your profession? What qualifications do you have?' Those who can, reply in German. The others explain in French. A deportee translates.

The ss officer questions a student from Versailles. He must be about seventeen years old. The boy does not answer. The officer becomes angry. Rozan, standing next to him, is acting as impromptu interpreter. 'And what about you, what did you do?' the officer asks Rozan. 'I was arrested at Clermont-Ferrand for acts of resistance.' Does his reply displease the officer? Did he find Rozan's manner insolent? He tells the soldier accompanying him to take down Rozan's number: 21161. The inspection continues. Rozan is disturbed. At Buchenwald it had been emphasized that you must not make yourself conspicuous if you wanted to survive. And here he was, on the very first day, in the notebook of an ss officer. Rozan, usually so circumspect, even secretive, was often rash simply to help a friend.

Roll-call over, we are sent into a cave down a little wooden staircase. To the right is a wooden barrack. It serves as the guard room. The ss are housed there. You cannot enter or leave the cave without passing the guards. The cave is immense, poorly-lit, twenty yards high. A locomotive travels ceaselessly around it, propelled by diesel. The driver is ringing a bell; the sound pleases him for he never stops. Much later that bell will haunt our few hours of rest. The railway track crosses the cave.

We go in. I wonder where destiny, in the green uniform of the ss, is leading us. After a hundred yards, we turn off to the right. The ground is not levelled; we descend into the darkness. The path takes us into another cave, through a small opening. The darkness gives way to the feeble glimmer of electric bulbs. We see that this cavern is to be our dormitory. We can make out bunks, positioned on four levels. There are ten bays. I am reminded of the tunnel in Fritz Lang's *Metropolis*, not a reassuring recollection. There is no escape today, even in imagination.

We return to the parade-ground. Soup. A vile gruel. I am amazed at the brutality of the cooks and Kapos supervising the distribution. It is a foretaste of what is to come. Dora was run by Kapos wearing the green triangle of common criminals, the worst of all. I was to see prisoners beaten to death by those Kapos for mild misdemeanours like, for example, not having understood an order given in German. I was to see the ss revel in these executions, then in a trance beat up any prisoner they came across. I have not forgotten a single one of those sadists' faces.

The next day, reveille at six a.m. We had found it difficult to sleep – the uncomfortable bunks, the humidity that literally froze our bones, the fear bred in that sinister, primeval place. Hostility on all sides. I am attached to Kommando Sawatski 4.[1] We transport all sorts of things – railway tracks, planks for the building of barracks, machines. We take the goods to the far end of the tunnel, where there is a station and railway. The machines arrive there. They are unloaded and put onto the little train.

We learn that these machines come from Peenemünde. We learn that the ss High Command has decided to install a factory in the cave to build secret weapons, weapons formerly made at Peenemünde. We also learn that the cave has to be shaped into a tunnel and other galleries have to be excavated. We, the moles, in the darkness, in the silence, came to know it all, by who knows what magic.

This first day is terrifying. The Kapos and ss drive us on at an infernal speed, shouting and raining blows down on us, threatening us with execution; the demons! The noise bores into the brain and shears the nerves. The demented rhythm lasts for fifteen hours. Arriving at the dormitory as the Kapos hurry us along with blows, we do not even try to reach the bunks. Drunk with exhaustion, we collapse onto the rocks, onto the ground. Behind, the Kapos press us on. Those behind trample over their comrades. Soon, over a thousand despairing men, at the limit of their resistance and racked with thirst, lie there hoping for sleep which never comes; for the shouts of the guards, the noise of machines, the explosions and the ringing of the bell reach them even here.

21161 is called for. Pierre Rozan's number. What awful thing is about to happen to him? Is he to pay for a peccadillo? I watch him as he prepares to go. What can I say? ... I learn later that he has been appointed Schwunk[2] to the ss camp commandant – a sort of valet, a Jack of all trades. I know he is unhappy about it. Most of the ss want the camp to be under the domination of the German common criminal deportees. They did not like to see a resister or political prisoner in an important position; and it was an important position that Pierre had taken, without wanting it. Of the political prisoners, only the Czechs were accepted because they all spoke German and – poor fellows – they had been deported longer than the other foreigners. Rozan feared that the Kapos and camp ss might harm him. But he did well in his job; when the camp commandant changed, he kept his place until the Liberation. And it was excellent for us that one of us had 'done well'. He was able to help us.

With extreme prudence, for he was closely watched, Rozan could sometimes give us a little food or information or act as a link in the beginnings of a resistance movement. His privileged position allowed him to sleep outside the cave. He slept in a barrack with the German Kapos who ran the camp. Thus, through his spontaneous intervention during roll-call, Rozan had been able immediately to improve his lot. Doubtless the ss officer had seen that he spoke German as well as he did French. 'One night,' he told me, 'I heard the most awful cries. I wondered what was happening. I was forbidden to leave the barracks. The Kapos told me that a young Frenchman, driven mad by thirst, had drunk some of the fuel used for the v2s. The boy was dying in terrible agony and no one would help him or put him out of his misery.... And that boy,' added Pierre, 'was the student I had helped the first day, at roll-call....'

The man in the bed next to Rozan was Kuntz, former Communist Deputy in the Reichstag. He had been a prisoner since Hitler's rise to power. Kuntz was *Bauleiter*, chief of construction for the camp. He was a remarkable man, very wise. He befriended Pierre. Kuntz' post was decisive; from nothing he had to build a full camp at Dora.

Through Kuntz, Rozan was to gain information, and information could come in useful....

# Chapter Eleven

# THE NIGHT OF THE MOLES

> Yes, how well we know
> one day we'll die in Dora.
> As the months go by
> months of work without pause
> under the bastards.
>
> *Anonymous poem*

We have to dig to enlarge and widen the tunnel. Scaffolding is erected. Day and night, the noise of the pick-axes is deafening. The locomotive's bell never stops ringing. The ammonia-filled dust from the explosions barely lets the weak light filter through from the electric bulbs. The Gummi blows rain down. 'Los.... Los....' Faster ... always faster.... The tubs stink. The men stink. The tunnel stinks.

Some deportees are too weak and collapse. They have dysentery. They foul their trousers. They no longer have the strength to sit over the barrels, even to get to them. The ss beat them. The blows are useless, they do not get up. They will suffer no more. Those who know in their hearts that they too are almost at the end of their tether watch in silence. Will they be the victims tomorrow? Soon? ... The 'Muslims' try to reach the queue for medical examination. Will they get a *Schonung* ticket for twenty-four hours' rest? Are they already fit for the crematorium? Woe betide the man who is turned away, not ill enough for the infirmary Kapo! His days are numbered. The Kapos in the tunnel will work him until he drops. As if we are not being driven to our deaths already! Often there are no mess-tins. Food is scarce and they cut down the number of rations. The total number of men does not increase, in spite of continual new arrivals.

I work. In the chaos, I try to think. Rozan's example spurs me on. We must find ways to get out of the tunnel. Roger Cinel speaks German. He should be able to get out, become an interpreter. If this hell goes on we wouldn't have the strength to try anything. I look at the men around me. Who will still be able to fight if the time comes? Who can be counted on? We must quickly get some of us to places where death is not lurking at every turn. But how? What physical state shall we be in tomorrow? Next week? In a month? A month! Shall we still be able to think or shall we only be conscious of our poor bodies and the sufferings they have to endure?

One deportee astonishes me. That is Jacky the sailor, whom I had first met in the trailer taking us to Dora. He had been an acrobat in a circus and had knocked about all over the world, amongst all kinds of people. I had already seen evidence of his courage. The day after our arrival at Dora, some Kapos were mercilessly beating two young Frenchmen in the dormitory. Jacky could not bear to see it. He ordered the Kapos – yes, ordered them – to 'stop mistreating those kids'. One of the Kapos, who was in his element, stopped, put on an angelic expression and said, in the deceptively sweet tone Germans use in films when about to deliver some awful threat:

'Certainly, sir ... you will beat them instead. Give us a rest. And if you don't, you'll get it yourself.'

He smiled. Jacky refused. He quickly threw a punch at the Kapo, who, taken by surprise, went down. Another Kapo joined in. Jacky, who knew how to defend himself from his experiences of street fighting, butted him with his head and the Kapo collapsed. To a man, the other bastards leapt on Jacky. He was driven into a corner. Murgia, Cinel, Princet, Lauth, Clervoy and I, and several others, ran forward to stop the carnage. Jacky cried out:

'Don't move! Don't join in! Keep out of it!'

Jacky took his 'punishment' without flinching.

Later on, the Kapos appointed Jacky the sailor to the transport of the dead and the dying. He was the *Totenträger*. At first on his own, soon he was in charge of several others attached to this horror Kommando. Their task consisted of taking the corpses and the sick,

and loading them onto hand carts. They went to collect those unfortunates who lay helpless on their bunks or in the tunnel. They
pushed the carts to the barrack near the *Revier*. The dying were
carried into the infirmary. The dead were heaped up in the barrack
on a pile of bodies. Every other day, since the Dora crematorium
did not yet exist, a lorry arrived from Buchenwald to collect the
bodies. Two Russians had the job of taking the corpses from the
barracks (sometimes the dead were left outside, if there were too
many) and, one holding the head and the other the feet, they threw
them into the lorry. The lorry was covered with a tarpaulin. There
were between fifty and one hundred bodies in each load. The heads
or feet could be seen sticking out. Much later, when the crematorium was built at Dora – a sign that the camp had become
autonomous! – Jacky the sailor took the martyrs there directly. The
crematorium Kapo put them into the oven and kept a register. The
lorry of the dead did not return.

Jacky, usually so talkative, never spoke to me of this terrible experience. Some memories are not easily passed on. We all were victims of, and witnesses to, vile and horrifying deeds. To whom can
we ever fully convey what it was like?

16 October 1943. We have been at Dora three days. Claude Lauth,
Max Princet, Pierre Clervoy and I are unloading goods. A young
*Rottenführer*, an ss corporal, appears. He is slim with broad
shoulders. He stands about 5 ft 7 ins high. His hair is brown, his
face tanned. This is our first encounter with Karl Multerer. I shall
never forget his sardonic expression. Alas! In spite of all our searching, we have never found him again.

This strutting corporal finds a little eighteen-year-old Frenchman lying against a pile of sacks of grain. Exhausted, he has fallen
asleep. Somehow the young man senses he is being watched: he
wakes, gets up quickly and goes back to work. Multerer goes into
a demented rage – he should have been in a mental hospital, in a
strait-jacket. He hurls himself on the young deportee. Frothing at
the mouth, he beats him with his Gummi, accompanying each blow
with harsh cries. Then he reassembles our Kommando and an infernal dance begins. He makes us carry the sacks on the run. Fatigue
and hunger have weakened us so much that the sacks seem heavier
than ever. They are piled up at the entrance to the gallery in a heap
five yards high. They have to be deposited in a niche in the tunnel.

Running with the sacks on our backs, Multerer beats our legs. As we run back, Multerer uses his Gummi on our heads and shoulders. This frenetic, insane, nightmarish ballet seems to me to be interminable. The running, carrying, beatings, running back ...

Suddenly, at the height of this furious frenzy, I say to Clervoy, who is running behind me: 'I shall go crazy. I'm going to kill him. I'll get his gun.' 'Don't be a fool!' cries Pierre. Multerer hears him. He rushes at him and beats him. Could this swine have had a mother? Is he made of human flesh? The little Frenchman, who was the cause of this saraband, collapses. His fall distracts Multerer's attention. He abandons Clervoy to devote himself to his prey. He beats and beats him. When he stops it is long after the boy's last movement. The corporal is covered in sweat. He must have enjoyed himself, his trousers are wet. With a grin on his face, he turns on his heel and disappears into the gallery. Calm is restored. We turn to the victim: he is drenched with blood. He was a hairdresser. He will never do anyone's hair again. He is dead. But we had much more to suffer from the murderous fury of Multerer....

We are exhausted, completely dehydrated: Claude Lauth pierces a hole in a pipe – it is a water pipe. We rush to drink. It is forbidden to drink in the tunnel; SS orders: the water is undrinkable ... We don't care...

I am tall, still fairly strong, but I am going to lose what strength I have. Fatigue saps the will. If one day the chance to escape or to hide should arise, would I still be able to take advantage of it? Swift action would be vital.

Pierre Rozan is trying to arrange for Roger Cinel to be an interpreter too. We must blaze trails wherever we can. This hope helps me to withstand the vice-like grip of despair which threatens to crush us all....

One Sunday, I go to the latrine near the guard room. Next to me is a man of my age, wearing a doctor's armband. His triangle shows that he is French. I see that he is number 20000. So he had arrived two weeks before I had. We chat. His name is Déprez. He is also a dentist. I ask him:

'Is there any way of getting a job in the infirmary? I was in the medical service in the navy.'

He answers me roughly:

' Are you stupid, or what? Do you think they need you when

there are real doctors, Poles, Czechs, Russians working in the tunnel. And they only want to be nurses! Everyone wants the nursing jobs. No ... there's absolutely no chance.'

I sense that Déprez is really sorry that he cannot help me. His rough manner is, under the circumstances, a sort of defence. We continue to talk. I like him very much. I had had to ask. I owed it to myself and to the others to ask everyone, try anything. Our survival depends on it.

Our work, arduous as it is, is nothing compared to that of the deportees who work with the pick-axes. These slaves of hell are perched on scaffolding ten yards high, enlarging the tunnel. I wonder how, with their strength weakening from day to day, they are able to hold their tools, especially since they have to hold them at arm's length above their heads. From time to time, exhaustion or the weight of their tools becomes too much and one falls to the ground. A cry, a thud, that is all.... Another man takes the victim's place.

Every morning, there is the long cortège of the dying. They drag themselves to the tunnel-exit in the hope that they will be taken to the *Revier*. Their haggard eyes blaze out of their drawn faces. They are nothing but skin and bone. Ravaged by tuberculosis. When I was a child, I was afraid of getting TB and here I am, surrounded by men coughing and spitting blood.

Time passes. Every day that goes by diminishes the possibilities of survival. I have hardly been at Dora two weeks yet I feel I have been here for an eternity. I always try, for the benefit of my friends, to seem full of hope. There are some subjects barred from conversation. To speak of food, of good meals we had enjoyed before disaster struck, is the worst. Mouths fill with saliva, stomachs begin to churn and cramps add to our misery. As for women, we are too weary to even think of sex.

And yet one good thing happens. Rozan has been successful – Cinel has become an official interpreter. That cheers me up! If we can only gain positions like that, our time will come. I imagine myself strangling Multerer.

One afternoon, we are transporting machine-tools. We are unloading a transformer with the aid of a little crane. With a friend, I am standing behind the transformer, which weighs about 1,000 pounds, to keep it balanced. The taut crane cable suddenly snaps. The arm rebounds like a spring and strikes the man at my side – Armand de Dampierre. He is thrown to the ground with his ribs broken. I stand alone; the transformer, off balance, threatens to crush me. I cry out. My friends run to help me. What a narrow escape. My legs are trembling. We go to help Armand. Thinking of him prevents me from dwelling on my own fear.

As for Armand de Dampierre, carried off to the *Revier*, where he was badly cared for as usual, he was assigned to light duties outside the tunnel. He did not ever fully recover. On 3 January, with 999 other deportees, he left for an unknown destination. We never saw him again ... but I shall return to those abominable, evil transports of the one thousands. ...

At Dora, as often in other camps, the Russians shared an extraordinary brotherliness, which allied them against all the other deportees. Some reproached them for it; for my part, I understood them. Their government gave them no help at all. Other prisoners, Belgian, French, English, Polish, Yugoslav and so on, only became deportees by an infinitely rare concurrence of unfortunate circumstances; the Russians were treated like mad dogs, even if they had been captured in combat and were regular soldiers. The Soviet Union had not signed the convention of La Haye nor recognized the International Red Cross. Whether prisoner or deportee, the Russians received no parcels, no mail. Nobody ever helped them. Reduced to the status of hunted beasts, they behaved like wounded, starving animals. The Germans, ignorant of the fate reserved for their own prisoners, avenged themselves on their Russian prisoners. The latter, able only to depend on each other, fought like wolves at bay. They stole anything they could find, from any prisoner, of any nationality: never in my life have I seen such patriotic people. Only being Russian mattered to them.

One of their thieving tactics was as follows. When a deportee slept, they went up to his bunk. They chose bunks high up, on the third or fourth level. One of the Russians stood at the sleeper's head, another at his feet. The man at his feet pulled the cover away gently. If the deportee did not wake, his blanket disappeared. If he woke and by reflex hung on to his blanket with both hands, sitting up, the Russian at his head would snatch the bread which the deportee, like most, kept in his mess-tin under his head. Once a day we got a ration of 9 ounces of bread. There were two alternatives: to eat the bread all at once and have no more to stave off hunger for twenty-four hours, or to save some and risk having it stolen. Thanks to their cunning, the Russians won either way. They carried off either the bread or the blanket, sometimes both. The deportee cried out, but the Russians, a whole gang of them in case they met with any opposition, cleared off. We had arrived at Dora with two blankets each. At the end of a week, very few had even one.

The Russians also practised what we called 'the lightning attack'. Later on, some deportees received parcels. They were given what was left after the ss and Kapos had helped themselves. The parcel was handed over undone. The Russians, always in a gang, lay in wait in places where the tunnels were the least well lit. When the parcel owner passed by, they leapt out, knocking the package from his hand; its contents scattered on the ground. Like looters, the Russians fell upon the debris. The poor man might try to stop them, to defend his goods, attempt to catch hold of one of his attackers, but he always failed. They took it all and ran away.

At Dora, no Russian became a Kapo. That cannot be said of the Poles, who, though victims of the Nazis as we were, often became, in time, their accomplices. And what accomplices! They went beyond even their masters' wishes. I do not like generalizations. I have known other Poles who were irreproachable. But the memory I have of them at Dora is not a pleasant one.

One morning, I am assigned to a Kommando that is to work outside. The idea of leaving the tunnel, even for a few hours, is a joy. I am part of the *Transportkollonne*. We have to shift panels which will be used for building barracks. These panels weigh two hundred pounds apiece. There are four of us. I am the tallest and take most of the weight. At first, that amuses me. Stronger than the others, I am happy to make things easier for my friends. But, eventually, my fatigue is overwhelming.

That night after roll-call, before going back to the tunnel, I have a moment's happiness. I meet Roger Cinel and Jean Kopf, whom I have not seen for a long time. Kopf comes from Alsace and speaks German. He works for the Kapo in the Kammer, distributing clothes. Is it the exhaustion, the emotion of talking to friends, misery at having to go back into the tunnel? I weep. I cannot stop. I am embarrassed. I weep for about a quarter of an hour, with Cinel and

Kopf trying to comfort me. I have never wept as much in my life. It was the only time in all those months at Dora. I said to them: 'I've got to get out of that tunnel or I'll die.' Kopf said: 'I think they need engineers to build barracks. I'll try to get you put forward.'

I go back into the tunnel. It has eased me to cry like a baby but at the same time I am ashamed. I, who am always a life-buoy for my friends, and now my nerves have given way. Am I, too, going to sink, like those lost souls around me? They still move, but it is clear that the spark of life has left them. Nothing attaches them to existence any more. They have given up. When I try to help them with a word, they just turn their eyes towards me and the look in them is no longer of this world.

As always we have to fight our way through the narrow opening leading to our dormitory past the shift coming out, one more effort to add to our exhaustion. That evening I fall asleep thinking of Jean Kopf's words: 'I think they need engineers to build the barracks. I'll try to get you put forward.' I have eaten my bread. The Russians might come to steal the only blanket I have left. I no longer care. Kopf's words have given me fresh hope. Am I about to escape from this wretched tunnel? ...

# Chapter Twelve

# WE PICK UP THE BBC

One evening, after roll-call, Jean Kopf brings me the news: 'You're on an outside Kommando. As engineer. You're going to build barracks at Illfeld.' Since I have been at Dora, I have lived only on hope. Now hope has given me a real sign. In the dormitory Murgia, Princet, Lauth and Clervoy congratulate me. One more of the Compiègne team who has got himself out of the tunnel.

In the morning Cinel comes. He is the Kommando interpreter. There are forty of us. Illfeld lies seven miles away. The first few days, they take us there by lorry; then, to save petrol, we travel on foot. Sometimes, when we finish very late in the evening, they come to collect us – not to conserve our strength, but to avoid escapes.

Illfeld. November 1943. A little village surrounded by woods. It is beautiful. So there are still people living real lives in real houses? The autumn is magnificent. There are all kinds of trees, each turning its own shade of russet. A feast for the eyes. Is it the change from Dora to Illfeld? The prospect of spending a day out in the open and not in the dank cave? The sheer absence of noise? ... I shall never forget the colours of that autumn. Sheer enchantment.

On the platforms of a little station adjoining the camp are stored the various materials for building the barracks. Two gigantic ss men are waiting for us. One, as if to keep his muscles in shape, is playing with a cudgel bigger than a pick handle, as an accountant might play with a pencil. He asks:

'Who is the engineer?'

That brings me down to earth. I had never built a barracks in my life. I had had thirty-six jobs since I was twelve, when I had begun to earn my daily bread; but building barracks?: never. My last profession, before the war, was journalism. I edited an economics journal.

'Who is the engineer?'

'I am.'

'Get to work.'

All the necessary materials are lying there. I think hard for a moment, trying to give the impression of a person who knows what he is doing. Play for time, that is the thing to do. I order the Kommando to begin sorting the various panels, joists, rafters and planks. . . . I feel as if I am in a Charlie Chaplin film – with me as Charlie. . . . The only trouble is that the audience consists of the two SS men, who have more in common with Primo Carnera and Max Schmeling than the little civil servant who goes to the cinema on Saturday afternoons.

I am handed the plans, written in German. Roger Cinel translates. Unfortunately he does not know the technical terms. He prefers the German of Goethe to that of cheap builders. I fear the worst; but, with animal instinct, I decide to live for the moment. And this particular moment is the autumn, the colours, fresh air and relative silence instead of the stench, gloom and racket of the tunnel. And besides, an engineer's pencil is a lot lighter than carrying the machines.

We sort the materials for two days. The SS site foreman becomes impatient. He insists that we begin the construction right away. After questioning my Kommando companions, I surround myself with men who know something about building. There are only Frenchmen in the team. Two of them claim to be carpenters. 'Saved!' I say to myself over and over again, to dispel my anxiety.

On the third day we begin to build the barracks. Quite quickly, we lay the floor. For forty-eight hours, we work on the panels and the carpentry. By the evening of the sixth day, the barracks are up.

On the seventh day we walk the seven miles from Dora to Illfeld and – catastrophe! The barracks are still standing, but completely awry, as if a Florida hurricane (a very gentle one) had blown during the night and given it a dangerous slant. I rack my brains; we must have forgotten to put up the wind-braces. It is too much for me: I want to laugh. The films again. What a joke. . . . But the SS foreman does not see it in the same light. He cannot have seen any American comedies.

'*Wo ist der Ingenieur? ... der Ingenieur? ...*' He shrieks fit to burst every blood vessel in his body.

'I am.'

I run up.

'Sabotage! Sabotage!'

He brandishes his immense cudgel. He swings it around his head. I try to stand out of its range. The desire to laugh has gone. I see myself dangling from the gallows – the accusation of sabotage is that serious. The foreman launches himself into a tirade of which I understand not one word. I say to Clinel:

'Idiot. You're the interpreter. At least tell me what he is saying!'

What Cinel tells me makes my blood run cold. I explain to Cinel that the building lacks wind-braces, that German technical terms have hindered our work and that he should assure the lout that we would sort it out right away.

Cinel translates this. The foreman orders him to help me. And there we are, Cinel and I, each at one end of a joist, darting every which way in order to avoid cudgel blows every time we pass our guard. In spite of our ducking, contortions, side steps, running and stopping short, the blows find their mark. Breathlessly, I say to the rest of the Kommando: 'Let's all do it, we must straighten this thing.' And, miraculously, we do. Once again, the barracks are upright.

When it is done, we have still to complete the fitting out, with the ss plying their cudgels to keep us on our toes. That morning there blew over Illfeld a wind of optimism. We were euphoric! We will all get out of the tunnel! This interlude was like a whiff of oxygen. . . .

In the Kommando, there is a pimp from Marseilles. I do not know why he was arrested. He has one peculiarity: he hates water. He can neither drink it nor wash in it. He is an odd fellow. Thanks to his allergy, his feet are disgustingly dirty, encrusted with a half-inch of filth. The ss have made him the cook. At Illfeld, he is the one who prepares their food. In revenge for being there, he soaks his revolting feet in the soup pot. Every meal eaten by the ss, he first infects with his feet. 'I'm giving them a few germs to kill them off,' he says to me. One day, one of the giants catches him rolling a sausage along the ground with his feet and spitting on it. All hell breaks loose. The guard picks him up like a wisp of straw and throws him out of the window. Hardly has he hit the ground than the giant is there, trampling on him and beating him. The pimp never recovered from this punishment for his attempt at revenge. A few days later he died, totally uncared for, without the least help to ease his suffering.

One evening when I return to the tunnel, I hear that Jacques Déprez is asking for me. I go to find him.

'There,' he says to me, 'I've done it.... I've had you made a dentist.' He is delighted with himself. The surly man I met in the latrine that Sunday has vanished.

'Dentist! You're joking! You might have had me taken as a doctor, I could have bluffed my way through that! But dentist! You have to know what you're doing, to work with your hands: I know nothing about it! Dentist! What a farce!...'

'Don't worry.... I'll be there.... It's my profession.... I'll show you ...' Déprez, as I have said, was both doctor and dentist. What was astounding was that he was doctor to the ss. Unbelievable though it may seem, it was he who examined the ss and declared them fit to leave for the various fronts or to stay in the camp.

When he was 'on form', Déprez was extremely cheerful. He was a man who could help others shake off their desolation. However, he also had days when, in the depths of despair, he became a prophet of doom. He would announce our impending death to whoever would listen to him: 'No one will leave Dora alive.' I tried to transmit to him my determination to live.

'But look around you, look at me, look at yourself; do you think the Germans will leave us to be witnesses for posterity?' he would reply.

His lapses didn't last long. He was as often on the crest of the wave as wallowing beneath it.

I saw Déprez play with fire and laugh until he cried at his own reckless impudence. During medical consultations, I heard him say, with a big smile, to the ss men he was examining: 'So, filthy pig, you're not feeling well? But you're fine, you bastard' – tapping them on the shoulder – '*Gut* ... absolutely fine.... It's a good season for shits. ... Bravo! ... In excellent health' – with a beatific smile – 'Well, you madman, off you go to defend your country out there in the snow on the Russians' doorstep.... It's an honour. A great honour. What terror you'll strike into their hearts! Ah! You'll make them all run. Your turn to suffer now. Good lungs, good heart, good legs. Away with you, you filthy bastard.... *Gut, gut....* Next.... Send me another stinker, I'll pack him off too....'

I had difficulty keeping a straight face but I also remembered the ss man who had advised me, in street French, to hide my watch on my arrival at Buchenwald. I warned Déprez:

'Shut up. One of these days you'll get one who can speak French and you'll find yourself on the gallows.' It was one of his good-humoured moments; he laughed at my warning....

So I become a *Zahnartz* (dentist) in mid-November 1943. We fit out an ss barracks and install instruments, drills and chairs. Nothing is missing; the surgery is faultless. I get to know another man who has been appointed dentist, a very dark man with jet black hair and a week-old black beard: Georges Croizat. He and a young Belgian, Albert Defroy, had escaped the bombing of Peenemünde. They arrived together at Dora on 28 October 1943. Croizat tells me of the raid and the extraordinary bravery and precision of the British pilots. 'Hell was falling from the sky. I'm still wondering how we escaped alive. They say the RAF lost at least 300 planes in that one operation.' We like each other on sight. Georges is a Basque. A deportee's thinness has not detracted from his lively, nervy agility. As we set up the dental surgery we discover some crusts of bread in a saucepan. A godsend! A feast! We know the ss have a passion for spitting in the pans. What does it matter! You have to have known hunger to know that nothing can be refused. We share out those crusts as if we are sharing the finest delicacies! I suddenly realize with amazement that I am longing for fat, though I have never liked it!...

Every time a little peace comes to this awful place, I am filled with nostalgia. How is my daughter; how is she growing up? And my wife? Have the Gestapo arrested her?... Claude Lauth has achieved the impossible: he has kept with him a photo of the woman he loves.... I have nothing.... Please God she too is not in a camp! ... At the end of October we are given permission to send our families our address and prison number on a postcard. On 5 November 1943, still on the same type of postcard, we are allowed to write at greater length. Will I receive a reply?

A new arrival wrenches me out of my melancholy: René Laval. 'No relation to the president of the Council,' he announces as an introduction. He comes from la Beauce. If Georges Croizat is a dental technician, Laval is a real dentist. 'And I have a practice in le Loiret,' he says. 'But back there I wear a white coat. I don't work in striped pyjamas.' René Laval has a cold sense of humour. He is also sometimes very disconcerting. I saw him slap patients because he was having difficulty extracting a tooth. 'I'm going to have to control myself. This holiday at Dora is driving me crazy.'

There is one other deportee attached to our surgery. A Czech dentist, Otto Cimek – there are four of us, like the Musketeers. Cimek was born in Prague. He was arrested in 1942. He has already experienced the ignominy of Auschwitz. He only knows a few French words. I am beginning to speak broken German, and a bit of all the languages used in the camp. We manage to make ourselves understood.

My role consists of questioning the men who come to the surgery and making out the index cards. In the beginning, this service was intended for the ss. Soon the ss only came in the afternoon, the morning being devoted to the deportees.

The fitting out of the dental surgery is supervised by *Unterscharführer* (ss Sergeant) Lorenz. He speaks to us roughly, arrogantly. He is forty years old. It takes us a few days to realize that Lorenz is an exception. For the ss we are *Stücke, Untermenschen*; but Lorenz lends us his razor, and asks us what we did before we were deported. Cimek is an officer in the Czech army, Laval a medical captain in the French army, and I a commander in the health service (quarantine service). Our ranks impress Sergeant Lorenz. (After the attempt on Hitler's life in July 1944, Lorenz will be sent to the front. The ss will shoot him for his anti-Nazi attitude.)

It is Lorenz who introduces us to our boss, *Oberscharführer* ss Michaelson, the ss adjutant who was a dentist in Oldenburg. He reminds me of Fernandel: long head and huge teeth. He is tall. His sang-froid will astonish me on many an occasion. His room adjoins the surgery. Always stretched out on his bed, he leaves us to do all the work.

23 November 1943. Monique's birthday. She is six. It is to be a memorable day. Michaelson leaves his room for Croizat to clean it and make the bed. Croizat takes advantage of this to turn on the

*Oberscharführer's* radio and tune in to the BBC. What an event! From now on we listen to the BBC every day. A historic date! I know that never again, for even one second, will I lose hope. I become resolute. We are no longer alone against the ruthless, unnatural SS! A voice in London tells us what is happening: the advance of the troops, the aerial superiority, the activity of the Maquis, the rout of the conquerors of Cherbourg!

Solitude is inventive. The hermit imagines more than the satisfied man. Look at de Sade in his dungeon, look at the priest, or the chaste old woman always ready to 'battle with evil' – their chastity fills them with wild sexual fantasies. As for us, destitute, abandoned, unhappy, we thought only of the war, of troop movements, of the victories of the men who must save us: the Allied armies, the Resistance.... Our imaginations flowed free. News took the place of the deportees' dreams. During the day, it spread like wildfire. Sometimes the news was optimistic: the Allies had landed, they had crossed the German frontier, tomorrow they would be here: the Russians were disguised as the SS, they were infiltrating the camp, tomorrow they would free us.... Sometimes the news was catastrophic.... But now we knew the truth we would be able to pass it on to our friends. Prudence was essential. When giving information, we were never to reveal its source. There were many informers in the camp.... If we were discovered listening to the BBC or spreading news, we would be hung.

While we keep Michaelson busy, Croizat, behind a paper-thin partition, continues to listen. He is to continue until the end.

# Chapter Thirteen

## ... AND STILL THE HUNGER
## AND THE FEAR

▬▬▬▬▬

But I have defeated hunger,
I shall hold out 'till the end
In the ice, in the mud ...
Dear God! I want to live too
not to die too ...

*Anonymous poem*

My new job as a dentist gives me the most envied of privileges –
sleeping out of the tunnel. I have a bunk in Barrack 14. That is
where the two doctor/surgeons for the deportees sleep. One is
called Ernst Schneider. His profession – stone mason. The other
– a stove-setter – is called Karl Schweitzer. They are German political deportees. They have been interned since Hitler seized power.

One evening, I assist at a surgical operation. Schneider and
Schweitzer are 'treating' a deportee for a purulent inflammation.
Without anaesthetic, without hygiene, without medicine, they open
the back of his right hand. The patient screams with pain. In his
eyes is the mournful and amazed look of a beast that cannot understand why he is suffering. To keep him quiet and put him to sleep,
Kapo Schneider hits him on the head. Medieval anaesthesia.

I cannot explain the very adequate fitting-out of the dental
surgery and the absence of even the bare essentials in that 'operating
theatre'. It is true that the dental surgery was intended for the ss,
but the deportees were allowed to use it. The Germans were often
disconcerting. One morning, for example, two mobile x-ray units
arrived at Dora. Ultra-modern. For three days doctors x-rayed
every single deportee. They took thousands of plates. We never
heard another word about this visit.

Schneider and Schweitzer, having absolutely no medical knowledge, usually kill those they operate on. The bandages are rolls of
paper. To be admitted to the infirmary you have to be running a
temperature of 104 °F. Few ever come out.[1]

The head doctor of the camp is called Otto Plazza, a tall man with
a brutish face. He rides about the camp on horseback. His was the
only horse I saw at Dora. Plazza is very dangerous when he is drunk.
He abuses the deportees and refuses to certify them ill though they
are staggering, exhausted, shaking with fever and vomiting blood.
He persecutes them, beating them with his own hands. A vile man.
He terrorizes us.

Fear is the dominant feeling at Dora: fear of beatings, fear of
illness, fear of the cold, fear of death ... until this last seems a welcome deliverance.


End of November 1943. Two young boys, aged perhaps about
twenty, are standing near the ss guard house on the slope leading
down to the tunnel. The wind is icy. They are two brothers, the
Belins. They have tried to escape. The ss have beaten them severely
and left them there for forty-eight hours: forbidden to drink, eat
or move. Did they die? We never saw them again....

One evening Pierre Clervoy brings me sad news. In the tunnel,
a deportee I had known at Compiègne has been beaten to death
by the ss. He had not understood an order. Charles Frémeaux had
been a major. He had worked in intelligence and lived in Boulevard
Saint-Germain, Paris. He had told me his life story. A warm,
friendly person. His body, beaten to a pulp, had been taken to the
*Revier*. Two days later the lorry came to fetch him. He went up
in smoke at Buchenwald....


We take full advantage of our position as dentists. That is the
law of the camps: those of each nationality who make it help
their brothers. Croizat, Laval and I hand out cards stating that the
deportees we examine must return for treatment. Thus they
can leave the tunnel for a few hours; the pit-ponies can come up to
the surface.

After negotiating with the cooks, I manage to obtain soup; a five-
gallon can every day. We share it out. There are plenty of clients
for the new dentists.

Claude Lauth often comes for a share of the soup can. He gives it to the men in his Kommando, which works outside the tunnel. He is very friendly with a deportee called Gadroy. This Kommando is mostly composed of Russians. (Later, during a quarrel, in another place and under different circumstances, the Russians were to attack Lauth and break his leg.) Claude looks like a tramp. He is dressed in a tattered pair of striped pyjamas and a torn winter coat. His face reminds me of a Mongol's. With his shaved head, his bulging high forehead, his small eyes, his round face despite near-starvation, he makes me think of Charlie Chan. He does not really look like him, but that is what I call him.

Since the Cherche-Midi I had thought only of escape. Any possibility of this was completely dependent on our physical condition, so my objective was to discover the means that would enable us to 'last'. The aim was to build up a team of trustworthy men from among those who had been friends from the start.

I thought of Déprez' prediction. When they saw that they had lost, the Germans would blow up all the camps and massacre all the deportees. They would not leave a single witness, a scrap of proof of their wickedness. They would lose the war. We had always known it, and now the BBC lent support to our convictions – the Allies were advancing. But we also learnt that Himmler had given orders to wipe out the inmates of the camps. Were we going to let ourselves be exterminated? The idea of starting an organization with the object of ensuring our survival, and harming the Germans, took shape.

Claude Lauth and I met one evening with Clervoy, Laval, Croizat, Rozan, Princet and a new friend, Doctor Maurice Lemière. We decided to keep in contact. Information obtained by one man could help another to find the weak link in this evil system.

Lauth, with amazing courage, was to leave the external Kommando where he worked, and go back to the tunnel. He used this catastrophe to initiate sabotage of the missiles of the Third Reich. In the worst possible living conditions Claude fought on – an exceptional man.

In February 1944, Doctor Jacques Déprez disappeared. He had taught me how to handle the instruments and the rudiments of dentistry. I could hold my own and be of use when Laval or Croizat asked me to treat a patient. Where was the Doctor? I learnt that he had been sent down into the tunnel. There he saw some Russians who had stolen potatoes from the ss and, as they were in the habit of doing, were cooking chips in motor oil. Déprez was hungry: he copied the Russians, and, still in the tunnel, he made some chips to a recipe that I do not recommend to anyone. An ss guard caught him in the act. 'Theft, sabotage,' he cried. Déprez spoke German; he was unruffled:

'Listen. I am a doctor. I often treat men with dysentery. I am trying to find out how they get it. I discovered that some deportees are cooking potatoes in motor oil. I thought I'd try it out myself and observe the results.'

The guard made his report. Déprez lost his post as doctor (Maurice Lemière replaced him). He became part of the *Strafkommando*, or disciplinary Kommando. Déprez did not stay there long. Intelligent and cunning, he got himself sent to Harzungen, with an external Kommando of which he became the doctor. He stayed there until the final evacuation of the camps. I rediscovered him at Bergen. Happily for me! But that comes much later.

I am in the infirmary in Barrack 14 where I sleep. As usual, there is a pile of corpses. (As I write these lines, where I want to tell not my own story, but that of all those martyrs at Dora, I wonder how I was able to survive that misery and, why not admit it, get used to the ever-present sight of death.) In a few hours the lorry from Buchenwald will come and those poor men will soon be nothing but calcium dust. On the pile of dead bodies is one which is completely naked. He has been shot in the head. A Russian. He tried to escape. The ss fired at him, stripped him and threw him there, thinking he was dead. He is brought, with others, to the corpse barracks. As it is full, he is left outside. The following day, just as he is about to be flung into the lorry, that naked man, who has spent the night in a temperature of less than 50 °F, sits up. Blood is clotted on his neck, head and face.

At Dora the inconceivable happened every day. This phantom is carried to the *Revier*. He is operated on in conditions that can only to be compared to the early days of surgery, and he recovers! I do not know if he lasted until the end. He may have been executed with the other Russians at the time of the mass hangings of January 1945. On 3 November 1944 – almost a year after his resurrection

– the day of my arrest in the camp, he was still alive. I saw him. I shook his hand.

2 December 1943, I at last receive a letter from Suzanne! She is safe! Monique is well! A flood of joy and emotion fills my heart. So the Gestapo have not arrested her after all. I long to jump for joy, to sing, to weep, but I keep my delight strictly to myself so as not to waste it or spend it too quickly. It must be savoured very gently, kept as the miser keeps his gold. I shall read this letter hundreds of times. I feel filled with immense strength. I am invulnerable. In the evening when we friends meet after roll-call, I feel as if I give them a transfusion of enthusiasm and hope.

A week later, a great commotion. Official cars arrive. The ss control becomes even more rigorous. They beat us twice as much and inspections are scrupulous. As always the rumours spread. Russian deportees in counter-espionage are dressed as German officers, they have escaped bearing the secrets of the v2s, the Allied armies have parachuted thousands of men who are approaching the camp, Hitler is dead.... It is only much later that we learn that German minister Speer had come to inspect the tunnel and see how the installations were progressing.

This was not to be the only 'official visit of inspection'. I remember the fuss on 25 January 1944. That time it took me more than twenty years before I knew the name of the visitor: Wernher von Braun.[2]

# Chapter Fourteen

# WERNHER VON BRAUN

If you have a taste for collective
massacre, but your own skin is precious
to you, become a scientist my son.
Today that is the only way to commit
murder with impunity.
  Nowadays to be a warmongering
politician is not a safe profession. If you
lose, they will hang you. If you are a
defeated General, you will go to prison;
but if you are a scientist, you will be
honoured, whichever side you were on.
Your enemies will covet you. They will
fight among themselves to have you,
without giving a thought to the number
of their compatriots you might have
killed.

*J. Joesten, The Nation*

In his memoirs, Albert Speer describes his visit to the extensive underground installations where the V2 was to be produced:

In enormous long halls prisoners were busy setting up machinery and shifting plumbing. Expressionlessly, they looked right through me, mechanically removing their prisoners' caps of blue twill [!] until our group had passed them.... The conditions for these prisoners were in fact barbarous, and a sense of profound involvement and personal guilt seizes me whenever I think of them.[1]

The official report is even more explicit:

On the morning of 10 December, the Minister went to inspect a new plant in the Harz Mountains. Carrying out this *tremendous mission drew on the leaders' last reserves of strength. Some of the men were so affected that they had to be forcibly sent off on vacation to restore their nerves.*[2]

General Walter Dornberger, Professor Wernher von Braun and the Peenemünde scientists must have had steadier nerves and stronger stomachs; from their pens can be found no allusions to the deportation camps or any concentration camp work-force. It was left to Speer, judged and condemned at Nuremberg, to reveal his feelings, and with a sentimentality that came rather too late. The conquerors of space were not about to tarnish their glory with such sordid details.

Let us take the example of Walter Dornberger. After the war, this general became a missile consultant to American aviation and vice-president of important companies in the US Aero-Space Industry, before enjoying a peaceful retirement in Buffalo He published the story of 'his life's work' under the title v2 *Der Schuss ins Weltall.*[3]

Though lacking literary talent, the general has an extraordinary memory when it suits him. He can recall his conversations with Hitler verbatim. 'In my life,' the Führer said to him, 'I have had to apologize to two men only. The first was Field-Marshal von Brauschitsch; the second man is yourself.' He remembers Himmler's every word. He dwells heavily on his dealings with SS Kammler and the services of Speer. If Germany did not win the war, it was because, he writes, of the 'lack of vision and lack of understanding of the leaders of the Reich'. The enthusiastic father of the v2 sings the praises of Wernher von Braun, Walter Reidel, Ernst Steinhoff (the head of guidance and control), and his assistant Helmut Gröttrup: 'young, enthusiastic and steadfast scientists, engineers and technicians in the most varied fields and providing scientific and technical installations on a generous scale, we successfully tackled, in isolation from the "dynamic of events" around us, problems whose solution seemed to lie far in the future.'[4] But the ardent soldier succeeds in the extraordinary feat of never once pronouncing the name of Dora, or even of *Mittelwerke.*

Here was a man who, according to historian David Irving, commanded 'the whole rocket programme, from factory to firing site'.[5]

Here was a militarist who himself specifies that he asked General Fromm, on 31 May 1944, that 'I be given unequivocal authority over the whole project from research to field operations.' Here was a peaceful pensioner who, having failed to prevent Kammler's rise, agreed to become, on 30 September 1944, his 'representative' in matters of research and providing the special units with missiles, which, as he says himself, 'enabled me to remain at my post'.[6] And yet, this matchless technician, this futuristic warlord was totally ignorant of the conditions of work on the missile for which he was responsible, a missile which was – remember – 'his life's work'! Forgive me, but even after so many years I cannot quote these extracts, repeat this calm insolence, this voluntary amnesia, without feeling anger and indignation!

If you wish to follow with what passion the researches at Peenemünde were conducted, if you wish to discover how 'with eyes filled with horror' Dornberger watched the bombing of 'his' secret base, if you wish to know everything about the way the missiles were tested at the SS practice ground at 'Heidelager' at Blizna in Poland, or how the special launching sites were built (Hitler wanted large sites which were later destroyed at Watten and Wizernes by the Allied Air Force: Dornberger, with good reason, preferred mobile platforms), you should read the V2s' father's own account. But you will soon make a sizeable discovery – there were miracles in the heart of Hitler's Germany, for there is not one word about Dora. The A4 was created by the intervention of the Holy Spirit. At the very most, Dornberger mentions – three times in four hundred pages and in a roundabout way – that there was an 'underground factory'. Modesty prevails. Or shameless cheek! The V2 was the 'Immaculate Conception' of the Third Reich.

The present generation of historians are not men to be believed. I read their books avidly to discover their conclusions. The result is edifying. It proves that silence pays whatever the nature of the crime. The old adage 'never confess' can be applied to even the most common crimes – those against humanity.

Michel Bar-Zohar is an Israeli, and as such more sensitive than others to the horrors of Nazism. In his book, *The Hunt for German Scientists*,[7] he claims to have seen survivors, questioned them, and consulted their own notes. He speaks of the 'laboratories at Peenemünde', of the 'fabulous factory at Mittelwerke', but he says not a single word about the deportations and nothing about Dora.

David Irving is English. He is, without equal, the greatest expert on the major military confrontations of the Second World War. His book *The Mare's Nest* is a haunting account of Hitler's secret weapons. It was written with reference to English and German archives. The technical and historical details he provides are of such value that they are quoted by Speer himself. Nevertheless, this master too avoids the cursed and evocative name of Dora. He contents himself with describing the 'factories of *Mittelwerke* and Nordhausen'. From time to time he refers to exhausted workers and 'slave labour'. When, twice, Irving mentions the presence of 'slaves' and 'convicts', we the deportees of Dora consider it to be insufficient.

Has the British historian been victim of a systematic falsification of the documents made available to him? As for the declarations made to him by German scientists and technicians, they are only a semblance of the truth. Sometimes a shell appears very beautiful although the interior is crawling with worms.

To read from the pen of a historian of his class that the *Mittelwerke* factory was 'constructed by *Waffen* ss labour battalions' is evidence of a sickening falsification – as sickening as the evidence of the flourishing streets of the new Germany where the mark is king. In short, the supreme fraud has been successful. Von Braun and Dornberger have perpetuated their lie: the hell that was Dora and the missile technology cannot and must not be connected.

Let the specialists on the deportation write their hearts out about Dora![8] Let them expose, in slim confidential pamphlets, the sinister reckoning of their dead and their sufferings! Their tiresome race will fortunately soon die out. While a few words are devoted to their mass graves, and fewer all the time, you may be sure that military historians, film-makers, and all those devoted to the popularization of science will be free to exalt men who, as Dornberger put it, 'tackled one of mankind's great tasks' and, 'proud of our technical achievements' had 'pointed the way to the future'.[9]

James McGovern is an American historian. In minute detail, he has reconstructed the operations of the Allied Special Services against Hitler's secret weapons. His approach is different but equally instructive.

A former Allied Intelligence officer, McGovern questioned the

US army officers who liberated Nordhausen and organized the departure of the German scientists for the United States. Brigadier-General Truman Boudinot was part of the US 3rd Armoured Division in Patton's army. He had crossed the Rhine at Remagen and wiped out the resistance of fanatical SS officers and their troops on the borders of the Harz. He was one of the first to enter the charred ruins of Nordhausen. Boudinot, according to McGovern, was driven into the concentration camp. There he saw 'hundreds of corpses lying out in the open and hundreds more in the barracks ... half stripped, mouths gaping in the dirt and straw; or they were piled naked, like cordwood, in the corners. The stench of decomposing bodies filled the air. Some living beings, ragged skeletons covered with skin, weaved and tottered forward.... Through interpreters, the two colonels heard that the skeletal figures wanted the Americans to know about "something fantastic ... underneath the mountain ... important ..."'[10]

Armed with as terrifying a testimony as this, James McGovern, unlike David Irving or Michel Bar-Zohar, was unable to see '*Mittelwerke*' or 'the factories of Nordhausen' as abstract entities of advanced technology. The dialectic by which he arrives at reconciling missiles and deportation is, however, as fascinating as the silence of General Dornberger.

Once again I beg the reader to excuse me here for entering into some details that are a little fastidious. If he has done me the honour of following me on my descent into hell, I am sure he will understand my motives. I have eaten too much of the dust of that tunnel not to continue to eat it and make a meal of it. Those who lived through the depths of Dora will soon disappear. There are few survivors. I must tell what I know. I must condemn the deception, the voluntary omissions, the untruths. I have a horror of grandiloquence. Yet I consider my decision to be a sacred duty.

According to McGovern, *first*: if there was a crime, it rests at Kammler's door, as he 'had organized and directed the use of concentration-camp labour in v-weapon production'.

*Second*: the concentration-camp labour was not the very essence of the SS empire of the *Mittelwerke*. It was only a subsidiary, almost incidental, element. 'German experts from Peenemünde, the universities and private industry directed production, assisted by some three thousand German technicians [let us note, in passing, the fine involuntary admission of the participation of the irreproachable

German experts!] ... The heavy labour was done by non-Germans. Kammler supplied the *Mittelwerke* with six thousand slave labourers from the nearby Nordhausen and Dora concentration camps.'[11] (Who is he trying to fool? These camps, in fact, existed solely to feed the tunnels. And it was not six thousand, but sixty thousand deportees who passed through Dora.)

*Third*: the deportees did not, in the final analysis, have so much to complain of: 'At the time (when the "*Mittelwerke*" were working at full steam) the prisoners had been *relatively well treated*, but *conditions* had deteriorated in the last two months,[12] especially at Nordhausen, which housed thousands of political prisoners and other "undesirables" who had not been assigned to v-weapon production.'[13]

Reading these lines, I was inclined to set little value on McGovern as a historian. I felt as angry as when I read from Dornberger's pen that von Braun and his consorts 'were using vast and perfectly conceived installations'.[14] It seemed to me scandalous that a historian who had himself fought against the Nazis could establish, for example, a subtle relationship between the ill-treatment and 'political prisoners and other "undesirables" who had not been assigned to v-weapon production'. Does one really only know about the events one sees oneself? Where did McGovern, a serious man of repute and integrity, find his sources?

My question was answered by McGovern himself. His sources are the declarations which von Braun and Dornberger made to him. All is explained. The fraud continues! The greatest scandal of all time! With one object – to conceal the truth! *Arbeit mach freie*, 'Work makes you free', we read at the gates of Buchenwald. Macabre humour knows no limits. And von Braun and Dornberger, through McGovern, still have the audacity to dish up a version of Nazi propaganda that an elementary sense of justice ought to make stick in their throats. Abandoning for a moment my personal experience, I shall let the American Public Prosecutor speak. Charged with trying the Dora executioners he, for one, did not rely on the testimonies of von Braun and Dornberger. He made investigations and established the facts for himself. His report is damning; a far cry from the cover-ups of the two scientists:

On the 1st November 1944, Dora became, on account of its importance, an autonomous camp with thirty-one sub-camps or

dependants. This was the beginning of the most atrocious period
in the entire existence of the camp. In January 1945, new guards
and officers arrived from the extermination camp of Auschwitz,
which had just been evacuated. These born criminals were the
cause of the deterioration of already appalling conditions. Dora
became a hell even more atrocious than before. The mass hangings began. Up to fifty-seven deportees a day were hung. An
electric crane, in the tunnel, lifted twelve prisoners at a time,
hands behind their backs, a piece of wood in their mouths, hung
by a length of wire attached at the back of their necks to prevent
them crying out. All prisoners had to watch these mass hangings.[15]

'Living conditions' says Wernher von Braun's spokesman.
'Dying conditions' would be more appropriate.

In January 1945, at the very moment when the murderers from
Auschwitz were flocking to Dora, the advance of the Red Army also
forced the Germans to evacuate Peenemünde. Now finally, Dornberger, von Braun, Reidel and Gröttrup could no longer pretend
to be archangels seated at timeless drawing-boards on the far-off
shores of the Baltic. The deception spread.

'Early in February,' writes Dornberger, suddenly laconic again,
'the move began. My own staffs also moved ... to the southern
slopes of the Harz Mountains near Bad-Sachsa.'[16] Wernher von
Braun is just as discreet. Certainly the presence of mind with which
he chose to carry out the order to withdraw to 'the centre of Germany' rather than kill himself on the spot – such things were not
uncommon at the time – is admired by his biographers. The guile
he deployed in decorating lorries, trains and materials with the fictitious, meaningless initials VZBV[17] to make the army roadblocks believe that the evacuation of the scientists was 'a top secret undertak-
ing ... ordered by Himmler himself',[18] forms a part of the myth-
ology of the man who lived with his head in the stars but nonetheless
out-did those 'great fools', the ss. On the other hand, the destination
of the convoy is still more mysterious. The scientists ended up, says
McGovern, 'in villages scattered around Nordhausen, with the
largest number in *the cotton-mill town of Bleicherode*', while Dornberger installed himself in 'the hot-springs of Bad-Sachsa'.[19]

'The Harz Mountains,' adds the American historian, 'were an

area of wild and melancholy beauty, of ravines, crags, dark green woods and snug little towns with ancient, half-timbered houses.'[20]

Romantic valleys. Scattered villages. Bleicherode ... Sachsa.... The American Public Prosecutor is more down to earth: the two names of Bleicherode and Sachsa figure amongst the thirty-one sub-camps of the Dora complex....

'Hot-springs resort?' A curious description. Deportees of Dora, you did not know how lucky you were! ...

Having arrived at this point in my attempt to dig up history, I do not wish my intentions to be misunderstood. I do not claim, as certain of my comrades have done, that Wernher von Braun was present at the mass public hangings of 1945; to us, the sub-humans of Dora who saw the bodies of our friends hanging above the machines in the tunnels and the workshops, nothing looked more like one well-nourished and self-confident German, than another fat and dominant German. I do not claim that von Braun, Reidel, Gröttrup or Dornberger personally brutalized deportees. I am even sure that the German scientists would have preferred to see their marvellous missiles made in more civilized factories and by a better treated work-force. They probably deplored the delays that our technical incompetence and our physical condition – not to speak of our sabotage – caused their programme.

I claim only that Dornberger, von Braun, Gröttrup and all those lumped together conveniently as 'the Peenemünde scientists', knew perfectly well what crimes were being perpetrated at Dora. Many fellow prisoners saw them in the tunnel and in the workshops. I claim that even before their final absorption by the sponge of Dora, in January 1945, the mass-production of a prototype which was far from ready necessitated a permanent contact between the researchers at Peenemünde and the executors at Dora. From conversations with present-day French missile experts and armaments engineers, I am convinced that it would have been absolutely impossible to produce the v2 without Dornberger, Wernher von Braun, Reidel, Steinhoff and Gröttrup maintaining constant contact with the technicians and work-force.[21]

What Speer saw, those men saw; what the civilians observed, they observed too.

Kurt Meister, inhabitant of Niedersachswerfen, testifies: 'One morning in the summer of 1944, I saw a transport arrive of detainees in open trucks who were headed for Appendore to work there. In the evening, when they returned, the trucks were filled with the dead and partly with the living who were dumped onto the ground for the evening roll-call. . . . An ss guard loosed his dog on the survivors and then forced the detainees to pick up the dead and carry them to the trucks. All this time, the Fascist dealt blows with his truncheon to the bodies of the detainees carrying the dead and set his dog on them. These facts,' specifies Kurt Meister, 'were known by the workers employed in the galleries.'[22]

And I claim that these facts could not have been unknown to Walter Dornberger, Wernher von Braun, Helmut Gröttrup and other scientists (including von Braun's own brother, Magnus) responsible for gyroscope mass-production at Dora.[23]

I do not reproach these men with not having made public confessions after the war. Speer's tears, the fuss and attention given to his memoirs – is 'dignified silence' really so out of fashion? – do not please me much and can do nothing to give life back to my dead companions. I do not hold it against the scientists that they did not choose to be martyrs when they discovered the truth about the camps. No. Mine is a more modest objective. I make my stand solely against the monstrous distortion of history which, in silencing certain facts and glorifying others, has given birth to false, foul and suspect myths.

When an otherwise most remarkable work, written by an author of repute in a prestigious collection, *Pourquoi la Lune?* by Jean E. Charon, offers France an evaluation of the conquest of space, it includes an enthusiastic chapter on the history of the v2. Such enthusiasm is usual in a work of popular science, but the substructure of the concentration camps is never mentioned.

When Hollywood decides to transform von Braun's life story, with the aid of the American defence department, into a Western, in which, despite a few tinges of conscience, the scientist appears practically innocent, I can only be indignant. This film – *I Am Aiming at the Stars* – is the more harmful because it is extremely cunningly made. But it is full of lies, passing straight from the bombing of Peenemünde to the Liberation, as if the interlude of Dora had never existed.

When Wernher von Braun's *Space Frontier* was published in France, the writer of the preface sang the praises of the 'father of astronautics' and, carried away by his lyricism, stressed the author's 'profound and benign sense of humanity'. Sense of humanity! It was as I read this that I decided once and for all to overcome the irresistible horror that Dora still instils in me and to write this book. Our consumer society has made for itself the heathen idols it deserves. Journeys to the moon ought not to force the sufferings of man on earth into oblivion. Though I risk disappointing the new science-loving generation, I conclude this perhaps austere, but in my opinion indispensable, chapter with two more passages.

The first is quoted by Michel Bar-Zohar from an article written by an atomic scientist:

> Scientists are the mercenaries of modern warfare. Almost wholly devoid of humanitarian impulses, they consider their cold and analytical search for scientific knowledge more important than any current affairs of mere mortals.
>
> If a scientist is given a chance to pursue his line of research unmolested, he doesn't care about the type of government he is working under, or the condition of the people, or anything else. Science is the thing, not people.[24]

The second is by Dornberger himself:

> ... I had made rockets my life's work. Now we had to prove that their time was come, and to this duty all personal considerations had to be subordinated. They were of no importance.[25]

Thirty thousand died at Dora. They were considerations 'of no importance'.

# Chapter Fifteen

# DREAMS OF ESCAPE

> They gave you a woman's name – 'Dora'
> You should have smoothed our furrowed brows,
> They gave you a woman's name – 'Dora'
> To deceive us once again
> 'Dora' – You were a woman of stone
> Thousands and thousands died in your arms,
> Thousands cursed your name
> Your breath was so cold,
> Your smile carved in ice,
> Your kiss deadly poison.
>
> *Stanislas Radimecky,*
> *Czech deportee at Dora*

Our lives as dentists continue. There are changes. A small annex to the infirmary is installed in the tunnel. I have to go there to fetch the patients. They are grouped in Kommandos and flanked by Kapos. As I pass the guard post I announce the number of men I am taking to the surgery.

Some of the ss amuse themselves by striking out at me with their Gummis. These men are definitely made up of a biology and chemistry all their own....

Beyond the prison camp, there were the barracks for free workers and the sto. The latter worked for Wifo, a private company for economic research I have mentioned before. They lived at the other end of the tunnel. They never penetrated the concentration camp proper. They always entered and left by the same passage, on the Sachswerfen side. Near this camp there was a liquid-oxygen factory, a refinery, an ammonia factory and a cemetery. As prisoners of war, those men saw us, lived cheek by jowl with us, but they were not allowed to speak to us. Officially – which was absurd – they were supposed to be ignorant of the very existence of the concentration camp. The camp stuck out like a urinal in a daisy bed....

In the daily life of Dora that I am here trying to recapture, the ignominy of the Kapos played a decisive part. As I have already said, we were above all ruled by the common criminals. Gallows-birds, corrupt, perverted sadists capable of evil-doing beyond belief; impunity liberated their innate instincts.

One was called Richard Kuhl. He wore the black triangle of the 'mal-adjusted'. It was he whom Pierre Rozan had involuntarily saved in a latrine at Buchenwald when a deportee was beating and strangling him. Rozan merely said: 'What's going on here?' The deportee stopped for a moment, an SS guard arrived and Kuhl escaped. Rozan did not then know that Kuhl was a Kapo, demoted following the evacuation of a camp; he had so oppressed the detainees that one of them had tried to take his revenge.

Strong, supple, swarthy and dark-haired, Kuhl was nicknamed the Gypsy Kapo. He thought of Rozan as his saviour. He talked to him, told him his life story. He said that he had been in the Foreign Legion. He bore the French a deep hatred. Kapo at Natzweiller, he had persecuted a French colonel. He regretted not having killed him. With jubilation, he explained to Pierre that he had made the colonel fill a wheelbarrow with rocks, then made him run. Without stopping. The torture lasted for three days. The colonel kept going. At this point in the story Kuhl would scowl. An inhuman sadness would appear on his face. 'Unhappily, they made me change camps,' he would say, 'I couldn't finish him. I'll never forgive myself!'

From time to time, he would shout at Rozan: 'I'll get you.' He would forget about Buchenwald. His ferocity, his need to kill, would take the upper hand.

The Russians in his Kommando took their revenge. Under his direction they had to empty sacks of potatoes. One of the Russians had the idea to hide a sack under Kuhl's bed; then they informed the SS. Richard Kuhl protested his innocence, but the proof of the offence was there – the sack under the bed. That day the Gummi and kicks took a new direction. Kuhl was on the receiving end.

At the Liberation, he was listed among the wanted war criminals.

He was arrested ten years later. The trial took place in France. Witnesses were called for from the deportees. When Pierre Rozan heard of it, he went to the tribunal and gave evidence against Kuhl. The ex-Kapo foamed with rage. He declared to the tribunal: 'Ah! If only I had got him at Dora ... at least, then, he wouldn't be here today to speak against me!' Richard Kuhl served a part of his sentence. Today he is free. Who is he victimizing now?

Another Kapo who wore the black triangle of the 'mal-adjusted' fitted in well with the leaders of this élite of villains. Right at the top of the pyramid of filth. His name? Kilian. He volunteered to hang prisoners. When Dora began, the executions were not public; they took place at the Holzhof, a wooden enclosure situated beside the *Revier* where the gallows were installed. Later, the hangings took place in front of the detainees. Some on the parade-ground, some in the tunnel. Kilian enjoyed these even more. He had an audience.

Of medium height, quite thin, with shifty eyes, he was himself a deportee of some years standing. He was a conscientious madman. To kill was a joy to him. (The example was set by the leading members of the hierarchy. I remember the trial of the last commandant of Dora: Hans Karl Moeser. He sometimes saw to it that the hanging ropes were cut – was it Kilian who carried this out? – while the victims were still alive. Then he finished them off with a bullet in the back of the head. When, at his trial, he was asked why he had done this, he replied: 'A hunter feels pleasure in shooting a buck. I feel the same with a human being. When I joined the ss and I killed my first three people, my food had no taste for three days. Today, it is a pleasure and a joy.' Moeser was condemned to death. Was he executed?)

The Kapos, though dressed in stripes as we were, ate better. After the ss, they had their pick of the deportees' parcels. I know that my wife sent me several packages through the Red Cross. After they had been raided, all I received was shaving soap, paper and string.

Among the Kapos' masters, two of the ss surpassed the others in their cruelty. Two furies, two bloodthirsty butchers. But how could they not show mercy when their victim had lost all his aggression, his last drop of strength, and showed only his weakness, his resignation to a death he knew must come but did not understand....

One was called Busta. He was nick-named 'Horse Face' because of the set of his features. Solidly built, with low forehead and a stupid face, he lorded it over the spectres. (We were so thin, however, that the least healthy man seemed a Hercules to us.) The other was Karl Multerer, called the Rumanian, whom I have mentioned before. Erzin Busta was brought to justice many years after. (I learnt from *Le Monde*, 10 May 1970, that he had been condemned to eight and a half years in prison.)

There is no news of Multerer. Perhaps he is living comfortably somewhere?

In this valley, three miles from Nordhausen, lay Dora, a blot on a desolate countryside. We never saw, or heard, a bird. The menu hardly changed: nine ounces of bread, beetroot soup, swedes, with sometimes some semolina (once a week the soup was sugared; I do not know what it was made of but we thought it was good). They served us these meals midday and evening. In the morning, with ersatz or barley coffee, we received a small roll and margarine and the bread ration for the day. (They weighed the bread on scales made with a wooden arm and a string. There were often disputes, some prisoners thinking they had been given short measure.) Sometimes, too, they gave us a ration of potatoes. The skin, when dried, was used to make 'tobacco'. Happily, I have never smoked. It was pitiful to see how some men suffered the lack of cigarettes. The deportees' thinness was horrifying. They were skeletons made to work at inhuman speed, while attempting to protect themselves continually from blows.

End of November 1943. The deportees are lined up on the parade-ground in absolute silence. In the middle, all alone, stands a Pole. He had escaped. They have recaptured him. The ss are making quite a ceremony out of his disaster. They are joking among themselves: here was a chance for a good laugh. One of them leaves his group. The Pole drops his trousers. According to the rite, he bends over a trestle. The ss chant:

'*Funfundzwanzig am Arsch, Funfundzwanzig am Arsch!*'
('Twenty-five on the arse, twenty-five on the arse!')

The tormentor waits. The camp commandant makes a speech. He tells the same old story. He says that it is useless to attempt to escape, that no one could get through the electrified fence and that deportees are always recaptured within the confines of the camp. 'Without exception, all deportees who attempt to escape will be hung.' The inevitable conclusion. Then the signal is given. Twenty-five blows of the Gummi, with maximum force. You can feel the hatred in each one. It is evening. A poor light illuminates this pitiable, poignant scene. If they could, I think the deportees would have torn the ss to shreds with their fingernails, like wild beasts sharpening their claws.

The pole will then be handed back to the ss who will beat him up, playing with him for fun. Attached to a disciplinary Kommando, he will wear on his pyjama jacket two little red circles with a white spot, like a target. One will be sewn in front, on the left; the other on his back. That was the costume. The ss always emphasized their vileness in every detail with the most repugnant precision. German organization! The deportee, in camp language, becomes a *Flucht-punkt*. He waits for judgement from Berlin, which invariably condemns him to death. Sometimes he does not have the time to hear his sentence; the ss and disciplinary Kommando Kapos are such monsters that the wretch dies before it arrives....

I remember that that evening René Laval and I planned to escape, with an almost demented determination. I kept touching my five-thousand-franc note in my belt, and in my trouser pocket my two rings and my watch, as one would touch good-luck charms. The following day, in spite of our lack of strength, we did exercises. We had to be ready for the running and long marches ahead.... The ss dissuasion tactics had the opposite effect to that intended. They only made us keener to escape.

We knew that an Italian called Robert de Varzala held a pass – it was a typed carbon copy, bearing the Hamburg district stamp. Robert's civil status was written on it. This rudimentary proof of identity had enabled him to move around freely in the region of Hamburg. I told him of our intention, Laval's and mine, to escape. I told him about our ridiculous sessions of gymnastics: we were not even strong enough to do one press-up! Our plan was simple. After roll-call we would hide in the attic of the dental surgery. We would make our move at night. We would have to find civilian clothes and passes for the identity control points when we got out of the camp.... I asked him to lend me his pass. I would try to find a typewriter and type out my identity and Laval's. The paper I would use would be a current type, easy to get hold of. As for the copy of the stamp, I had an idea for that. De Varzala entrusted me with his treasure, as long as I didn't lose it! In the evening, after roll-call, I explained my plan to Louis Murgia....

Murgia's experiences are without a doubt the most fantastic in the story of Dora. His life's obsession? – not to work! To achieve this end, he showed unparalleled ingenuity, drive, common sense and intelligence. He had succeeded for six months, all while being in the depths of the tunnel. Yes, at Dora! Later, he was in charge of micrometric control in a division of civil engineers. I am sure that numerous v2 parts, passed by him, caused quite a few irreparable accidents.

But how had he managed not to work while being a prisoner in Dora's tunnel, when the ss and the Kapos were constantly on the prowl, relentlessly plying their truncheons? Work in the tunnel never ceased. When one team left the dormitory for its twelve hours' grind, another returned to rest. The dormitory was never deserted.

Murgia's tactics were simple. In the morning he left with the Kommandos going to work, and at the point where the outgoing file met the incoming file, he slipped from one to the other and returned to sleep on his bunk. He devoted most of his energy for those six months to not being noticed. Neither too taciturn, nor too talkative, he did his utmost to pass unseen. The Russians didn't steal his blanket or a morsel of his bread! He was far too clever; vigilant, he slept with one eye open like a cat. He had known the jungle as a small child ... 'I'm not physically tough ... if I hadn't learnt how to manage, I wouldn't have lasted this long,' he said to me.

Murgia was extraordinary! What he did at Dora is unique! And when he tells his story – if he tells it, for he never commits the sin of bragging – it all seems rather ordinary....

So I explained our project to Murgia. I asked him if he thought he could make us a stamp, like the one on Robert de Varzala's pass. I knew that he was capable of such a job, but at Dora the tools did not exist. He said he would try. We stole a raw potato, and cut it in two. Murgia endeavoured to imprint the stamp on it. With a razor blade, he set about carving the characters in relief. He pegged away at it, using every ounce of his dexterity, meticulousness, skill and virtuosity. He applied the result of his carving talents to the sheet of paper I had procured. We inspected his work. It was not very successful. He lacked the tools necessary to bring it off. He apologized. I showed the effort to René Laval. 'Too risky,' he said. We had to give up the plan. Once again, escape had been only a dream....

# Chapter Sixteen

# THE DEATH OF MAX PRINCET

---

Dora, Dora, devourer of Life, of cursed name,
Hewn out of suffering and cemented with blood.

*Extract from Chaines et Lumières*
*by l' Abbé Renard*

The SS summon us to the morgue. They order us to extract gold teeth from the corpses. We know this is common practice. We even know that if you have a gold bridge it is better not to let it be known, for the SS will order the Kapos to execute the owner of the treasure. This collection represented several hundred ounces of gold.

In the morgue is a foul odour – the unbearable stench of bodies that had died of dysentery and the other maladies that decimated the camp. To the stink of decomposition is added the foul smell of excrement. An SS officer supervises the tooth-pulling. Armed with a chisel, a Polish deportee opens the corpse's jaw. The officer looks to see if there are any gold teeth. If there are, the Pole, with a hammer and pliers, smashes the jaw and extracts the teeth. When the operation is completed, he kicks the corpse away and passes to another. As the dead are in a heap, the bodies all slide down. A scene of abomination. And am I watching all this? It's a nightmare! I must surely wake up! The gold teeth are in a corner. The SS guard, sentry of horror, watches over his plunder.

We leave without waiting for the order to be given: the officer and the Pole follow. We refuse point blank to pull out teeth. We would rather go back to the tunnel. We would rather die.

Miraculously, the officer, who has made us watch the operation

to edify us and teach us how to do it, does not insist. When we
return to the dental surgery, we are green in the face. It is a long
time before I cease to wake during the night, moaning and crying
out: I dreamed that I was in the Pole's place. Today, like an halluci-
nation, that image still sometimes comes back to me. I chase it away,
as one shakes off the memory of some shameful event.

If the deportees had a right to summary care, the ss had a right
to full treatment, including fillings. Sometimes the rules were
twisted. When we received a visit from a Kapo or ss guard who
had beaten us (alas, Karl Multerer never came to the dentist's surgery!) we took our revenge with the means at our disposal.

At the moment of anaesthesia, the injection was given in such
a way that the liquid went into the mouth and did not desensitize
the gum. Drill, polishing-wheel and forceps made the bastards
scream with pain. 'That's for us! That's for our friends you torture
all day and all night!' We knew how to make it hurt. Our smiles
were angelic, full of compassion. 'Would you like another injection?
You have such a robust constitution, the anaesthetic hardly takes
on you,' Cimek, the Czech, explained in German. My efforts to
make myself understood were getting better and better. I even
translated Croizat's and Laval's excuses. When we told them they
were too strong, that they were out of the ordinary, the ss were
so happy. Men are so often flattered to be singled out. To feel
different...

For several days, Max Princet has seemed to be in a worse state
than usual. I speak to him. I try to give him a little strength. His
eyes tell me that he has given up, a look of such sadness that it forces
me to share his unshakeable presentiment. I try to say the useless
words one says in desperation. Lies! He who had known how to
overcome the effects of the war, cured of his wound, by what miracle
could he continue to live? No, it was not possible! Princet! Princet
whom we loved so! Nothing will reconcile me to the Germans. I
pretend to have forgotten, but deep in my heart the terrible crimes
of the ss at Dora will always be there. As long as I live.... Max
shook my hand, turned, and I saw his walking corpse disappear into
the hole of the tunnel....

The following day Princet is not at roll-call. I run to the infirmary.
He is still breathing but he can no longer see. On 20 December
1943 he died. I was at work, I did not even see his remains. Already

gone with the others.... To the morgue.... To Buchenwald....
Up to heaven.... Into the very air we breathed....

Right until the end, the Germans made him work. When he ran
a temperature, for days and days, of 102 °F, they would not take
him in at the infirmary. He was beaten. At 104 °F, they let him lie
down. It was too late.

That evening, we are all silent, Clervoy, Murgia, Cinel, Lauth
and I. No one dares say the first word that might start a conversation. Death has struck the group of seven from Compiègne. Max
is the first. We feel a deep despair.

Christmas 1943. We work until the evening. We no longer sleep
in Barrack 14 with the 'doctor-surgeons' Schneider and Schweitzer.
We sleep in another barrack with some Dutchmen – nurses and
Doctor Essel, who is one of the new doctors assigned to the deportees.

The Dutch prepare a little Christmas celebration with their
parcels (what is left of them). It is not sumptuous, but all the same,
they do have something to eat.

Croizat, Laval and I have nothing left. Not even the morning's
bread ration. The Dutch eat, trying to amuse themselves as one does
at Christmas, joking. We try not to look at them, to think of other
things. They offer us nothing, nor do they invite us to join them.
That makes us sick. We would not behave in such a way. One thing
consoles us: the belief that we will be spending Christmas 1944 at
home, at our own fireside with our families....

We were mistaken.

# Chapter Seventeen

# THE HEAVEN KOMMANDOS

A wisp of smoke
Vanishes into the sky
The last farewell
Of the unknown dead.

What was going on? The ss had announced to the sick that they were to leave Dora in order to go to rest in a special camp. This camp was depicted as almost idyllic. There, they would only perform light duties. The promised climate was ideal. 'A sanatorium,' concluded the ss, pronouncing the word gutturally, in the German fashion.

On 2 January 1944, with Doctor Lemière, I had seen Armand de Dampierre and Ambassador Dumaine. Armand was not recovering from his broken ribs, broken by the arm of the crane when he was working with me in the tunnel. Dumaine was exhausted. Two and a half months at Dora had almost destroyed him. They had come to tell us they were leaving. The ss had promised them a veritable Garden of Eden. 'What do you make of it?' They were so disillusioned they could not believe that their luck had changed. Our scepticism was obvious. But we knew nothing. What could we say? We wished them luck. 'Let us know how you are.' We never met again.

Dora's *Revier* was full to bursting. The beds of the dying were on four levels. Each bed was always occupied by three patients, head to foot, despite the awful gaps caused by a rate of death no civilized human being could conceive (which is in a manner of speaking when one considers the crimes committed by civilized human beings). The sight of those men suffering from pneumonia, oedemas, cachexia, erysipelas and dysentery, had to be seen to be believed

– a painting by Bosch, in which the bodies suddenly groan and come to life.

On 3 January 1944, in the middle of the night, Jacques Déprez witnessed horrible, frenzied scenes that he will never forget.

His barracks is suddenly invaded by an ss company, armed with machine-guns and flanked by their infamous dogs. With shouts, oath and blows, the Kapo leaps into action to please his masters. The ss give the order '*Los, los, aufstehen*'. . . . The sick, all running temperatures of at least 104 °F, rise from their beds. They are like phantoms. Where do they find the strength to obey, to fall into rank in the space between the bunks? They are given wooden clogs, we called them the *claquettes* – and the hysteria begins anew: '*Los, los, alle raus*'. . . .

They exchange their rags for even older, dirtier clothes. '*Los . . . los . . .*'

Now the bedridden are outside. It is winter. A terrible winter, as it so often is in times of overwhelming misfortune. Nature seems to be hand in glove with the murderers. The searchlights have been turned on. On the parade-ground in the dead of night, standing to attention in a mire of ice, mud and snow, the temperature well below zero, the sick men wait for the thousand to be counted, to be chosen, and for their numbers to be called. The ss have prepared their list for the 'sanatorium'. One thousand! A number dear to the hearts of the ss. Can this atmosphere of terror really be the prelude to the dream camp held out so temptingly to the dying? Already the first deaths occur. Bodies fall to the ground. Sufferers have suddenly ceased to suffer. They are dead. The ss run back to the *Revier*. More deportees must be dragged from their beds, for the number must be exact: one thousand! Otto Plazza, the camp doctor-in-chief, has said so. At last, there are one thousand. '*Die Rechnung summt!*' (Long live the Reich!)

Like a rabbit confused by the shouts and the lights, Doctor Jacques Déprez huddles in a corner. He longs to shrink, to make himself tiny, like a circus contortionist. He only hopes the all-powerful Kapo has not written his number on the fateful list. Fateful, for now Déprez knows that the promises made to the sick were lies. But where are they taking them? What more odious and horrible fate has been dreamed up by the paid assassins of the land of Heine, Kant and Beethoven?

At dawn on 3 January 1944 – hours after the ss had burst into the infirmary – the sufferers are still there, standing stiffly to attention, any movement punished by blows or bites from the dogs.

The commander of the *Arbeitsstatistik* sends for Déprez. After a swift visual examination, the doctor is to supply the list of those fit to travel. Those who are not will be replaced by other deportees.

Déprez runs to another barrack. He goes to ground. They cannot be searching thoroughly, they are in such a hurry for the greater glory of the German Reich! Déprez even runs across the parade-ground, passing *Unterscharführer* ss Lorenz, the man who ran the dental surgery. Lorenz who was later shot by his peers because he was too human, who had been kind to us but had never dared confide in us for – you never could tell – informers were everywhere, the man whose family we would dearly love to find, to tell them that amongst those legions of bastards there was one man who was not contaminated. Lorenz makes no sign. He does not shout out: 'There's Déprez! I've found him. He was trying to hide from us, the bastard!' No. His eyes red and full of tears – is it the cold? – – he says to Déprez: '*Jack, schau nur, das sind tausend Leichen*' (Jacques, take a good look, that's a thousand dead men).

Déprez no longer has the shadow of a doubt. The exterminators have triumphed yet again. Cynicism and horror joined hands to bring about the systematic destruction of the weak and the sick, in the name of selection. It all obeyed an insane logic, but a logic all the same. The doctor's head was buzzing. Was this the beginning of another civilization sweeping everything away before it? Had a rule of terror been decided, by those at the top of the hierarchy, for the men who were to do the work? Were they going to use an endless stream of slaves, each replaceable with shocking ease? Jacques was dazed. And yet his brain still functioned. As he witnessed the tragedy he felt unreal.

That was the day that Déprez, arriving at Dora, had had the chance to obtain the post of nurse – Déprez who washed the floor while his superiors, Ernst Schneider and Karl Schweitzer operated on the deportees; Déprez who recorded how the mason and stove-setter complemented each other so appallingly when amputating – moreover, if their surgical intervention, by some miracle, succeeded, the ss, who refused to be hampered with an invalid, would have assassinated the patient immediately; Déprez who had seen so much, learned the gentle-sounding word *Himmelkommando* –

'Heaven Kommando'. In this way were described the sick men destined to be liquidated. Heaven Kommandos. . . . The Kommandos that went up in smoke.

And so, the sinister farce has been played. The transport of 3 January 1944 is ready to get under way. Jacques manages to catch that the thousand are headed for Lublin Maideneck, classified *Vernichtungslager Stufe Eins* (first-class extermination camp – the class signifying the speed of extermination).

But how did we know what became of the victims?

Firstly, a deportee in the *Kammer* (clothes store) thought to mark some of the clogs set aside for the transported. The clogs returned. Well, well! . . .

Then, one day, Pierre Rozan met a drunken guard. Rozan would have happily avoided him, but the guard hailed him and clung onto him. At first Pierre cursed the ill-luck that had set him in this fool's path, but the story the guard had to tell was so gripping that he soon no longer regretted the meeting.

He was bemoaning his fate. He told Pierre that he had accompanied the convoy of 3 January. 'It makes me sick; I have such a revolting job. Might as well make me work in the latrines, knee deep in shit. I had to take care of the ones who were too ill to get out of the truck. They didn't want to get up, I had to stamp on their throats to finish them off.'

He felt absolutely no remorse. What upset him was the messy work they made him do, and he a member of the ss, too! He went lurching off. Rozan wondered who had really said 'All men are brothers'. . . .

Roger Cinel managed to speak to the only man who escaped these transports (for there were others: 4 February, 23 March 1944 and more than that came later, but I do not know the exact dates). Cinel has forgotten the name of this survivor. Here is his account:

'Having left Dora, we arrived at Bergen-Belsen. We were put into barracks. We were woken at six a.m. – to get up, and roll-call. As we stood there, in mid-winter, when they considered the ranks in straight enough lines, they hosed us with cold water until we were well iced-up. The ss were giggling. "You're ill. You have to be cared for, disinfected, given exercise and cleaned up." As not one of us had a temperature below 104 °F, this treatment was perfect! But we were not dying quickly enough for the ss' taste, despite their exceptional efficiency. So, after the ceremony, the Kapo in charge designated fifteen of us to make room for the others. The Germans were always obsessed with "living space". The orderlies seized fifteen men and gave them an intravenous shot of petrol. There was chaos in the barracks in those few moments. Each man, with desperate energy and all the strength he had left, tried to get away. We hid under the beds, anywhere we could. The Kapos and the orderlies caught and beat deportees until they had their number of victims.'

On 3 January 1944, there were about four thousand deportees at Dora. One thousand were transported to the extermination camp. One in four.

One of the men most responsible for this act of genocide, and all those which followed, was the ss *Obersturmführer* Otto Plazza.

After the war, along with Jacques Déprez, I gave evidence at the Dachau tribunal, where the trials of the war criminals were held. Otto Plazza was not in the box with the accused. He was never found.

# Chapter Eighteen

# GASTON PERNOT'S ESCAPE

If only someone would send us arms! If only the English would parachute in some Thompsons! Those who still had the strength dreamed of merciless revenge. We saw ourselves machine-gunning the ss, attacking the barracks where they had taken refuge, lying in wait for them in the tunnel. Not one escaped us. To our own lives we no longer gave a thought. We might all die, if only the ss died first. And we'd take a few alive so that they would know what it was to suffer, and learn that suffering was not an abstraction inscribed on the emaciated bodies of others. When there is nothing left to hope for and the fanaticism of destruction is rife, hatred reigns. The torture and death machine engenders another machine of torture and death.

Dora was a cancer of damnation from the first to the last day of its existence. But there are degrees to horror as to everything. The worst period lasted from October 1943 to March 1944. The camp was getting into working order. Despite malnutrition, decrepitude, death, Dora settled and grew.

At the end of March or beginning of April 1944, with the barracks completed, the deportees – some of whom had not seen the sun for months[1] – were at last able to sleep outside the tunnel. The tunnel was now only used for the factory, the laboratory and storage. (The work of enlarging and fitting out was continuing elsewhere in the anthill of the Harz.)

The v2 missile, of which three had come out of the tunnel on New Year's Day, ran into serious hold-ups during the winter and spring. Nevertheless, the ss took a new step forward in their construction of an empire of secret weapons. On the 3 March 1944, Hitler decided that the Luftwaffe's flying bomb, the future v1, which had made great progress, would no longer be produced at the Volkswagen factories, but at Dora.

If the camp was organizing itself, so were we; modestly it is true, with the means at our disposal, but our state of mind helped and gave us courage. We tried to make a 'life-line' around those who seemed to be going under. We were fighting back as best we could. I continued signing vouchers for consultation, so that French deportees could escape their exhausting work under the Kapos' yoke for a few hours. To those we felt we could trust, we passed on the news we had heard on the radio. We tried to find less tiring methods of getting deportees out of the tunnel. And in the evening, after roll-call, in Barrack 26, we held our councils of war. We learned that Rozan had also managed to tune in to the BBC, but as he worked for the camp commandant, he had to be twice as careful. He listened in less often than Croizat who managed to every day.

In the month of January, I received a second letter from my wife. One passage made me smile: 'Pierre has recovered the bike.' She was referring to Roumeguère. The day of our arrest, an eternity ago, in another world, Pierre, who had arrived at the rendezvous in the Rue Hamelin by bicycle, had pushed it to Schnell's where the Gestapo had caught us. From the letter I now knew that he had returned to the corridor of the building and collected the bicycle. (In fact it was my bicycle. I had lent it to him.) I replied to Suzanne at once. My writing was naturally quite large, but the size of the cards they gave us made me write microscopically small.

I meet a boy of about twenty. Tall, handsome, blue-eyed and of Germanic blondness, he is called Gaston Pernot. If many are at the end of their mental and physical resources, his energy seems rather to increase.

He was born in Russia, where his ancestors had emigrated at the time of the revocation of the Edict of Nantes. His mother is from Alsace. His father, who had returned to France, is a lawyer. He is fortunate in being able to speak German, Russian, English and French like a native. Called up in 1940, at the fall of France he was demobbed in Clermont-Ferrand. Since 1942, he had been a member of the Mithridate circuit. Arrested in 1943, after being interrogated in Clermont-Ferrand and Paris, Gaston Pernot was sent to Buchen-

wald. He arrived there on 16 January 1944. Transferred to Dora
on 8 February, he obstinately and tirelessly plots to escape.

The following story, which is something not far short of miraculous, I would not learn until some months later.

15 March 1944: a hanging in the camp. A public hanging for
attempted escape. That is the moment Pernot chooses to make his
own attempt. With him are three other deportees, Yves Sentis,
Rousseau and another, whose name I have forgotten. Call him 'the
fourth man'.

They avoid the obstacle of the barbed-wire fence by leaving on
the side where the tunnel opens onto the little station. They climb
into a wagon. It is full of empty crates. They hide. They hear the
ss checking the train. They are not discovered. Then the train sets
off in the direction of Nordhausen station, where it stops for three
days. For food they have their bread ration, but nothing to drink.
The wait seems interminable. Thirst causes delirium and discouragement. Finally the train sets off again, but in what direction
they do not know.

In the evening the convoy stops in the middle of the countryside.
Pernot and his companions emerge. They try to work out in what
direction the train is heading: Czechoslovakia! They decide to abandon it. On foot they head west, into a little wood; they will be under
cover. In the morning, desperately hungry and thirsty, they spot
a farm. They hurry to it, knock, push open the door. A woman is
there alone. Seeing four unshaven men in striped pyjamas burst in,
she cries out in fright. Despite their beards, dirt and all the signs
of men on the run, they manage to calm her down. 'Something to
eat and drink, that's all we want.' The woman feeds them, begging
them to leave as soon as possible. Harbouring a deportee, a prisoner,
a 'misfit', is severely punished, sometimes by death. They go on
their way.

One morning, at dawn, they see a cottage. It is unoccupied. Obviously only used at weekends. They break down the door and spend
the day there. They will set off again at night, which is what they
have decided: to rest by day and travel by night. In the house they
find some food and civilian clothing. They change and leave their
prison suits, taking care to remove the numbers and triangles. At
least, so they think! (Pierre Mussetta had been wiser when he
escaped from Buchenwald. He had changed his clothes, but had

hidden his own quite far from the place where he had stolen new ones.)

That night, they follow the railway track. They reach a station. They hide inside a goods wagon, the only one with its door half-open. Destination – Frankfurt. A good run if they can get there! They close the door. The wagon contains ore. They are pleased because the train has started to move, but the cargo gives off toxic fumes. They cough, their eyes run, they are choking. They open the door to breathe. The convoy is depressingly slow. After three days, it stops. They are at Weimar, point of departure for Buchenwald. They think that odd, the more so as the train continues to stand. They evacuate their train and find another with no direction-board. Rousseau and Pernot go to scout for one marked for the French border.

Suddenly, they hear regular footsteps. A German patrol? You have to have lived such moments of harassment and tension to understand the terror that gripped the fugitives! They lie down under the train, between the tracks, holding their breath, suppressing the coughing caused by the fumes. The soldiers march past. Rousseau decides to return to the others. Gaston Pernot continues the search.

More footsteps. One man this time. Gaston slips onto the rails. A railwayman. He stops. 'Did he see me?' Pernot wonders. No! The railwayman drops his trousers and Gaston finds himself watching a natural enough sight, but one that usually takes place behind the door of the smallest room. Crude comedy relief. Pernot waits, the railwayman's arse at eye-level. Suddenly, the man turns around; crouched down like that he sees Pernot. This unexpected presence, in such a place and in such circumstances, frightens him. He screams. Before he has time to get his trousers back on, Pernot runs back to the wagon as fast as he can. He tells his tale. Nobody laughs. The less determined of his companions are already losing their nerve.

The train sets off again. Time passes. How long since they left Dora? A week? Longer? They have no water, no food, they are numb with cold. The wagon is loaded with printed matter destined for the Wehrmacht quartered at Forbach. Forbach! France! They are heading in the right direction! The convoy stops in open country.

It is snowing. Crouched down and huddled together, they try to keep each other warm. What has happened to the train? How long are they stuck here in the middle of nowhere? Two days? Three? They dare not even catch snow to drink, for fear that their hands might be seen reaching out of the wagon. They decide, cautiously and temporarily, to leave the shelter of the train. If they stay any longer, they will die of starvation. They leave under cover of darkness. The ripple of water – a brook! They drink delightedly. Further on, they find silos of beetroot. They eat their fill and gather potatoes too. Laden with provisions, they return to the wagon.

There is some disagreement between the fugitives. Sentis and the other young man want to leave the train. They are in such a state that they threaten to make a noise unless the others agree. Pernot and Rousseau calmly advise them to stay in the wagon. 'The convoy is headed for Lorraine. You saw those leaflets for Forbach,' explains Pernot. 'Once there, I know people. They'll help us.' The two others do not give in. And so, all four of them set off on foot. It is night. After following the railway tracks for some hours, they arrive in Fulda. At the station, they search for trains heading westward. In vain . . .

Dawn. For one whole day they keep to the shelter of a wagon. Thirst and discomfort add to the worsening atmosphere. The opposing points of view are becoming irreconcilable. His spirit worn down by fatigue, the fourth man now resembles an operetta fugitive, suddenly facing reality. Pernot feels that he could reach France alone, or with Rousseau. But Sentis, and particularly the other man are exhausted. In the early hours, they set off across the fields.

Near one place, a policeman challenges them. He orders the four men to follow him. The fourth man, exhausted, cadaverous, is suffering from dysentery. He can barely move. Rousseau, Sentis and Pernot confer and escape. Taken by surprise, the policeman cannot stop them. By the time he has drawn his revolver, the three are already far away. They hide in a forest, trying to cover their tracks in the hope of fooling the police dogs. They continue on their way, reaching a barn, where they find some potatoes, a pan and some matches. At last they have hot food! It has been three weeks, more or less, since they left Dora, three weeks of fasting or raw, cold food. At night, they leave the barn. They continue for fifteen miles. They are suffering terribly from the cold. But they still have hope. Now three, they feel closer, stronger and think their escape is going to be successful.

In the morning, a peasant finds them. He is dumbfounded. In German, Pernot explains that they want to get back to France. The peasant takes pity on them and hides them in a barn. He lends them a razor and gives them food. Yves Sentis – who must be about eighteen – is complaining of frost-bite in his fingers. In this relative calm, his nerve cracks completely. Worn out, he weeps, calling for his mother, whining and saying he cannot go on.

What is to be done? Rousseau and Pernot are perplexed. Abandon him? Go on with just the two of them? They are sure they could go it without him. They hesitate, torn. In the end, they stay with Yves Sentis for three whole days, trying to comfort and restore him. After three days and nights the peasant returns and seems terrified. 'You must go! You'll be arrested, and for my pains I'll be arrested too.' Pernot and Rousseau apologize ... and go on their way.

Yves Sentis is totally spent. It is agonizing to see. They stop. In the forest, they cook some potatoes they have taken from the barn. Perhaps the halt will enable Sentis to get a grip on himself? He cries and cries for his mother. He is delirious. At the other end of the clearing three peasants with a cart appear. They are collecting firewood. Pernot, Rousseau and Sentis hide. They think they have not been seen. Alas! One hour later, a policeman and two peasants leap out of the bushes. Their adventure has come to an abrupt end. They have been on the run for a month, perhaps longer.

They are taken to a farmyard. Three armed men are standing guard. Peasants and children come to stare at them as if they are zoo animals. The peasant who helped them is there too. Of course they pretend not to recognize him. The worthy man leaves in relief. The policeman must have had orders from Fulda. He handcuffs them. They set off on foot.

They are four miles from the police station. Now that hope no longer gives them strength, even Pernot and Rousseau are exhausted. The efforts of these long days has made their legs as heavy as lead.

Pernot advises his friends to say nothing, he will speak for them. He will say that they are British, escaped prisoners of war. At the police station, the tragedy becomes mixed with comedy. Pernot can easily understand what the policemen are saying. He replies in English as if the German's questions are incomprehensible. They are convinced. They become kinder. They even go as far as to attend to Gaston's sore feet: basin, hot water, clean towels. A privilege of being British?

As the interrogation was practically in dumb-show, they are taken to the prison at Fulda. Here, the subterfuge collapses. The fourth man is there before them. Terrified, abandoned, he has confessed everything. Disaster! They are put to work sewing buttons on to tent-cloth. Then they are taken to be disinfected.

Three days later, they and other detainees are collected, handcuffed, and escorted to the station. Destination – Weimar. It is all over. Buchenwald awaits them. They are haunted by the inscription *Jedem das Seine* ('To each his due'). Is this to be one of their last days alive, in this locked wagon?

At Buchenwald, they are shut up in a prison cell near the entry gate. They are amazed: the ss do not beat them! They are in transit and belong to Dora, of no interest to their guards....

On board a supply lorry, they arrive at Dora, handcuffed, on 21 April 1944, Adolf Hitler's birthday. Their reception is worthy of this event. The ss and Kapos, with Gummi and kicks, propel them into the room that serves as a prison. (At that time – the bunker not being completed – this room, adjacent to the ss HQ, was right at the entrance to the deportees' camp.) The fourth man has not even the strength to weep, Sentis no longer complains about his frost-bite, no longer cries for his mother, Rousseau and Gaston are no longer angry, thinking that they would have made it on their own. The beatings have emptied their minds. They have been beaten so much that there is not a fibre of their beings that is not painful.

In this room, face to the wall, arms in the air, feet tied, are twenty prisoners – all condemned to death.

They are ordered to take off their shoes. It is terrible. They are not allowed to lean against the wall or to go to sleep. The least slip is punished by a beating. There is a large empty tin for their needs.... This calvary lasts for an eternity.

Some days later, they are taken to Niedersachswerfen, the Gestapo centre for the region. Gaston Pernot is surprised, agreeably surprised, to find that the interrogation is not brutal. In reply to questions, Gaston says that he is a French officer from Alsace, a qualified lawyer. The Gestapo agent tells him he would have done better to have stayed in Alsace, then he could have joined up with the Germans. Pernot is careful not to contradict him. After this conversation, back to the prison: half a pint of soup a day, three ounces of bread and the agony of the cell. But there is one improvement. They can sleep at night, though on the floor without covering of any kind.

On 6 June 1944, they are taken back to the Gestapo. Have their death warrants already been signed by the office, in Berlin, as requested by the authorities at Dora, in accordance with *Jedem das Seine*? It is there, from a conversation among some of the ss, that Pernot hears that the Landings have happened. The ss are confident. 'They have only gained a little ground. We'll throw them back into the sea,' they say. Pernot passes on this news to his companions. Must they die now that the end of the Nazis is in sight? Once again, the interrogation is routine. What is going on? What does this enquiry mean? After this dialogue with the Gestapo, they are not returned to the prison. They are attached to the *Fluchtpunkte* Kommando (or escapees Kommando) to await Berlin's verdict. The discipline is merciless. Their physical condition now borders on absolute collapse. They are at the mercy of the green Kapos – the common criminals.

At the end of June, their four numbers are called out. They are taken back to the prison. Is this it? As time passed, they had begun to hope. The return to prison is like a shower of cold water. Is it the gallows?

Once again, they are taken to Niedersachswerfen. The attitude of the inquisitors has changed. The four men, always interrogated separately, are threatened with worse treatment. 'Where did you get the clothes you were wearing when you were recaptured?' It is from the ss that Gaston discovers that the police had found out that Sentis had forgotten to remove his prison number from his deportee's uniform when they changed clothes. So it is impossible to deny that they were inside the house. 'Did you break down the door?' Hoping that the others would not contradict him, Gaston maintains that the door was open and that the theft was a petty larceny, since the clothes were only second-hand. The ss insist: 'What about the sheets?' Gaston feels at his ease, as the lawyer in him takes control. 'Seriously, what on earth do you expect us to have done with sheets?'

The ss are eventually convinced that there was no housebreaking and that other bandits must have taken the sheets. This round leaves Gaston perplexed. Why are the bastards wasting time on these trifles, these 'peacetime' details? Especially as, in conclusion, the ss says: 'You have escaped from a secret camp. The penalty is hanging. We are waiting for orders from Berlin.' This is an insane world we're struggling in, thought Pernot. Perhaps this madness, this passion for collecting useless details, will give the Allies time to reach Dora. . . .

After having emphatically pronounced this expected sentence, the Gestapo agent leaves the room. The secretary remains. She looks at Gaston with compassion. She offers him a piece of cake. 'Take it,' she says, 'I made it myself.' Pernot is astounded. Does this humane gesture hide something? The secretary does seem sincere. 'I will do all I can to save you,' she whispers. 'I have been moved by your statement and your perseverance.' Her voice may be low, but her conviction is strong. Pernot looks at her as at a spring in the middle of a desert, an angelic apparition among a legion of monsters. He thanks her. As he speaks, he wonders if his words convey everything he feels, the intensity of his gratitude. When they come to find him, he once more looks into the secretary's eyes. His fate, and that of his companions, is in the hands of this young woman he does not know. . . .

The return to the camp plunges them into despair. They are not sent back to the Kommando but to the prison, where the routine of suffering and starvation continues. Every day, the number of detainees diminishes. Each departure is terrible: it is for the short trip to the gallows.

Pernot thinks back to the secretary's words. Did he dream them? In his reduced physical condition, he can no longer distinguish the real from the unreal. Soon, all those who were in the prison before them have gone on their last journey. Yves Sentis weeps. The fourth man is only a bare shell.

One morning, the *Rapportführer* comes in. He lays his machine-gun on the table. Their feet are untied. 'Get ready. Put on your shoes.' There is a deathly hush. Not a sob, not a tear. It is the end.

Gaston considers the situation. His mind is made up. He is in the grip of a cold fury. He shall not be hung. Before they handcuff him, he will seize the machine-gun from the table. Mow them down. Better to die armed than to hang like a scarecrow from the end of a rope. But what is this? The *Rapportführer* disappears while they are getting ready. He returns. He announces that they are to go back to the camp. They are to be assigned to the disciplinary Kommando once more. What joy! Is this the secretary's doing? Did she not send their files to Berlin? Will they be back in prison again tomorrow? Is the nightmare over at last? All is forgotten – the beatings, the suffering, the torture, the endless standing without sleep, without leaning against the wall.... They are going to live!.... Even in Dora!...

# Chapter Nineteen

# DEFIANCE

_Revier_ ...
A whole continent,
many nations of pain.

_Anonymous poem_

At the beginning of 1944, Roger Cinel is hospitalized in the _Revier_.
He has a fever, an enormous boil. His neighbour is a young man.
He has a gangrenous leg. Everyone knows he will not recover. The
other patients shower attention and kindness on him. The young
man is touched. He says happily that his leg does not hurt anymore.
The gangrene has risen to the thigh. The infection has taken hold.
Some days later, he dies....

One evening, the ss bring in a deportee covered in blood. They call
for the orderlies. 'Take this one, we'll be back for him tomorrow
morning.' He is a Pole. He has escaped and been recaptured. The
dogs have torn him to shreds.

In the _Revier_ barracks, most of the orderlies are compatriots of
the wounded man. They give him an injection to ease the pain, bathe
his wounds, make a fuss of him. They put him to bed next to Cinel.
Everyone offers something to the unfortunate man. Did he escape
from the prison? Has his sentence come from Berlin already? What
is certain is that in the morning he will be executed.

Efforts are made that the night should not be like the eve of a
funeral. As the time passes the agony of waiting becomes unbearable. The man does not want to sleep. He wants to talk and talk, for
the last time. At about four in the morning, noises and conversation

can be heard around the gallows set up near the *Revier*. The condemned man goes on talking as if the murmuring outside does not concern him.

At dawn, the ss come to fetch him. The Pole waves to his friends. He leaves calmly. From what depths of their beings do men summon up such dignity? The victim's farewell was sublime, its simplicity was heart rending. Afterwards, the silence was terrible.

In early 1944, I meet André Méresse again. At Dora! An emotional meeting. He is still as ardent and caustic as ever. Perhaps the reader will remember that it was through him that I joined the Resistance at the end of 1941. Founder of the *Armée des Volontaires* (AV), Méresse was arrested, along with most of the circuit, in November 1942. Something in him has changed; it is as if an unknown force has come to his aid and bolstered his already great courage. He tells me: 'Since we last saw each other I have been ordained.' Where? In which prison? Which camp? How could the Germans, who hounded priests, have authorized such a thing? Imbued with a deep, secret mysticism, Méresse gives me no details. He behaves as if motivated solely by goodness and generosity. He is charitable to those less fortunate than himself. He shares his meagre ration of food. He turns our imposed starvation into a voluntary asceticism.

By the wondrous means of communication that triumph in even the most severe conditions, the deportees know that he celebrates the mass and hears confessions. The Catholics are comforted by his presence and his words. As for myself, who had become an atheist from contact with the church in my youth, I observe how faith supports those who have it.

André Méresse was later to develop a mastoid infection, some said a tumour. He was operated on in the infirmary. I do not know if it was the doctor or divine intervention which performed the miracle, but he recovered and continued his mission in the camp.

At Dora, priests often kept their holy orders secret, for the ss put them into suicide Kommandos in order to exterminate them. There was one who impressed us a great deal. He was called Jean-Paul Renard. His conduct was exemplary. Always ready for a discussion or provoking one, using language everyone could understand, he was a permanent source of aid. There was unanimous affection and esteem for the man.

What remains a great mystery, a mystery which explains Méresse's strange behaviour, is that he was not a priest. He had invented a role for himself and he stuck to it. He carried the deception as far as to have invitations printed at the Liberation which announced that : 'Colonel-abbé André Méresse will celebrate a mass at Saint-Sulpice in the memory of those who disappeared in the concentration camps.' In the presence of his friends and many of the faithful, Abbé Méresse performed this mass. When the bishop realized that he was a fake priest, there was a scandal.

Méresse then became even more mysterious. 'As I have heard quite a few confessions, I have learnt many things, I fear that one day some people are afraid that I will divulge their secrets or try to blackmail them,' he said to me.

Later I heard he was drowned in the sea off Brittany. Two days after, his friends received printed cards announcing his death, but he had ordered them himself. That was very much in the style of that remarkable man.

It is Jacques Poupault who operates on André Méresse. At Buchenwald, he had been assistant-surgeon to the Czech doctor, Horn, interned since 1941. On 13 May 1944, he arrives at Dora. He is made chief surgeon of the *Revier*. Poupault is tall, strong, a cultivated man. He is as I imagine a *condottiere* to be. His knowledge and his will to challenge impossibilities work wonders.

The *Revier* now consists of seven barracks : one for consultations, two for surgery, four for medicine. The surgical equipment is fairly complete. Lacking are bandages, anaesthetics and materials for sutures. The staff comprises four French doctors : Morel; old Giraud; Lagey; Lemière; a Dutchman, Essel; a Russian whose name I forget and a Czech, Jan Cespiva. This last named is to become Poupault's assistant. The orderlies are mostly Germans, Czechs and Poles. There are also some French and Dutchmen. In the consultation barracks is a radiography room, equipped with French field apparatus. A pharmacist from Strasbourg, Ebel, is in charge of this. Marcel Petit, a professor at the veterinary college in Toulouse, is his assistant. A German Kapo, Fritz Preul, a Communist interned for eight years, controls the *Revier*. He must be about thirty-five. He is blond, fine-featured, of average height.

The ss doctor, Karr, is the overall boss. He does not look Poupault in the eye when he is introduced to him, he even pretends not to

have seen him at all. He just orders him to assist at a hernia operation. Karr, according to Poupault, did no other surgical operation.

Right away, Jacques Poupault is accepted by our group. He tells
us how he was arrested in Paris just as he was getting ready to travel
to London with three suitcases full of documents. He was the leader
of the north zone of the Brutus circuit.

Jacques becomes part of our group. The numbers have increased.
There are Croizat, Laval, Lemière, old Giraud, Turk, Cales,
Lacoste, Ziller, Leschi, Herpin, Leroy, Petit, Le Lionnais (called
'Cosinus'), Hémery, Sadron and Pescadere. There are to be General
Dejussieu (called 'Pontcarral'), Colonel Cazin d'Honuncthin, Cap-
tain Cogny, and those who had been there from the beginning:
Lauth, Rozan, Cinel, Murgia and Clervoy. A White Russian joins
us: Nicolas Hronstein. He has beautiful hands and white hair. He
is gentle, calm, intelligent and courteous, smiling in the face of
adversity. He is forty years old. He has lived in France since 1924.
He expresses his love for Paris so well that it intensifies our nostalgia.
He has studied in Berlin. His mother was dressmaker to the
Empress of Russia; he fought for years, before the Russians agreed
to let her leave. He was living with her in Paris, in the happiness
they had found at last, when the Germans arrested him.

Our meetings take place, after roll-call, in Barrack 26 where we
sleep. Deportees who have been working all over the camp reassemble. In this way, we are able to collect information. We always
talk about the news we have heard on the BBC. It restores our optimism. We talk of life, of literature, of the cinema. That may seem
childish and pointless. But these conversations about our lives when
we were free, about books and films, help us to carry on. These
conversations enable those who still work in the tunnel to forget
for a moment the beatings and the insults. The beasts of burden
become men again.

Sometimes we break one of our rules and talk about food. Our
state of collapse prevents us from even thinking of women. We do
not experience sexual frustration.

The day's work is often discussed. There are those who have
suffered too much and feel the need to say so, to re-enact and thus
exorcize their pain and fear. There are those who have noticed some
detail; one day it might be of use.

Jacques Poupault describes the coldness of ss Doctor Karr the day he met him. Karr replaced Otto Plazza in March 1944. He is a descendant of the *ancien régime* who has not reneged on his origins. He is distinguished, very handsome, with aristocratic manners: a squire. His wife, very beautiful, an elegant thoroughbred, lives with him at Dora. They have a dog – a schnauzer. Karr became the camp doctor because he cannot fight. He was severely wounded on the Russian Front. Though his deep-seated sense of superiority makes him antipathetic, he never strikes the deportees. This is a welcome change after the terrible Plazza.

A reversal of Karr's attitude towards Poupault is worth noting. This reversal dates from the day when he watched the French doctor-surgeon perform a trepanation, with the limited facilities available. This operation was carried out with such skill that Karr, from that moment on, showed in his manner his respect for Poupault. Could such psychological observations of one of the key men of the camp be of any use to us? Who can tell? ...

On 2 June 1944, Jacques Poupault learns that Boyer, his boss in the Resistance, leader of the Brutus circuit, is at Dora.

André Boyer is in a pitiful state, emaciated, filthy, totally exhausted. Jacques is moved. The two men fight back their tears. Poupault approaches Schneider: he manages to convince him. Boyer is accepted by the *Revier*. Showered, shaved, he looks human again. He is admitted for a serious case of nephritis; a pretext found by Poupault.

A lawyer from Marseilles, André Boyer joined the Resistance early on. Fourcault's right-hand man, he took over the circuit after his chief's arrest by Vichy. Twice, Boyer was called to London.[1] Twice, he insisted on rejoining his post in France, in the heart of the difficulties and dangers. He has extraordinary determination and much courage; a man of medium height, dark with sparkling white teeth, he has a smile that restores confidence to those around him. Nothing undermines his morale. He wears huge thick-lensed glasses. He wonders why the ss did not break them.

It was in trying to organize Poupault's escape that Boyer was arrested in Paris. He was denounced by a Gestapo spy, a Frenchman, who had infiltrated his circuit. Like Roumeguère and I, Poupault and Boyer found themselves handcuffed together in the Black Maria taking them to the Rue des Saussaies. Later, like Poupault who stood up to the 'specialists' for eight days, Boyer was tortured. He had to hold out for forty-eight hours in order to give his group

time to organize, to cover their tracks, to find new hiding-places.
That was the plan. Boyer would hold out.…

He has been beaten so severely that Poupault is concerned for
his health. He installs Boyer in the VIP[2] room, where he has a bed
to himself. Jacques asks Fritz Preul to make his friend an orderly
when he recovers. Preul says he will think about it.

André Boyer brings news of the Resistance. It is catastrophic.
Pierre Dudreau, Poupault's replacement in the north zone, only
lasted three months. The southern groups (Marseille, Toulouse,
Bordeaux) have been wiped out. The few members who managed
to escape the Gestapo were 'burnt'. They rejoined the Maquis. 'Our
network is too old,' comments Boyer. 'We have held out for too
long. But relief is assured. There are other groups still going strong.
Germany has had it.' André expresses neither bitterness nor discouragement about the fate of the circuit. He intends to carry on
the struggle, here, at Dora.

'Rest. Conserve your strength. You must. The fight isn't over.
Here too we're waiting for the chink in their armour. No suicide
squads. We're just patiently putting the pawns in place,' says Poupault.

One morning, Pierre Rozan finds some horrifying photographs in
one of the camp commandant's jacket pockets. He can hardly believe
his eyes. In one, an SS officer is standing with one foot on a deportee's
body, as if it were a big-game trophy; doubtless the result of a beating after escape. There are other pictures: torture sessions and
hangings. Rozan wants to show us this evidence, but how can he
get the pictures out of the commandant's room? He thinks of the
camp cleaners. He decides to send the jacket to be cleaned. He will
say that he had to empty the pockets. He comes to the dental surgery. Doctor Lemière is there, with Laval, Croizat and me. With
the jacket over his arm, as a safe-conduct, Rozan continues on his
way. The photos stir up our hatred.

Suddenly, the camp loudspeakers call out: 'Detainee 21161, to
the camp gate immediately.' 'That's it, they've caught me,' thinks
Rozan. It's the death sentence for me.' He feels strangely calm: 'At
last, I'm free, I can see the sky, tomorrow I shall be hung.' '*Haftling*
21161. … *Haftling* 21161.' The loudspeaker continues its chant.
'What's the point in trying to gain time,' says Pierre to himself. 'I'd
better go.' He makes his way slowly to the gate.

'21161? We sent to Buchenwald for your watch. Here it is.' Pierre is delirious. In a daze, he grasps the object they are holding out to him. He does not understand.... And then, suddenly, he remembers. When the camp commandant demanded something at an exact time, Rozan would say that it was difficult for him to comply: 'I have no watch, it was taken away at Buchenwald.' So the commandant had insisted that they send the watch back. He has it now, back on his wrist.

More than thirty years have passed; Rozan has not forgotten that moment when the Dora loudspeakers repeated his number, over and over again....

Georges Croizat is very depressed. We try to comfort him. He has received a card from his wife. It comes from Ravensbruck. His wife has been deported too! What happened? Each one of us identifies with Georges. I imagine Suzanne in a camp. I try to be as nice as possible to my friend.

It is not until his return that he discovers that to avenge him, to punish the Germans for having arrested her husband, she had joined the Resistance.

There is trouble in the dental surgery. The Czechs are trying to take our places. They complain of the quantity of consultations granted to French detainees. The ss come to make enquiries. I have to argue our case. I hold up a graph of the consultations with different colours for each nationality; I can prove that the French are not more numerous. Exactly five per cent of our compatriots in proportion to other nationalities come for dental care. What is not shown on the graph is the number of times the French deportees return. That is the trick.

Otto Cimek does not press his point. He has no desire to collaborate with the ss. It was not he who alerted them, but we know he wished them on us. The Czechs have not forgiven us for our non-intervention in 1938 when the Nazis invaded their country. Our boss, ss *Oberscharführer* Michaelson, puts an end to the incident: he does not want any trouble: all he wants is to do nothing, and pick up young girls, when he can. They come to join him in the barracks. One afternoon a girl came, young, sixteen at the most, very pretty. How can that far from attractive man succeed in seducing them? Money? Fear? Food? The grim lure of power?

Michaelson's nerve always surprises me. One day, an ss general
was inspecting the camp. I warned Michaelson: '*Der General ist
da.*' As usual, he is lying on his bed in slacks and a sweater. Without
moving, he answers me: '*Tur zu!*' This 'Shut the door' takes my
breath away. That Sybarite has nerves of steel.

From walking about in deep mud, I sprain my ankles. Doctor
Lemière eases the pain with injections of novocaine. For a week,
I suffer terribly, working, walking. But I am determined that no
stranger to our team shall lay his hands on my graphs and records.

If our existence can be called living, life went on ... In constant
danger, under the yoke of chastisement, with the petty rivalries
and tokens of friendship, all those little buffers against the unbearable ... In return for our labours, we were offered the choice of
dying of hunger, dying from ss beatings or dying at the end of the
hangman's rope. Of dying ...

# Chapter Twenty

# TO RESIST IS TO HOPE

Although Poupault does not hand out *Revier* admission slips, he does do his best to try to prevent deportees being chosen for Ellrich, which is like Dora at the beginning; Ellrich, where the work is infernal, Ellrich the horror camp.[1] He also puts many resisters forward for the *Arbeitsstatistik* Kommandos, which are commanded by *Oberscharführer* Simon, an ss adjutant who directs the whole work programme. There, we number those friends who speak perfect German: Pierre Ziller and a priest, Alfred Untereiner, known as 'Brother Birin' whom I have already mentioned. Other deportees, whose services we can call upon, trustworthy men, work there too. I know a Red Army lieutenant there, Nicolas Petrenko, who speaks German and with whom I have established a permanent contact. Through him, I know how the preparations of the Russians are going. All nationalities stand together against the Nazi monster in a sort of spontaneous alignment. The slaves of the Dora Tower of Babel have no intention of dying like lambs led to the slaughter.

I make contact with a young man of twenty-two, Floiret. He belonged to the sr Air 40, then to the Marco Polo circuit. Arrested on 10 August 1943, he spent six months at Fresnes. Interned at Compiègne, he arrives at Buchenwald on 24 January 1944. At Dora, he wears number 41640. He works in the tunnel: Kommando BMB, super-control. The tool of his trade is a pair of Zeiss electronic micrometer callipers. A German civil engineer supervises the sector. He confides to Floiret: 'I am working on research into a super-bomb. Dropped from a high altitude, it will totally demolish enemy air-bases.' Is he bluffing? Is this the boasting of a man who wants to seem important? ...[2]

As I keep Floiret informed of the Allies' progress, he decides to commit several acts of sabotage. A few days from certain victory, we are not about to let the enemy turn the tables! The fear of the German secret weapons is so great that the only thing to do is to devote all our efforts towards delaying their manufacture.

Floiret and two of his friends, Boulardeau and Paterson, set about placing ill-matched parts on the assembly line and putting the good parts to one side. Imagine their surprise to see two Yugoslavian students cancelling this out by removing the defective parts and putting back the good ones. Did they see what Floiret, Boulardeau and Paterson had done, or are they bent on sabotage too, not knowing the French have struck before them? How can they find out? To tell the truth would be too dangerous. Floiret chooses to catch them in the act of changing a part. He acts outraged, saying 'You'll be tortured and hung for this!' The Yugoslavs treat them like filthy traitors ... so that's it! They're up to the same game. Sabotage begins in earnest ...

On 14 July, the members of Floiret's Kommando decide to demonstrate. They will not sing *La Marseillaise* or *The Internationale* but *Le Chant du Départ*. The news spreads through the camp. And sure enough, Kapos and SS see coming out of the tunnel, marching in orderly ranks, deportees of every nationality. They are singing and followed by the guards from the tunnel interior. The Russians, who had insisted on participating in this 14 July and who are gifted in choral singing, give the scene great majesty. The SS react predictably, and the distribution of blows reaches a rare intensity. The armour-plated discipline has not been penetrated. The destiny of the camp has not altered its course. It is like a student demonstration but its daring is its strength, and it comforts us. Deportees, filthy men in striped pyjamas, in rags, pitiful and starving, have made some sort of stand. ... It is overwhelming. Floiret and his friends have celebrated 14 July 1944 in their own way.

We are gaining Otto Cimek's confidence. It has taken some time. His spell at Auschwitz has made him a man without hope, and nothing will ever cure him. He, like Déprez, thinks that the Germans are going to kill us all. Those are their orders. Not one of us will be left to testify against them. When he speaks French, even when being serious, his extraordinary accent always makes us want to smile. He tells us of the day he saw a pretty girl on a station platform.

'I go up to her, say: you a whore? She slaps my face. I say: Can't I even ask?'

His obsession? What the ss will do when the Allies are near. The camp will be burnt. We shall all be for the crematorium or the flame-throwers. I tell him that we have decided to defend ourselves. We shall take arms from the racks by the barracks near the dental surgery. I tell him we plan to seize the garage. We shall try to kill the men on the watch-towers, to get hold of machine-guns and sub-machine-guns. We have the materials to make Molotov cocktails. Then he admits that he is in touch with a Czech group who are also thinking of attacking when the moment comes. He is in touch with Cespiva, Poupault's assistant.

I tell him that sabotage of the v1s and v2s has begun in the factory. I do not name Claude Lauth, Leschi, Leroy, Hémery or Murgia.

I explain to Cimek that the service of the *Arbeitsstatistik* is very valuable, but I do not name Pierre Ziller or 'Brother Birin'. Nor do I speak of Nicolas Petrenko, my Russian friend, nor of my contacts with the Russians. I have Nicolas' respect and he mine. I am the only Frenchman he sees while organizing internal resistance and, perhaps one day, insurrection. He has asked me to keep quiet about our meetings. I am not going to betray his confidence, even for a man as worthy as Cimek. If Nicolas wants to reveal himself to the Czechs, he will do it when he chooses. Perhaps he already has.

'Thanks to the *Arbeitsstatistik*,' I say to Cimek, 'we know every day which Kommando our friends are in. It's practically indispensable.'

The Czech approves.... Perhaps now that all mistrust has vanished we can join forces? The moles' work is not only carried out in the tunnel....

Shortly after his arrival at the camp, Jacques Poupault had received a visit from Petit, whom we nicknamed 'Father Petit'. He was the radiography laboratory assistant. He said:

'Dora is classified as a *Geheimlager*, a top-secret camp.... You are aware that there are among us many mathematicians, physicists and chemists. They all know the secrets of the v1s and v2s. The ss will let no one escape. They will exterminate us when they see that they have lost. I put to you that, because of your membership of the bcra and the ties you have with official people, you should set up a group for self-defence. I lack influence,' he added. 'You are a source of energy, of fire. People have confidence in you. But take care! No idle talk! Here it's the rope for the least mistake.'

Poupault accepted this proposal. He began by searching out trust-worthy men in the various barracks: Ziller and his friends in the *Arbeitsstatistik*, despite *Oberscharführer* Simon, would try to have them appointed to useful posts. He thus made the acquaintance of Colonel Gentil, a former graduate of the Ecole Polytechnique, tall, skeletal, very dignified even in his ragged clothes. He declared him-self to be totally devoted to our organization.

Every evening, after roll-call, we would meet. 'Father Petit' explained that we must note the exact location of the necessary tools for cutting down trees. At the chosen moment, the felled trees would crash down on the barbed-wire fences, crushing them. He said that he had collected a small stock of petrol and empty bottles. That many of us would die did not matter. What was important was that a few should survive to escape and bear witness.

During those days that we were stepping up our efforts, we felt that our slow and derisory labours were beginning to bear fruit. I learned with pleasure that newcomers were hatching plots. Clervoy, Lauth, Murgia and I listened to them all. We said little. Our own work was much more advanced. Our projects had the advantage of having matured longer. But I had no wish to reveal everything that we had done, or the relationships we had forged. In those cir-cumstances, the slightest error, an imprudent remark could have wiped out months of effort. We said only what we judged necessary.

Petit confirmed to Poupault what I had learnt from Otto Cimek: the Czechs had organized themselves. Petit declared that the Rus-sians were equally structured and ready for action. Prudently (as advised by 'Father Petit') Poupault questioned his assistant Cespiva,[3] who finally confided in him. The Czechs' aim, their first objective, was to build a short-wave radio transmitter using parts stolen from the tunnel factories. He also said: 'I am not authorized to let you know the head of the Russian organization. They are ex-tremely cautious. But they are working too.'

The radio transmitter was soon ready to be used. It was hidden in the *Revier*. How could we communicate with the Allies? We would have to send out messages in clear, not code, and know which waveband to use. The risks were enormous. Poupault was both excited and anxious to keep the Czechs on their guard. 'The Germans will pick us up before the Allies can hear us.' Despite Jacques' reservations, the Czechs persisted in their intention. Poupault informed Marcel Petit of the mad ambition of Cespiva's companions. How on earth were they to dissuade them, and by what authority could they force them to be silent? Perhaps they were right to stake everything? ...

Jacques kept André Boyer informed, from the moment he arrived at Dora, of what the Czechs were trying to do – make contact with the Allies. André did not find the idea absurd at all. He proposed that they transmit in clear and in code if the ss decided to liquidate the deportees. Boyer had a prodigious memory. He recalled certain code phrases that were transmitted in English. Perhaps we would be heard?

This excitement that I am trying to describe lasted, for some of us, for months. Everyone was busy discussing plans and all the time taking every precaution not to be found out, for the ss and the Kapos did not relax their vigil.

When 6 June 1944 arrived, they were under the impression that they held only the winning cards.

6 June! It was eight a.m. Cimek, Laval, Croizat and I were in the surgery. Michaelson had slept out, probably with some girl. Suddenly, the BBC! 'The Allies landed last night. The landing has been successful. The troops are holding their ground and progressing on French soil.' At last! For two months we had waited for this. We jumped for joy, and hugged each other. We were trembling with delight. Our eyes full of tears. We explained what had happened to Cimek, for he had not understood. That inveterate pessimist joined in our celebrations. 'It's over. In a month they'll be here!' We were the first to hear the news and we were eager to pass it on. Our struggle to survive, to help, now seemed less hopeless. No longer were we clutching at straws. Reality was on our side. The Germans would be beaten. Every day that passed brought them nearer to their end.

Even today, when I remember that moment, my eyes fill with tears, my whole body shudders with joy, a lump forms in my throat. Was that the happiest day of my life?

The ss looked odd that 6 June. At least, our optimism made them uncomfortable. The invincible Third Reich did not seem quite so invincible to them now.

René Morel, a solid Breton, defensively surly, a doctor and vet, burst into the operating room. He shouted out the information we had passed on to him. Happily, Karr was not there – it wasn't 'hernia day'. Morel said to Poupault: 'They landed between Caen and le Cotentin. The air force has command of the air. The Maquis has gone into action.'

Poupault could not reply. He was thinking: 'If I open my mouth to speak I shall burst into tears.' Boyer, forewarned by Jacques, kept calm. 'The Allies have prepared for everything,' he declared. 'They will hold firm. You can have no idea of the amount of material they have amassed. It's the end of Nazism.'

Boyer had been at Dora for only four days. He had not had to wait long to know the joy of that day. There were others who would never know it, for they felt, deep in their hearts, that no good could come to them now. They carried on automatically. For them it was all over. Death had taken a hold of them for ever. They had seen so much, and for so many years. . . .

# Chapter Twenty-one

# FRITZ PREUL

No sun, not a star,
hope is extinguished
No apostle will come.

*Stanislas Radimecky*

One hour after the Landings were announced, Fritz Preul, *Revier*
Kapo, sent for Poupault. He arrived in Preul's room, where no one
had set foot before. This room was in the block where the consultations were held. It contained a studio couch, a wardrobe, a cloth-
covered table, two chairs, a comfortable leather arm-chair, a carpet
on the floor. This décor was surprising in a concentration camp.
Fritz smiled at Jacques' amazed expression. Then he broke the
silence:

'I was deported eight years ago. I have had time to settle down,
to learn to settle again when I changed camps.' He added: 'You
know that the British and the Americans have landed in France.
It's said the Maquis will go into action, if they haven't already. ...'
Poupault did not know what Fritz Preul was getting at. He waited
prudently before replying. Preul, as if invested with a mission, declared:

'I asked for you to come to congratulate you in the name of my
German Communist comrades. The action of the French forces in-
land gives us new hope for the future of France. You may repeat
my words to the comrades of whom you are said to be leader.'

Jacques was more and more astonished. His head was spinning.
Were we about to work, hand in hand, with the German Communists in the camp? He knew he had to say something.

'I am no one's leader. There is no French group.'

Preul seemed to appreciate his caution. He continued:

'Leader or no, group or no, go back and tell your friends what I have said. And then come and see me this evening at about eight o'clock. I shall show you something that will interest you.'

Jacques Poupault left the room. He was shaken, anxious. What was Fritz up to? If he was so well informed, surely the ss were too? He thought about this meeting all day and did not speak of it to anyone. If Fritz was watching him it would be better for him not to be seen hurrying to repeat their conversation to other Frenchmen.

Jacques arrived on time for his second meeting with Fritz. The latter offered him a cigarette and a glass of schnapps. Poupault felt as if he were at a friend's house, at a party, not at Dora in the heart of a repulsive world, a blot on humanity.

'It's not a patch on cognac,' said Preul, 'but one must take the rough with the smooth, as they say.'

Previously Poupault and Preul had spoken German together, now the Kapo began to speak perfect French.

'I didn't know you spoke French,' said Jacques.

'I learnt it at grammar school. I went to grammar school,' replied Fritz. He seemed to be lost in this memory of his past. A desperate sadness appeared on his fine-featured face. He was silent for some time. Jacques, though still on his guard, felt drawn by the sadness that emanated from Preul.

'I even studied medicine for two years. At the age of twenty-one I was arrested for spreading Communist propaganda.'

Poupault made some mental calculations. Fritz must be twenty-nine, as he had been a deportee for eight years. Fritz seemed to read his thoughts. He said, this time in German:

'I know. I look much older. The camp ages you terribly, and the first years were atrocious. More friends died at Buchenwald than have died up to now at Dora.'

Poupault thought of the struggle of the German Communists against the Social Democrats during the rise of Nazism. They obeyed orders from Moscow which considered the Social Democrats to be prime enemies. He thought of Stalin's toast to Hitler: 'I know how much the German nation loves its Führer. That is why I shall be happy to drink to his health.' That was on the eve of the German-Soviet pact. How could the poor German Communists navigate the treacherous waters of politics? There has rarely in history been a group of men so greatly sacrificed. Jacques felt moved, but was still wary. He said: 'I have heard about that time.' He did not add, 'I also know that the Soviet authorities handed over to the Nazis the German Communists who had escaped to Russia.' He merely said:

'Soon you will be free.'

A look of utter despair then came into Preul's eyes.

'Free to do what? After eight years behind barbed-wire will I know what to do with freedom? Go back to the "good old days"? I have organized my life here, what could my life be out there? Soon I'll be thirty. I know nothing of the world, nothing of life. How would I manage? Here I am somebody, what would I be out there? Nothing.' The despondency and helplessness of this man were overwhelming; a man who must daily have had to display so much courage, tenacity and heroism.

Preul must have felt that he was arousing the other's pity. He shook off his black thoughts. He said:

'I did not bring you here to philosophize to you.'

Jacques realized that he had forgotten that he was at Dora.

The German lifted the cloth from the round table. A wireless set appeared. 'It works well,' he said, 'you will be able to hear the French broadcast by the BBC.'

He placed covers across the window and door. Everything had been scrupulously prepared: the openings were completely obscured. He turned on the set.

'Find the station. I don't know exactly where it is,' he said.

Jacques found it easily. He listened intently to the news. It was an extraordinary moment: to be in the heart of a concentration camp, listening to friendly voices coming from London, watched by a German Communist Kapo.

When the broadcast was over, the set was covered again.

'You must have guessed that the real hiding-place is not under the table cloth,' said Preul. He went on:

'The place is secret. It cannot be found. Four of us know the existence of this radio. I don't need to tell you that we are all for the rope if the SS find out. And give me your word that you won't tell Petit or Boyer.'

'So Fritz knows of "Father Petit's" involvement and Boyer's importance in the Resistance, though he's only been in the camp since

2 June,' thought Poupault, 'but he obviously doesn't know that Croizat listens in every day, or about Jean Michel's tireless efforts, or Lauth's action in the tunnel or the Czechs' plans ...' He wrenched himself away from these thoughts to reassure the German: 'I give you my word,' he said, 'I shall say nothing about the radio.'

This was the first broadcast that Jacques had actually heard since his arrest. He had a moment of euphoria, of well-being, as if he had just had a shot of heroin: that was how he put it, as a doctor. He had never given up hope but at that moment he was filled with an intense joy. Almost at once, like the threat of a storm, he was paralysed with fear of an accident, a mistake: what if the ss, the camp Gestapo, were to find out what was going on? ...

We follow the Allies' fortunes through Croizat: the quantity of weapons landed, the troops who set foot in Normandy, the joining up of the forces from the different landing points, the fact that the Allied combined air force is practically alone in the sky, the action of the Underground.

Croizat is playing a game of cat and mouse with Michaelson. Laval, Cimek and I detain the ss officer on the most slender pretexts. We have to get him out of his room as often, and for as long, as possible. Croizat's skill would merit a standing ovation. The greatest comedy actors are not in the theatre. It is in real life that comedy is at its best and Croizat is a real star!

Now, in the evening, Jacques Poupault goes regularly to Fritz Preul's room. Together they listen to the BBC. The broadcasts by Maurice Schumann delight Jacques. It must be very hard for him not to break his word and tell his friends. He learns that the four men who knew of the existence of this radio are Preul, the Kapo Schneider, Cespiva and himself.

Two Germans, a Czech, a Frenchman. ... The survivors of the camps know of this kind of communion, as do the relatives of the victims. When peace came, a mother who had lost her child was to say: 'I want ashes from Ellrich. I know that they will not be my son's, but they will be just as precious....'

# Chapter Twenty-two

# WAITING FOR RESCUE

Two weeks after the Landings of 6 June, the Germans are searching for all skilled men capable of speeding up the production of the V1s and V2s. The tunnel is teeming with them. It swallows up more and more victims. I am summoned to the *Arbeitsstatistik* by *Ober-scahrführer* Simon. I go, wondering why they have sent for me. At Dora, to be called for causes instant fear. There are several SS men there. One of them questions me: 'What do you want?' I reply: 'I was sent for. I am a dentist.' 'That's not true, you are an engineer.' It's Simon. He shows me a photograph of myself – head shaven, smiling (yes, I was) – taken at Buchenwald. I am surprised to see that I looked so well. Weeks, months have passed since that day. Dora has changed me. As I look at the photo from Buchenwald I say calmly: 'That's true. I am a dental engineer. That's what it's called in France.' The lie was so outrageous I thought perhaps they might believe it. Simon takes a swipe at me and shouts: 'Get out!' I do not need to be told twice. I have no wish to lose my place with Laval, Cimek and Croizat.

The SS must have thought that the French accorded grades to the dental profession. They must have put away my photograph and file. I escape the tunnel. I had begun to fear I would be sent back to that hellish place.

Soon, all the same, there is a change at the dental surgery. Happily, it does not involve Croizat. He is able to continue to listen to the BBC. In the surgery, we treated the SS and the deportees at different times. As the camp grew in importance, a new dental surgery was created for the SS.

With Laval – towards the middle of June 1944 – we leave our barrack for another. We are to treat only deportees. The new barrack is not in the ss camp but inside the perimeter of what we called 'the big camp' – the concentration camp proper. *Rottenführer* Maischen, the ss corporal in charge of us, was a zealous cretin. That was a change for us from the sensual and indolent Michaelson, but Maischen was not really that bad.

Our two new dental technicians are called Pierre and Jean Galliot, two extremely nice brothers. They were in the convoy before mine, the 'Twenty Thousand'. They are nineteen and twenty years old. They are always together. It is touching. They speak of their parents with emotion, thinking only of the anguish they must be feeling. 'We had never left them. When they went on holiday, they took us with them. Now we are the cause of their pain!' Pierre and Jean were dental students when they were arrested. Before getting this job, they suffered a great deal; particularly in the winter of 1943-4 when, equipped with crampons, they had to climb posts and instal the camp telephone wires. 'That's a terrible job when the lack of food has sapped all your strength and gives you no protection from the cold.' And yet the Galliot brothers still speak calmly, never complaining. Their sense of family and love for each other gives our new home a warm and peaceful atmosphere. . . .

Jacques Poupault was to have two terrifying experiences.

One day, in the tunnel, a Russian, who is one of the seven 'Bible Forcers' of the camp, refuses to make weapons.

ss Busta, whom we called 'Horse Face', one of the worst of them, orders the detainee to work. The Russian refuses. An empty stomach is usually persuasive, but the 'Bible Forcer' sticks to his refusal. Busta draws his revolver (a 6.35 mm) and holds it to the deportee's head, right between the eyes. He says: 'If you do not work, I'll fire.' The Russian does not budge. Without showing the least sign of emotion, looking his victim straight in the eye, Busta pulls the trigger. The shot rings out.

As if nothing has happened, the Russian advances on the German. Flabbergasted and doubtless terrified, Busta retreats and does not fire a second time. The scene is haunting. To see that deportee, in rags, half-starved, a hole through his skull, standing up to the German, advancing on him, is something of a miracle. Busta is absolutely petrified. He must think the supernatural has taken over. Finally, the Russian collapses. He is taken to the *Revier*. It is there that Poupault sees him and hears the unbelievable story.

But that isn't the end of it! By an extraordinary twist of fate, the bullet has not harmed a single vital organ. It has travelled along the base of the skull and lodged itself in a muscle at the back of the head. Jacques removes the bullet and the Russian makes a rapid recovery.

Another day, a Czech who has escaped and been recaptured is brought to Poupault. He has been caught by a *Volkssturm* who has shot him. The poor man's arm is riddled with shot, bloody, the flesh in shreds.

Poupault examines the wound; there is only one course of action: amputation. He operates. Despite the complete absence of anti-biotics the Czech makes a good recovery from the operation. When he is completely well, the verdict from Berlin reaches Dora: 'Condemned to be hanged.' Poupault was deeply discouraged: 'To have saved a man's life for the gallows, it's absurd!' But Poupault can do nothing when the ss come to fetch their victim. Must it always be so, that in every country in the world the condemned must be cared for so that they go to meet their maker 'in good health'?

One morning, Cespiva has a word with Poupault. He speaks quietly. He is afraid they might be overheard.

'Did you hear the BBC yesterday? I am worried. London was bombed by the v1s. The British are very concerned. We must use our transmitter. It can't be put off any longer. We must warn the British that the things are being made at Dora.'

In spite of the circumstances, Jacques once again opposed Cespiva. 'We haven't a chance of being heard,' he said. 'We're 900 miles from the front. It's not that I'm afraid they'll destroy Dora, and us too. I would accept that sacrifice if I were sure the English could hear us.'

'The Czechs will send the message. Even if the French don't agree.' Cespiva's reply was rough, cutting.

Poupault, very calmly, asked his assistant to wait: 'Give me until tomorrow to think about it.'

That evening, Jacques discussed it with Petit and André Boyer. André, who had favoured the Czech's idea if the decision to kill all the deportees was about to be carried out, agreed with Poupault:

'The British learnt about the existence of Peenemünde from the Polish Resistance. Doubtless they know of the existence of Dora.[1] But how could their bombs reach the v1s and v2s built in the tunnel?

An air raid, important as it is, would be useless. Their attack would be better directed against the launching pads, which are not in the camp. If we act now, without thinking it through, the ss will discover us at once. They'll hang us. Dead we'll be of no more use to anyone. We would have made a startling gesture, but one which would have no lasting effect on the hostilities. . . . A shot in the dark. . . . Worse, an error!'

'Nevertheless, Cespiva's ready for anything,' retorted Boyer.

'That's true,' replied Jacques, 'but I'm not sure of his nerves. He's been in concentration camps for a long time. He's had typhus. Several times I've seen him in a state of near total collapse. I fear for him, and for us, if the worst should happen.'

In the morning, Poupault took Cespiva aside and explained patiently to him the reasons why he persisted in his refusal. The Czech heard him out. The launching-pad argument impressed him.[2] Finally, he agreed.

A Frenchman 'extracted' from the bunker is brought to the dental surgery. He is escorted by two ss men. The deportee tells us that he had escaped, been recaptured by the ss and beaten. His jaw is broken. Laval starts to patch him up. The ss are waiting to take back their prey. At that moment, Karr passes by. Enraged, I explain to the German doctor, without raising my voice but with my anger barely under control, what is happening. Karr says to the ss: 'I forbid you to make martyrs of the deportees.' He does not shout, but articulates each syllable with cold fury. He emanates authority. The ss leave, penitent. Despite his haughty and insolent demeanor, Karr was human. He did not really belong to the race of torturers and madmen whose uniform he wore.

The Nazis try out a new diet on the deportees, based on synthetic protein. They must think this might combat the vitamin deficiency which is giving the prisoners enormous oedemas. These they scratch, and they become infected. Then scabies and phlegmons follow, usually fatal. The new diet proves ineffective.

In July, another transport of an ailing thousand is decided on; these were the most atrocious moments in life at Dora and its thirty-one dependent temples of atrocity. The selection took place. It disqualified from the rank of men those ss who took part with such enthusiasm, such sadistic pleasure. They were abortions of humanity, obsessed with aberration.... The same horrible scenes were enacted again.... Doubtless the July thousand went up in smoke like the preceding 'Heaven Kommandos'...

Karr is becoming friendlier and friendlier to Poupault. Does he forsee the German defeat? Is there no one for him to talk to among the ss? Is he ashamed of belonging to that fraternity of murderers? Does he feel more and more respect for Jacques?...

The ss doctor has just taken a week of leave in Berlin. He returns in a thoughtful frame of mind. He confesses to Poupault: 'They told me Berlin was fifty per cent destroyed. I walked from north to south, from east to west of the city and I only ever saw that fifty per cent.'

Jacques draws on his store of expressions for one that is suitably distressed.

*Unterscharführer* Lorenz, of whom I have already spoken and to whom we owed some recognition (the only blameless ss officer or soldier we ever met) is once again put in charge of the administration of the *Revier*. He questions Poupault closely about the medical profession in France.

One morning there is a buzzing in the sky, which grows louder and louder. We run out of the barracks. The sky is blue. Sparkling in the sun, thousands of little white specks float gently down like garlands of silver paper. Thousands! Millions! They are decoys to block the radar. Bombers are heading east. There are so many it is impossible to count them. Lorenz says to Poupault who is standing beside him: 'The Americans! I hope they're not headed for us!' And he glances at the derisory shelter dug out beside the *Revier*. Jacques asks him: 'But where are the Germans?' Lorenz gives him a funny look. He is wondering if the question is a trick. He replies, half-smiling, half-serious: 'How could they find room in such a crowded sky?'

Croizat hears on the BBC news of the attack and advance of Patton's army. The Allies are making great strides. There is no need of a map to follow the offensive. Dora holds deportees from every region of France. Each contributes his knowledge of the lie of the land.

Doctor Lemière receives a postcard from his wife. It brings him news of the bombing of Condé-sur-Noireau, where his family lived, and the death of his brother-in-law. Lemière has seven children. His brother-in-law the same. Here he is in a concentration camp, head of the family, with fourteen children in his care. He waits until he is alone to give way to his grief.

In addition to the actual tragedy of deportation, the constant humiliation of each day, there is always this private concern for those who are far away. Often a letter comes which proves the concern justified and sometimes, alas, insufficient.

'You have been gone for months. I am tired of waiting. If you are not back in a week I'll go off with someone else.' This is the laconic message, with the dubious merit of being frank, received by one deportee who is very ill and hospitalized in the *Revier*. He reads and re-reads the postcard. Yes, that is his wife's handwriting. Already very weak, these two lines plunge him deeper into the despair that often precedes death. He shows the card to everyone. The French, unlike other peoples, often make fun of the cuckold – in life as in the theatre. Here at Dora, the joke is unthinkable. We try to cheer up the unhappy man, and certainly do not joke about him behind his back.

15 August 1944, Georges Croizat pays us a visit. He has tried not to run. On his face is written the good news. 'They have landed on the Mediterranean coast.' We embrace joyfully. The information spreads throughout the camp like wildfire.

Karr is making himself even more agreeable. He confesses to Poupault: 'I have always been opposed to the creation of a gas chamber at Dora. As long as I am here it will never happen.' Would he be able to engineer his own future?

Fritz Preul is becoming freer with Poupault.

'We German Communists count heavily on French support,' he says. 'We must keep in close contact. I don't trust the Russians, who are not, for the most part, real Communists. I fear their violent and tactless reactions in the last days, in the sole aim of settling personal scores.'

'I understand them,' replies Jacques. 'The Russians have suffered even more than the others. It's only natural that they want to make the ss and the Kapos pay.'

Preul explains that the political prisoners who are trying to con-

trol the camp would prefer the action to be led by thinking men.
'We mustn't let ourselves be over-run. We must unite our efforts.
We have made preparations for the liberation of the camp. Let's
work together.'

For a long time I had known that the Russian Communists themselves feared being overtaken by an impulsive action which risked
hastening the extermination of the deportees. I also knew that the
German political prisoners ran the camp; the Kapos in the tunnel
were their men; little by little, they had taken the place of the green
triangles. Preul and his men might well fear that the Russians,
blinded by hate, would indiscriminately assassinate the organizations' Kapos as well as the others. Particularly as, in order to mislead
the ss, they were not always 'gentle'. I was happy to see that the pact
that had been made as a result of our agreement with the Czechs
and the Russians was functioning well. I could not tell everything
to the other Frenchmen who came to our meetings. Lauth, Clervoy
and Murgia were the best informed. We had been together from
the beginning.

When Poupault saw Preul again, he told him: 'We've counted.
There aren't enough of us.'

At that time, Jacques did not know the full extent of our organization. This organization, despite the Czechs' advice, preferred not
to work with the German Communists; as the Russians and the
French were in the majority, the Czechs were keen to do so. It was
for that reason too that Fritz Preul, who had suspected that we
existed, did not know exactly our potential in action.

'It is too soon,' commented Preul. 'Take care. The Gestapo has
spies planted among the deportees. We have already eliminated
some of them. There are others. I shall soon be able to tell you who
are the French agents for the Gestapo.'

26 August 1944. Another visit from Georges Croizat. This time he
cannot help breaking into a shuffling run. When he arrives there
are tears in his eyes. Tears of joy ... Paris is liberated! He heard
the re-transmission of the event. There we all are – Laval, the
Galliot brothers and I – too moved to speak. Paris liberated! We
savour the words. Repeat them to ourselves, over and over. In my
mind's eye, I see the town where I was born, its streets; Clichy,
where I lived as a child; Suzanne; Monique, my daughter; Pierre
Roumeguère, my friend ... I can imagine the crowds in the streets.

Patriotism is a warped sentiment. Suddenly, in moments like these surrounded by tragedy, this love of a country is an emotion of sincerity, elegance, dignity, nobility and freshness. An emotion that could never have served to subjugate those loyal men who simply love the land of their fathers without denying others a right to that love of their own lands.

From the beginning of September 1944, Jews and gypsies arrive at the camp. They have been evacuated from Auschwitz.

Some time afterwards, Rozan discovers that the members of an SS general staff from outside Dora are assembling in the commandant's barrack. He learns that they are forming a court martial. They have come to pass judgement on two of the SS who, completely drunk in a café in Nordhausen, kicked up a row and summoned the waiter, saying: 'If you don't serve us quicker you'll find yourselves at Dora. You'll be laughing on the other side of your face then. In two weeks you'll go up in smoke.' They were trying to be clever. Their words had been reported, the Gestapo have ears everywhere. Dora is *Geheimlager*: nothing was to be divulged of what went on there. Summoned before the court martial, the two macabre boasters are condemned to be shot.

As soon as the judgement was passed, this fine gathering returns to the commandant's rooms to 'celebrate'. Officers from the camp and from elsewhere help themselves to drinks. Over the public address system the former musicians from Auschwitz are ordered to report to the camp gates immediately. Rozan sees a troop of vagabonds, dressed in rags, suffering from pellagra, more dead than alive, in calf-length trousers and dilapidated shoes. Pierre is appalled by the distress and misery emanating from these human wrecks. Among them are gypsies, musicians who used once to play at the *Opéra*: they are all in a state of physical collapse with one foot in the grave. Rozan wonders how on earth they manage to stay upright.

They had arrived at Dora with those from Auschwitz in a succession of goods trains. These convoys were made up of categorized trucks; for example, one of spectacles, one of children's boots, one of adults' shoes, and so on, including one of musical instruments. You could never define the limits of the Nazis' passion for organization.

Since the camp commandant and his guests feel the need for a little music, an SS officer orders a soldier to take the musicians to the store to select an instrument and bring them back to play under the window.

This was done.

The orchestra assembles and the pitiful, emaciated, filthy little musicians, fingers stiff and sore, play to order while the officers drink, bellow and laugh. The contrast is greater than anything the German expressionist cinema has ever shown. Sometimes an officer cries: 'Play better, you slovenly bastards, you sub-humans, *Stücke*.' The ragged musicians try, desperate to prevent the threats from turning into blows. The cheerful music is cruelly in contrast to the desolate scene.

That concert, in broad daylight, a concert that lasted for hours, is deeply embedded in Pierre Rozan's memory.... To have to stand by and watch that masquerade and be powerless to stop it!

# Chapter Twenty-three

## A BROTHEL AT DORA!

One autumn evening, Fritz Preul brings Poupault three prison numbers. 'Memorize them,' he says, 'destroy the paper and keep an eye on the men wearing these numbers. They are three Frenchmen whom we suspect. In our opinion they are Gestapo agents inside the camp.'

From Ziller, at the *Arbeitsstatistik*, Jacques learns the names of the three men. The first, a Kapo in the tunnel, is called Naegele. The second, D,[1] is a *Schreiber* in the tunnel (he wrote out reports). The third is a charming story-teller, Deglane.

Until now, except for Deglane, there has been no French Kapo who has come straight from Buchenwald. Naegele is the second. The moles decide to exercise surveillance.

Naegele speaks freely to the deportees. He criticizes the ss and the German Kapos. He acts prudently, trying to gain the confidence of the detainees, saying that he only accepted the job as Kapo to make things easier for them. 'At least, with me, there are no beatings or punishments.' Naegele passes on information about his contact with the resisters. He cites names and places that he would have to have known to speak of so precisely. He is exact and at the same time too 'open'. The detainees do not know what to think.

Naegele constantly asks if there are important members of the Resistance in the camp. He tries to find out any contacts between deportees. He preaches the execution of the ss as soon as the opportunity arises. He claims he belonged to the Buckmaster circuit in Orléans. He gives the names of the leaders. By cross-checking, those who question him discover his facts are true; and yet, they are still wary of him. If he is loyal, he is still behaving too imprudently.

We were to learn later that he really did belong to the Gestapo.

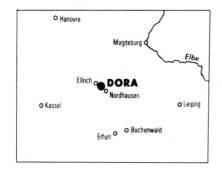

In the summer of 1943, after the destruction of their installations at
Peenemünde on the Baltic coast, the Nazis decided to set up a new
installation in an area to be called 'Mittelbau', the central point of which
was Dora, situated in the Harz hills near the town of Nordhausen. The
installation, set up to develop V2 bombs, would be controlled by General
Walter Dornberger and the scientist, Wernher von Braun.

The project map for the building of the railway through the Helme
valley which would act as a transport system for materials for Dora,
Ellrich and Nordhausen. Dora is not named on this German map drawn
by Helmut Meyer, but the tunnel system is mentioned between Ellrich
and Nordhausen on the detail in the upper left-hand corner.

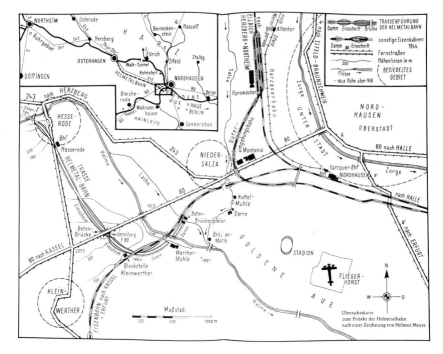

Dora was a complex system of galleries and tunnels running through the Kohnstein hill. Until the beginning of 1943 the deportees had to dig and enlarge these tunnels in order to create a subterranean factory. In appalling conditions, sleeping in overcrowded bunks on four levels (*left*) with no sanitary facilities, the deportees worked with bare hands and few tools, the bodies of their fellows hanging from the roof of the tunnel (*below left*) as a warning. These two woodcuts were made in Dora by a deportee, Dominik Černy.

One of the V2 rockets ready to be fired.

Prisoners approaching the camp at Dora (*above*) and a midnight outing from the eastern end of the tunnels (*below*). Very few of the prisoners who worked in the tunnels saw daylight more than once a week; they were shut up in the darkness of the galleries and forced to do a 12- or 14-hour day. Nearly 100 men died each day.

Sabotage on the production line of the V2s was very successful at Dora,
yet bombs *were* made. The drawing shows the mounting of the
propulsion unit into one of the rockets in B-tunnel.

The welding on of the outer skin of the rocket.

After 1 November 1944, Dora ceased to depend on Buchenwald and became an independent camp.

From 1 April 1945, with the approach of the Allies, the ss began to evacuate Dora, taking the prisoners northwards, particularly to Bergen-Belsen where many died. This photograph shows one of the galleries in the tunnel.

A v2 which was found in the tunnel when Dora was liberated.

Piles of bodies in a courtyard at Nordhausen, after the American air force had bombed the town on 4 April 1945.

In the summer of 1948, the buildings at Dora, already gutted by the Soviet occupation forces, were finally destroyed.

Nothing of the camp of Dora now remains except the crematorium with its ovens.

He had participated in the arrest of all the members of the circuit whose names he cited. If the Germans had sent him to a concentration camp, it was because he had cheated the Gestapo in dealings on the black market. But right up to our arrest, despite our doubts, most of us believed that he was a resister. Too talkative – and he was not the only one – but a resister all the same ...

Deglane is an extreme case of mythomania. Amazing! What was true was that he was the oldest of the deportees. He said he had been a captain in active service in Intelligence, arrested by the Germans in 1941 and condemned to twenty years confinement in a fortress. He said he had been wounded by the ss while trying to escape. As punishment, they had put him into a concentration camp. His green triangle, which had intrigued me, was soon removed and replaced by the red triangle of the political prisoners. It must be said that despite Fritz Preul's suspicion we never had any cause to reproach him. Always smiling, he tried to be of service. Numerous deportees owe him for some kindness or help. German-speaking, he had been made a Kapo and wanted to remain one. It gave him advantages and enabled him to help his friends.

After the Liberation, he returned with us to Paris. He wore a captain's uniform and worked for some months in the social work of the Resistance. One day he was arrested. He was found guilty of fraud – the illegal wearing of a uniform. He was not a captain. He had never done a single day of military service. As for his belonging to the Gestapo, we never had any proof of it.

The third man, D, is a living enigma. He passed through our lives like those characters in the films symbolizing Destiny. The Man of Tragedy, fascinating in his precision, terrifyingly mysterious. A conjuror of genius, he played with events, made secrets vanish by inventing others. Almost religiously suspect, he would destroy our suspicions just when the desire to condemn him was strongest in us. Hand in hand with intrigue, Fate's acolyte, he laughed at the quirks of history. He fought neglect and destruction when we thought him an accomplice to evil. His mask never slipped.

This character of fiction was a man of superior intelligence. He spoke eight languages, rolling his r's in French. A Russian by origin, he was driven by a deeply-rooted anti-Communism – the Nazi camps were only following the example set by Lenin in the Soviet

Union, from the days following the October Revolution. Hitler considered Stalin his master, but the pupil did not have the teacher's cunning; he did not know how to found a religion ...

Yellowish complexion, a round head, thick glasses, a high forehead and of average size, D looked about forty years old. He said he was an engineer. Had Fritz Preul fingered him so that we would rid him of a man who knew far too much about the Soviet Union? But the German Communist Kapos could just as well have beaten him to death without our help ... Besides, they would have had right on their side – the unwritten rule of the camp! And why was D there at all? Why had he been imprisoned by the Nazis when he could have fought on their side at the Russian Front? ...

'You must understand, I hate all totalitarian régimes,' said D when I asked him this question. 'I'm not going to ally myself with one because I consider it less dangerous than another ...'

Though the deportees used the familiar *tu* to each other, he addressed me as *vous*. A strange man, unique, who seemed to know what other men – for the most part – did not. He discussed problems; unlike most people, he seemed to see every side of them.

D and Naegele belonged to the convoy of the 'Seventy-Seven Thousand'. This convoy had left Paris on 17 August, just before the Liberation. The Resistance had attacked it. A few detainees had been able to escape. After travelling for six days the convoy had arrived at Buchenwald, and on 15 September, at Dora.

General Dejussieu (Pontcarral to all the resisters), Debaumarché, Cazin d'Honuncthin and René Cogny, who became General Cogny, were all part of this convoy.

Jacques Poupault was busy. Dejussieu had slipped him a list of numbers. Each one corresponded to a deportee who belonged to a Resistance general staff. The struggle must continue. It was Jacques' mission to have men capable of fighting attached to less perilous Kommandos than those in the tunnel. The choice tore Poupault in pieces, particularly as the unfortunate men who were not chosen left for Ellrich, where they had to dig, enlarge, shore up and widen the tunnel in the same awful conditions that we had known.... The death rate there was terrible. After the Liberation, it was estimated to have reached ninety-five per cent.

When Poupault had completed his mission he saw that Dejussieu was to leave for Ellrich. He had not been put on the list. Jacques had him admitted to the *Revier* for nephritic colic. To keep him as long as possible, he even operated on him for two hernias, one after the other, depriving Karr of his favourite operation.

Jacques Poupault informed Dejussieu of his contacts, the good-will he had encountered and the organization which was taking shape. I had already made friends with Cazin d'Honuncthin, colonel in intelligence. I had spoken to him of our work, of the slow construction of a circuit which could go into action when the time came. He was happy to be one of us. Then I met Dejussieu. He was the head of the *Armée Secrète* (AS). He had succeeded General Delestraint, creator of the AS.[2] I asked him to become the head of our organization. He accepted. He approved of my discretion, which I had maintained from the very first day. He was very interested in my contacts and told me I was right to keep the various groups separate. To Dejussieu, who had been my 'patron' in the Resistance, I explained everything, omitting nothing.

In July 1944, Hitler's interest in the secret weapons manifested itself in the creation of quick courses for the deportees. In order to be assigned to increasingly more delicate work, they had to pass examinations – the *Prüfungen*. Once their education was completed, they handled the precision instruments necessary for the manufacture and checking of the parts for the VIs and V2s.

In October 1944, Dora became an *Arbeitslager*, a work camp, as if we had not slaved hard enough up until then! Did they think the diseased deportees would overnight be transformed into healthy, skilled workers? There was one difference, however, the food improved: slightly thicker soups and an extra two ounces of margarine. At work, the SS and Kapos still supervised but struck us less often. Hitler and his experts thought this régime of milder slavery would improve the work – which was not solely physical effort – and prevent eventual sabotage.

The mutation of Dora into an *Arbeitslager* brought other changes. They installed a crematorium oven. Thus we now had the joyous prospect that our rotting remains would not have to be shipped off to Buchenwald on the back of a lorry, but could be incinerated at Dora.

Then they created a canteen. So that we could get extra trifles there – mussels in sauce, for example – they gave out 'camp marks' to the deportees; one or two marks a week depending on their work. In November 1944, one of the barracks was turned into a cinema.

But the SS reached the height of absurdity when, a few days later, they opened a brothel. Yes! A brothel at Dora! For men who needed all their will-power to keep on their feet, whose systems were crumbling under the onslaught of disease and vitamin deficiency, bedridden invalids wondering what had become of their loved ones, wondering what their families would do when their turn came to die, men who thought of everything from hope to despair, everything but physical love. All they could do at the brothel was to take their camp marks as a gift to the poor girls, but nothing else which could justify the ladies' function.

The *Puff* was not receiving any clients. Teutonic sensitivity to returns could not bear such waste. As there was a brothel, the brothel must be used. The brothel had to be justified to Hitler and his henchmen. Are we organized or are we not? We Germans are kings when it comes to organization. Are these sub-human deportees going to sabotage our *Puff* and ruin the prostitutes' 'yield'? Of course not!...

The girls were controlled by an SS woman. Among them there were deportees or condemned prostitutes who worked in these brothels in order to obtain, after several years, some remission. It would seem that their profession would facilitate their rehabilitation. They were better fed than in a camp or prison, did not have to work (that is, not in a factory or an office), they were allowed to keep their hair long, wear powder, lipstick, in short – retain their femininity.

One evening, the camp authorities, exasperated by the detainees' 'sulking', decided that things were going to change. The Kapo in charge of a Kommando where a friend of mine, Delaroche, worked, reassembled the deportees after work, and bellowed, as if he were giving the most terrible order: 'You are not going to the tunnel!' What was going on? There was rising panic. Every time the SS organized what we called a '*Sonder-truc*' (special event), deportees wondered if it was to watch a hanging or suffer reprisals. The Kapo quickly allayed their anxiety.

'Good news! You're going to the brothel!'

The men were stupefied. There they were marching in ranks towards the barrack which had been transformed into a house of ill-repute. The poor fellows were drunk with fatigue and only wanted to sleep after twelve hours of work. The first line was put one in front of each door and commanded to drop their trousers. The doors were still closed. The girls must have been inside. The second order was given: 'Enter!' They went in, trousers lowered, feeling as much like making love as an ailing octogenarian. Delaroche found himself face to face with a woman who was waiting. He was worried and blushing with confusion. How could he manage it? The 'little Frenchies' were about to fail to live up to their reputation. That is how legends are destroyed!

Suddenly there were shouts: stop everything! The ss had realized that the water was not connected, so there was no hygiene. The rules. Always the rules. When you think that these miserable men lived in the tunnel covered in fleas, vermin, boils and shit!... 'Trousers on!' shrieked the ss man. And so the men of Delaroche's Kommando went back to their putrid dormitory in the tunnel, without even having shown those ladies a glimpse of their manhood....

It must be added that after a while the brothel began to justify its creation. The ss had access to it. But they were not supposed to sleep with a girl who had been in contact with a deportee or a deportee Kapo.

Everything in accordance with the imperial order of the Third Reich!

# Chapter Twenty-four

# DESPAIR

Croizat continued to keep us up to date. Alas! When France was almost liberated, the advance of the Allied troops came to a halt....

This halt disturbs us and stretches our patience to the limit. After the early offensive, it is as if there is a stalemate. For us, rotting in the depths of the Harz, the waiting is cruel. André Boyer explains that, as the advance has been swift, the troops have to re-group.

Cazin d'Honuncthin is working in the tunnel with the Scherer Kommando, a Kommando of engineers. This group have built themselves a radio set. On 15 October, Cazin appears at the dental surgery. He is excited: the BBC have just sent out an appeal. The British are asking all prisoners to sabotage the German war industry at source.

For some months, at great risk, Claude Lauth has been working to this end. He has organized deportees around him. And Louis Murgia, in quality control, deceives his department with that easy manner only he possesses. He and Floiret, the 14 July demonstrator, reject perfectly good parts and keep the bad ones. The Russians too are systematically sabotaging where they can.

Have I said enough in this rambling narrative about the nature of the tunnel? Have I adequately described the evolution of that 'circle of hell', a 'circle of hell' beyond even Dante's imagination? The cold, the sweat, the putrefaction, the noise of machines that crushed men and matter, the yellowish mud in which exhausted beings lay, the bellowing of the *Lagerschutz*, the dust which clung to men deprived of their dignity, to their skin, in their lungs, the explosions, the feverish *Schicht* – changing of shifts. Have I made you feel the uneasy companionship of friendship, death and fear?

Claude Lauth is one of those who lived the longest in the tunnel.

There was reveille, when the *Stubendienst* made the men get up, the cries seeming to come from another world. The agony of the blows made you aware that you were still alive. There were those who could not open their eyes, the eyelids stuck fast together by the damp dust. There was the stench of the corpses – ten, twenty comrades who had not survived the night. The survivors, dressed in their damp rags, shod with their wooden clogs – the memory of these sliding on the ground will haunt them to the day of their death – filed past the rows of bunks, hardly able to see so quickly did they have to move, past the bodies overcome with fatigue and weariness, eyes open, for death had surprised them not in their sleep but as they were still struggling to survive. Was that a friend lying there? A friend destined for the common grave or the crematorium? … Then it was time for bread. They hurried, pushed and shoved, for they were starving. With Gummi blows the *Stubendienst* kept order. He is happy to see their fall from grace. He is happy to see the phantoms quarrelling, protesting, fighting over crusts. When some of them fall upon the 'greasy margarine papers' he is in seventh heaven. He will be better able to judge the suffering of others when, a few minutes later, the long column of starving men rejoins its Kommando and he, with his equals, will feast on stolen lumps of bread and fat, before going back to bed. His work is over until the next shift has to be woken. Claude Lauth lived through all this for a long time; in the beginning, when the deportees slept in the tunnel; later, when they slept outside in the blocks, where they heard music over the loudspeakers. 'You could die to music at Dora. There was even a Gypsy Orchestra.' Lauth lived through the relative comfort (!) of summer 1944. Then once again he had to share his four-foot bed with another man when evacuees from other camps flooded to the *Mittelwerke*.

There was the moment when the column, after passing the SS barracks, 'their kitchens, their cinemas, the parks where the bodies and tails of the v2s were kept', once more descended into the bowels of the earth. Lauth trod many times 'the path of gravel and stones brought out of the tunnel'. He knew the difference between the night shift and the day shift – twelve hours for each, two weeks nights and two weeks days – the night shift being preferable because it was slower. He knew the effort that had to be made when after twelve hours of calvary he still had to carry 'a girder, some bricks or cement for the construction of the camp'.

Then the tunnel became a colossal factory with 'its blast-engines, diesels, electricity-generators, stores, kitchens, canteens, infirmaries, ss barracks'. Lauth saw the endless assembly lines, the mixers churning out cement, and on the still wet ground the bustling carpenters, boiler-smiths, solderers, electricians and labourers installing the machines – ss booty stolen from the four corners of the occupied countries. He watched for anywhere that the various German workers were lacking; here our organization could step in and slow down production, commit sabotage, pretend to work, cut several sheets when one would do, punch holes that had been punched already, thwart the surveillance of the Kapos and Polish *Vorarbeiters* who were so eager to speed up production as soon as the civil engineers or the ss put in an appearance. The boiler-smiths adjusted the shells of the missiles, 'the weakest men cleaned the sheets with emery-cloth'. The clacking of pneumatic scissors was answered by the clattering of the electric welders. The racket was deafening, the frantic movement mesmerizing. The missile tail-fins slid by on trucks. They were on their way to be attached to their respective shells.... The electric arc-lamps burned the eyes. The light-blue vis took shape. It was at that point that sabotage could be quite effective.

They were not to speak, not to go from one hall to another, not to go to the toilet more than twice in twelve hours, paying for the visit with different-coloured discs. A *Schreiber* kept a scrupulous record. Only deportees who were electricians and those employed in the various tool shops were privileged. The former were allowed to cross the tunnel to repair machines, the latter to go to the store to fetch necessary tools. Brief moments of respite ...

Underground, even deeper, were the v2 halls. Hands bleeding, deportees 'rubbed down the missiles with steel wool'. Others painted, tested pressure, tuned the jet-engines. By its smell or sound, Lauth and his fellow slaves could recognize which hall they were in: the forging hall, the assembling hall, the riveting hall, the central hall where, when the v2 body was put together, a false movement could crush the already soiled and burnt men. Others replaced the dead. Other martyrs from Russia, Belgium, Poland, Czechoslovakia, Yugoslavia and France, who were soon to know the vermin of the blocks, hunger, torture, blows, forced labour. 'It was at Dora that I realized how the pyramids were built.'[1]

20 October, Claude Lauth is caught red-handed by the SS. In agreement with Dejussieu and Cazin, he has intensified his sabotage. He has sabotaged 152 parts in one day. He is taken to Niedersachswerfen, Gestapo centre for the region, situated six miles from the camp. It is Murgia who tells me of the disaster. It is impossible to know if Lauth is still alive, and if so, in what condition. Everything seems gloomier than ever. I am divided between despair and anger. If they have assassinated Lauth, I know I can wait no longer. I will take a machine-gun and mow down the SS until they mow me down. I go to see Dejussieu. He tries to calm me down. His conversation does me some good. We must wait; come D-Day I will lower myself to the murderers' level and display a wickedness equal to theirs.

I shall learn during the night of 3/4 November that Naegele is responsible for Claude Lauth's arrest. That bastard was told by the Gestapo to unmask the resisters in the camp. Lauth and Debaumarché trusted him, because he named contacts they knew. This confidence was not absolute, for Naegele's insistence in trying to find out the French leaders of the Dora organization annoyed Lauth and Debaumarché. Nevertheless, it was sufficient for the Gestapo agent to inform the SS about Claude's sabotage....

That month of October is a month of despair. The Landings had raised our hopes that we would soon be free. Time drags. Days and nights when waiting is constantly unrewarded, are endless. The *Revier* is overcrowded. Sick men who were being kept alive by hope, saying to themselves 'in the morning we'll be free', have no more strength to carry on. They cannot bear the thought of spending one more winter at Dora. They die in silence. I see death in their eyes forty-eight hours before it comes.... I feel that their will was broken....

Since Dejussieu has taken over as head of the organization, I am in charge of maintaining contacts within the camp. My dentist's armband permits me to circulate without the SS challenging me too often. I learn that although Lauth has been arrested, Leschi, Leroy and Hemery, who are also engaged in sabotage, are not worried for the time being. The camp resembles a cemetery peopled by ghosts. The standstill on the front engenders an atmosphere of surrender.

# Chapter Twenty-five

# THE MAN OF DESTINY

2 November 1944. D asks me urgently to come to a meeting after roll-call in Barrack 15. Cogny, *Schreiber* of the barracks , is there. Also Leroy and other Frenchmen whose faces I know but whose names I have forgotten. We listen to D.

There is nothing very new in what he says: the French must group together, accept jobs where they will be in the best positions to act when the time comes, even if those jobs are compromising – head of block, Kapo and so on. Our frequent meetings over the months are as much to help each other keep going so that each individual might not feel alone in the face of the Nazi machine as to collect information, tiny fragment by tiny fragment.

After, D addresses himself personally to me: 'You who are one of the oldest members of the camp, who know most of what's going on and the most people, trust me. We must organize more rapidly than in the past. Time is running out.'

This meeting leaves me with a bitter taste in my mouth. I share my feelings and suspicions with Cogny. I decide to speak of them to Dejussieu. He does not know how to advise me....

3 November 1944. Pierre Ziller, very worried, comes to see me in the dental surgery. It is three o'clock in the afternoon. He opens the door quietly. He looks to see if I am alone. Ziller is a man I respect a great deal; he is extremely useful to the organization. He closes the door behind him. He shakes hands with Laval, who is there with me: 'Jean,' he says, 'hide everything you have; the Gestapo came to pick up files, including yours, at the *Arbeitsstatistik*. I don't know why. But it's very, very serious. I'm sure of that. If you have any papers, notes, destroy them. These people really

know how to search. I must go. I'm afraid I may have been followed.'

When Ziller has left, I ask myself questions. Is this threat of the Gestapo because of yesterday evening's meeting with D? Or Claude Lauth? Even if they have tortured him, he cannot have talked, for it is now more than ten days since his arrest. So what has happened? What can they have found out?

After roll-call, I seek out Nicolas Petrenko and another Russian whom I nicknamed the 'Asian'. Others thought that Petrenko, a young man of twenty-two, was the leader of the Russian organization. He was my contact. We spoke German together. Nicolas translated for his companion. Instinctively, I realized that Petrenko was only second-in-command. The head of the Russian circuit at Dora was the 'Asian', always silent, impassive. Future events proved me right....

I tell Nicolas that the Gestapo have taken my file. He knows, since he also works at the *Arbeitsstatistik* with Pierre Ziller. I ask him if he knows the names of the other deportees whose files have been taken. He replies that he did not have time to see the names, and that he could not remember the numbers. He does not seem worried, in fact he is very optimistic. The Russians are making great advances, amazing offensives. So, all is well! And then, as he leaves, he says '*Nitchevo*'. His good humour does not reassure me.

I join Pierre Clervoy between two barracks. He is waiting for me accompanied by Roland Deyssier. Roland is a real Paris street arab, brave and funny. Arrested at the age of fourteen, he has been in a concentration camp for over two years: a strange education for a child!... Roland Deyssier has a surprising gift for languages. He speaks Russian, German and Polish and has a repertoire of swear words which would enable him to be at his ease in any slum in the world. He works as a *Laufer* (errand boy) for the Kapo in charge of clothing.

I speak seriously to Clervoy: 'I have been warned that the Gestapo are looking for me. They're looking for other deportees too, whose names I don't know. Tell the others not to worry. I won't talk if they arrest me. Try to find out what has happened to Claude Lauth.... I'm going to give you my rings and my watch, I've managed to keep them hidden since Buchenwald.'

Then I change my mind.... My optimism takes command again. Perhaps it is not as serious as Ziller has led me to believe. I shall keep my watch. As for my belt with the five-thousand-franc note, I shall not part with that either. I hand Clervoy a notebook in which I have written down, in number code or a shorthand all my own, my impressions of Dora. This journal, if I come out alive, will be the basis for a book about the camp. I was already thinking of it then.

After this conversation, I return to my barrack and go to bed.

Still 3 November 1944. At D's instigation, there is another meeting after roll call, but with Poupault this time. Jacques is ill at ease. As he enters Block 15, where the meeting is held, he sees and hears a man who is speaking Russian with the Russians, German with the Germans and who greets him in French. It is D. He takes Jacques into his room in the middle of the block. He offers him a cigarette.

'Forgive me for making you come here so late. I cannot move around. It's easier for you with your doctor's armband. I am so pleased to meet you. I have often heard about you and the work you are doing in the camp.'

The politeness, flattery and use of the formal *vous* which was un-usual in the camp, upsets Jacques. He puts himself on his guard, wondering what is behind it all.

'I can tell you,' continues D, 'that tonight the Gestapo will mount a massive search throughout the camp. There will be arrests. I don't know what the Gestapo are looking for. If you have anything to hide, if you are in possession of any forbidden article, get rid of it at once.'

Jacques is stunned. He automatically says: 'I have nothing.'

D goes on, as if Poupault has not spoken: 'Keep no papers, no lists, no secret apparatus.'

'I don't understand what you mean. I have nothing to hide, I have never had anything to hide. The Gestapo can search where they like.'

'It's said you are the leader of the French.'

'That's ridiculous!' protests Poupault. 'Many people talk about me because they all want to rest and come to the *Revier*. A few days in the infirmary or hospital are always welcome in their miserable lives! Obviously, I do what I can, particularly for the French....'

D becomes annoyed at Jacques' caution:

'You don't trust me because I am in contact with the engineers in the tunnel through my job as *Schreiber*. But you, you also put men in jobs where they run less risk of dying and where they can be more useful.... I suppose those German Communist bastards warned you against me?'

'No one has ever mentioned you....'

'Listen. I trust you. I am going to tell you what I have done and what I know. Since the attempt on Hitler's life on 20 July 1944, the German people has been divided. The attempt failed, but it did have the merit of opening some peoples' eyes. These people, who have kept quiet up to now, have had enough. They want an end to the war, at whatever cost. For them, Nazism is finished. In the tunnel I know of German engineers, in touch with the ss, on whom I can rely. They are ready to completely sabotage the constructions in the tunnel and to give us certain advantages from now on. They want to make contact with the leaders of the French Resistance who are at Dora. That is their primary objective. They fear Communism like the plague, for they have no wish to pass from one totalitarian régime to another, without even a transition period. They wish to be in a position to negotiate an agreement with the Resistance. This is a proposition of extreme importance for them and for you, I would say even for the future of the war. They ask that you agree to certain conditions: firstly, to protect them from the Russians when the camp is liberated; secondly, to clear them with the Allies, for whom they will facilitate the advance across German territory, and to whom they will hand over the plans of the secret weapons and various other projects that are under way....'

This proposition, with its possible enormous repercussions if it is not the result of the onset of mythomania, astounds Poupault. He is even more surprised than on his first visit to Fritz Preul. He is being asked 'simply' to establish contact between the Anglo-Americans and the German engineers, the self-same men who held in their hands the Nazis' ultimate means of action, the plans of those secret weapons on which Hitler was counting, those weapons that so worried the Anglo-American general staffs! He looks around him: he is in a concentration camp, a scarecrow in striped pyjamas, talking with another scarecrow in striped pyjamas! He must really be in his bunk dreaming that he is the hero on whom depends the fate of the Dora detainees and the speedy end to a war that is dragging on and on! But he is not dreaming! There is D standing before him with his high forehead, his pebble glasses, his yellow face, rolling his r's....

'You are more powerful than Machiavelli or Talleyrand,' says Poupault ironically, coming down to earth again.

'I would not make these proposals to you if it were not that there are important members of the Resistance at Dora, capable of discussing matters at the highest level with de Gaulle, and through him, with the British and American governments,' D replies dryly.

'Here you are only in contact with a tiny number of Germans. How can that tiny number have so much influence on the course of events?' asks Jacques.

'Firstly, this tiny number holds the key posts at Dora. And don't lose sight of the fact that Hitler has staked everything on Dora and the secret weapons, against the advice of certain members of his General Staff.... Then, these people I'm talking of are in contact with influential members of that General Staff which, in Berlin, realizes that the party's over and their leader's lost his head.'

Poupault does not smile at D's turn of phrase.

'You say the little nucleus here includes some members of the ss?'

'Yes.'

'But why did you choose me as your spokesman? Why not send an emissary, or radio messages, to the Allies? Why don't you try to negotiate, with the neutral countries acting as intermediaries?'

'The contacts that the General Staff tried to make were not successful.... The neutral and Anglo-Saxon countries were sceptical. The engineers, in agreement with the members of the General Staff, are now directing their interest towards the French Resistance....'

'But why me?' insists Poupault.

'Because I am certain that there are among your groups men who are important spokesmen, as I said.... And because I inspired this plan.... At least, some of it ...' adds D with a little smile.

'Your idea is tempting, but it is too romantic. It can't possibly relate to the real facts. I am in no position to help you. I am a surgeon. I try to save the maximum number of lives. There is no clandestine organization in the camp, at least as far as I know. As for important leaders of the Resistance, I don't know of a single one. In my opinion, the leaders were not arrested. They were in London;

now they are in Paris. In France our work in the Resistance was, I hope, effective, though hardly professional, but all those who fought underground did not necessarily rise to the rank of important leaders.'

D is becoming increasingly irritated with Poupault's denials and evasiveness.

'You are wrong to continue to doubt me. I know the action you are taking. I know that you have not stayed inactive at Dora. If we stay alive you will see that you will be obliged to turn to me. As the first tangible proof of my sincerity do not forget the Gestapo. They will search here tonight.'

Confused, Jacques Poupault leaves D. The conversation has lasted over an hour. He does not know what to think or what to believe. The man's vehemence, his assurances, the logic of his deductions are almost convincing. But the whole project is on far too great a scale! Too extraordinary! Why did he speak to him? Why has he not tried to meet Dejussieu at the *Revier*? If D is so well informed he must know that General Dejussieu was the leader of the *Armée Secrète*! And yet, his story oddly holds together. Incredible, but its logic is irrefutable. It would not be so surprising if with his intelligence, his personality, D has managed to persuade a number of the engineers supervising the tunnel of his own importance and influence. It is true that the German leaders must now be doubtful of victory. It is true that they must unhesitatingly prefer an invasion by a democratic country to a Russian invasion; but they have other means of contacting the British and Americans than via Doctor Poupault, inmate at Dora! Jacques smiles to himself. The whole thing is too far-fetched, too absurd, too crazy.... And yet ... why not agree to the proposition, even if only to save the deportees, who, on Himmler's orders, are all to be exterminated before the arrival of the Allied troops? ... Poupault's head is buzzing. He goes out of the barracks thinking that D is not a traitor. Fritz Preul's suspicions are totally without foundation, he says to himself. Yet what is D really plotting? Is he mad? Is he a pathological liar? That could be very dangerous! Even saints can be dangerous!

Poupault decides that he should speak to Boyer, Dejussieu and Fritz Preul about this conversation. (Though I knew about all Jacques' activities since he arrived at Dora, he did not realize my role in the camp Resistance. He knew from various signs that there must have been a French organization when he arrived, but he did not suspect its relative importance. He believed it to be only embryonic, a muddle of good intentions, and, he thought, good intentions mainly directed to helping friends in need. As for Dejussieu and Cazin d'Honuncthin, they were too experienced. Experts at intrigue, they considered it pointless to let people, even friends, into the secret unless it became absolutely necessary.)

It is late. It is impossible to move around the camp without being stopped. When Poupault enters his barrack, Morel and the two Czech orderlies who share his room are asleep. Jacques goes to bed. He is so preoccupied and excited by D's proposals that he lies awake for some time. Then he falls asleep.

# Chapter Twenty-six

# IN THE CLUTCHES OF THE GESTAPO

Suddenly, Poupault is rudely woken. The room is brightly-lit. Three ss officers are standing at the foot of his bed. Karr, the head doctor, is with them. He is very pale. His arrogance has vanished. He even seems overcome and ill at ease.

'These gentlemen wish to interrogate you,' he mumbles.

René Morel and the two Czechs are looking on apprehensively. It is never reassuring in a concentration camp to see the Gestapo burst into a room with interrogation on their minds.

'Where are your things?' asks one of the ss officers.

'On the shelf.'

Poupault has two shirts and a woollen pullover.

'Search them, search the bed, search everything,' says the ss officer who seems to be in charge of the group.

A soldier obeys. Poupault is not worried by the search: he possesses nothing compromising. Ordered to by the leader, Jacques dresses. Before he has finished, the officer says: 'Follow me.' As Jacques leaves the room he is stopped by Karr. 'Here, take your jacket. It's cold tonight.' Karr is tense. He is uncomfortable, uneasy. Jacques, still half-asleep, cannot really take in what is happening to him.

The corridor of the barrack is full of ss soldiers armed with machine-guns. Jacques makes his way between them. At once he is flanked by two armed men. At the same time he finds Cespiva the Czech, and Schneider the German Communist Kapo, escorted in the same manner. He is now completely awake. The nightmare is real! Things are looking black. 'I must act brave,' he says to himself. 'A bit of bravado!' He remembers his first arrest, the torture he endured for eight days, the lies he was able to invent to throw

them off the track, the suffering he underwent when the Gestapo
angrily set about him again. Eight days! He held out for eight days!
'This time we're for it. They're really going to put us through it!'
He smiles like the Hollywood hero about to face the 'baddies' again.
The officers and soldiers look right through him. His smile does
not impress anyone. Poupault thinks of D's warning.

At the same time, I wake with a start. An electric torch is shining
in my face. I sit up. I see three SS soldiers with machine-guns.
'*Schnell*. Get dressed.' It is almost midnight. The room is silent,
lit only by the torch. I wonder why there are three soldiers for one
man alone and then I wonder why this stupid thought is the first
thing to come to mind. Suddenly, I realize that I looked at my watch
in front of the SS and that therefore I have kept it and not left it
with Clervoy. Perhaps it is such a mechanical gesture that the
soldiers did not notice it. If they are taking me to Gestapo HQ things
will be different. There I will get a thrashing to remember.... On
top of the beatings already in store....

I ask one of the soldiers permission to go to the latrines. I get
up, dress, unfasten my watchstrap. The torch is shining towards
the door. I place my watch on the table. (This watch was returned
to me in Paris, after our liberation, by my friend Doctor Lemière.)

At the point of a machine-gun, Cespiva, Poupault and Schneider
are marched right across the camp. They arrive at the guard post,
where the SS administration barrack is also to be found. They enter
the room. Jacques catches sight of André Boyer among the thirty
deportees already gathered there. André gives a wry smile and pulls
a face as if to say that now things are going to get rough. Jacques
wonders why Boyer is there. He had believed that nobody knew
about Boyer. An order cuts across his thoughts: 'Face the wall!'
An SS man. Jacques tries to see if there are other friends there besides
Boyer. He recognizes the tall outline of Colonel Gentil. To one side
stands a Frenchman with a Kapo's armband – a handsome, tall,
strong boy. 'That must be Naegele.'

After a visit to the toilets, I am taken to the SS barrack at the point
of a machine-gun. I am told to face the wall and put my hands up.
I am scared stiff, but sure that it does not show. This is serious!
So many people! What are the bastards up to? What do they know?

I quickly try to see who has been arrested; that way I can make a few deductions. We are all with our hands up, noses to the wall. I think of everything that has happened these last few months when the resistance movements had organized. I hope that Dejussieu has not been arrested....

'Turn round!'

This is shouted by an SS officer. He has just come into the room. 'No talking. You will get into the lorries when your number is called. The soldiers are under orders to shoot the first man who disobeys.'

I look to see who is there. There are Poupault, Boyer, Pernot, Cespiva, Schneider, Nicolas Petrenko, Brother Birin, Gentil, Naegele and D. I do not see Murgia, Croizat, Cazin d'Honuncthin, Cogny or Cimek. There are altogether too many men I am in contact with. The presence of Cespiva and Petrenko disturbs me the most. The Germans have thus connected Czech, Russian and French.

We shall learn much later that the Czech organization who slipped the net the night of the 3/4 November burnt the radio set in the crematorium oven. The Kapo did not inform on them, perhaps out of fear of being knifed. The SS searched for the radio for ages in vain. Gone up in smoke, like so many men....

We shall also learn, from Ziller, that Kuntz, political prisoner and chief of camp construction, had forewarned Fritz Preul. When the SS had come to arrest him, he had killed himself. After so many years in detention he no longer felt he could stand up to interrogation and torture by the Gestapo.

More men arrive. There must be forty of us. They call out nine numbers. I climb into an ambulance with Poupault, followed by Naegele. He sits down next to Jacques.

'See where your stupid sabotage has got us? Didn't you have enough to do at the hospital? You had to go and get involved with these bastards.'

Poupault replies: 'Are you mad? Don't you feel well? You're imagining it all!'

'Imagining it! Suppose they shoot us?' exclaims Naegele.

'Well, we'll see! Meanwhile, shut up, for God's sake! It's the middle of the night....'

There are nine of us in the ambulance. It is past midnight. I avoid Naegele like the plague. After travelling for twenty minutes, we stop. Niedersachswerfen. I recognize the place. We used to go through it on our way to Illfeld when we were building the barracks and I passed myself off as an engineer. I was with Cinel.... I know that Niedersachswerfen is the Gestapo HQ. Seat of the reign of terror. Blows are going to rain down like hailstones. I am filled with dread.

They make us get out. The usual reception: the ss and machine-guns levelled unequivocally. What power there is in a weapon! A thing like that in my hands and I could do anything! But we are on the other side; we are the victims. Once again, they put us against the wall, arms in the air. The Frenchman next to me, as bald as Max Princet, murmurs: 'I hope they know how to use those things, those idiots, and they're not going to shoot us where they shouldn't.'

'*Maul zu!*' bellows an ss man.

Everyone knows that to sit is less tiring than to stand, and that for relaxation it is best to lie down. For those who have never experienced torture, I hope that they never do. For their personal experience, I suggest to them that, in the privacy of their own rooms, they simply stand up, facing a wall, touching it with their noses, but not leaning against it, put their feet together, raise their arms and wait and see what they feel. I challenge them to stay in that position for long without having cramp and, if they do hold out, hallucinations. Particularly as, in our case, the ss' boots were ready to kick us for the least movement. It's a position that drives you to beg all the saints' forgiveness for sins you've not even committed.

I think of Pierre Ziller. If he had not warned me I would have been irredeemably lost. Arrested with ring, watch and notebook, I would have been for the gallows right away.

Naegele is not with us. We had hardly arrived when he slipped calmly away from the rest of our group of nine. So he is the filth, the Gestapo lackey. The eight of us are left waiting. Perhaps one day I shall get my hands on Naegele. If, thanks to him, something bad has happened to Claude Lauth, I shall find him ...

After a moment, the ss call for Nicolas Petrenko. Ten minutes pass. Suddenly, screams! 'That's it,' I think, 'the fun's beginning. Nicolas must be getting it....' Of the other deportees whom they arrested not one comes to join us. (We shall later discover that they were taken directly to the prison at Nordhausen.)

For the moment, only our group of nine had been taken to Gestapo HQ.

Time passes. Nicolas returns. They put him back face to the wall.

He is groaning, try to keep one hand on the wall. The SS lever him off with their cudgels. These Russians have to be taught good manners. . . .

They call another man. A Pole. He was a paratrooper in the army. They arrested him as a resister. The sinister routine is played again. It is Brother Birin's turn. Every time a friend comes back into the room you can hear his painful breathing, his groans of agony. Every time the SS cudgels force him into position against the wall.

I am nothing but solid fury. I swear that one day, if I get the chance, I shall repay their little reception in kind. Brother Birin returns, Jacques Poupault is called. When he comes back to his place he is twisted with pain. How can you stand upright against a wall when you are twisted with pain?

They bark the number of the bald man next to me. (He is called Puppo. He is there solely because his name in German is pronounced like Poulpault's. So as not to let the Poupault they wanted escape, the SS took them both.)

Soon it will be my turn. I try to concentrate, hide my fear, feed my fury to give myself more courage. In such circumstances, being last on the list drains your strength. You hear nothing but shrieks during the interrogation, groans and the thudding blows of the cudgels afterwards.

I am called. I enter a very well-lit room. The Areopagus is arranged in a circle. I recognize some of those evil rattlesnakes. There is Detmers, young SS camp lieutenant. There is Hazel, who boasts the fine title of Gestapo Commandant. There is Sander, quite fat, tall, well-built; he holds the rank of *Haupsturmführer*, but that means nothing here, for the Gestapo can give orders to generals. There are seven or eight SS officers and, in the corner, a civilian. He is a Czech called Appel. He is there for the interrogation of the Czechs. To one side, two detainees in striped pyjamas. One is Naegele. The other, a Russian, there to interpret for his compatriots. To the right is a magnificent radio set such as I have not seen in a long time. It is playing gentle music. The atmosphere is unexpectedly mild ... I spot that at once. 'Be careful, Jean, be very careful, think before you speak, try to keep calm. You saw the others: they are going to give you the same treatment. Try not to think about it.' To help me clarify my thoughts, it is the same old story of two fellows slapping me about the face before each question.

The SS officer presiding over this family reunion asks me who I am, in German. I do not answer. Naegele translates. This'll give me some respite, I think. I reply: 'Jean Michel.' Profession. Same procedure. 'I am a dentist.' 'You are a captain in the French army!' shouts the officer. Silence. Naegele translates. The ss officer gets furious. They are making him stay up all night and here is one of the men responsible for his forced insomnia being pig-headed! 'You speak German, it's written down here!' He flicks through the report in front of him; but he flicks through it at random, very quickly, not stopping at any particular page. I think: 'It's all bluff. If that was a real report he wouldn't need to look for the page.'

I still do not reply – the complete confusion of a man who cannot understand a word that's said to him, nor what he is doing there in the first place. Naegele translates. 'I speak camp German, but just a few words for my work as a dentist. I am incapable of following a serious conversation.' My explanation. Naegele translates. The officer seems pacified by this reply.

'Do you know Rogny?' I still wait for Naegele's translation. 'Rogny? I don't know him.' I know they mean Cogny, but I am not going to make their work any easier for them.

'You are a member of the camp resistance organization. You have launched a programme of sabotage. Where is the radio set?'

Naegele's translation. I look as if I have no idea what they are talking about. They are not convinced. Slaps, punches and cudgel blows rain down on me. It is painful, but I stand my ground well. Perhaps they are tired out by the preceding interrogations? They stop.

I find myself back in the room where my friends are assembled. I go back to my place, face to the wall, feet together, hands in the air. I have not come out of it too badly. They hit mostly my shoulders, arms and back. My back is to hurt for quite a while.

Time passes.... The standing position becomes unbearable. I feel myself going mad. If I lean on one leg to rest the other, the cudgel goes into action. My shoulders no longer support my arms. They feel as if a thousand ants are crawling in them. Ankylosis. I am going to crack. But I mustn't crack. When the ss are watching the deportees have no right to crack. I try to think of anything, anything at all. It is impossible to fix on any idea, any image – nothing but the wall an inch from my nose that I am not to touch. It would be so good to lean on it a little. Just a little. I begin to pitch forward ...

I am going to fall. Forbidden. My mind is on fire. How long must this agony go on? In the interrogation room the radio is playing Gershwin. It reminds me of the music that accompanied the documentary about the *Graf-Zeppelin* crossing the Atlantic.... Those bastards are so relaxed! As if they were at a tea party! That's not the same music they were going to play for me! I'm going, going ... too bad, I'm touching the wall, just the tips of my fingers ... Aargh! That bastard has eyes everywhere!

The purgatory lasts at least three hours. The door opens. On the threshold stands an ss officer who shrieks: 'Join hands. Outside.' Puppo takes Poupault's hand, Poupault Brother Birin's, he mine.... This is ridiculous! Out we go. It is dawn. It must be after six. A fine rain is falling. They march us around to the back of the building. 'Face the wall!' It's a mania with them! We take up the same position. My ankylosis has diminished a little, but my arms are heavy and my hands are numb and bloodless. Icy November rainwater drips from the gutters and down our necks. I am frozen, at the end of my tether. I do not feel in any state to spend another three hours standing with my hands in the air. It was not yet midnight when they came to wake me.... Nearly seven hours have passed since then....

Six ss guards are there to watch us. We hear them load their machine-guns. All this behind our backs. It is an awful feeling. Are they about to shoot us like fixed targets in the fairground? The tension is becoming unbearable. We feel that something terrible is about to happen. Are we going to die here, riddled with bullets, against a wall, in Niedersachswerfen? Poupault breaks the silence: 'Goodbye, everybody,' he says simply. He feels death is imminent. I reply: 'You lot can all die, I'm not going to!' It is not bravado. It is a certainty that I would live. Brother Birin murmurs: 'No, no, it's not possible.' Puppo has only one thing to say: 'Oh shit!' He is fantastic! (Jacques will later tell me that he was waiting for the first shot to be fired. 'Hurry up!' he thought. In a few seconds, he had prepared himself for death. He was afraid that his acceptance of the inevitable would desert him and that he would be seized by terrible gut fear.) As for me, I refuse to accept that they have lined us up to machine-gun us. I feel invincible. I am not boasting, I really did feel that. The seconds tick by. We forget the pain in our bodies. Some, like Jacques, tense their backs, in a defensive reflex, as if the contraction of their muscles could prevent the penetration of the bullets. Puppo, in his Miramas accent, even says: 'They're stupid to leave us out in the rain. We'll all get pneumonia!'

'*Maul zu!*' Puppo's reflection and the German's shout wrench Poupault out of his sensation of impending death. Against orders I look round. Jacques too. The ss are sheltering from the rain. They are chatting and smoking. They seem to be waiting for instructions. Did they knowingly play out the comedy of the firing squad?

Later, in prison, Jacques Poupault told me about his interrogation. When he entered the room, it was Sander who addressed him. Jacques replied in very shaky German, although he could speak it very well:

'I don't understand your language well enough to be interrogated in it.'

'You will understand when we read out your death sentence.'

The whole gang of them burst out laughing. Sander's reply was so funny. The ss found humour in the sufferings of others. Jacques did not laugh. He was one of the others. But he would not have laughed even if the situation had been reversed. He was not cut out to be a member of the Teutonic élite. He was not bloodthirsty by nature.

Sander called for a *Dolmechter*, an interpreter. It was not Naegele. It was a civilian, young with a shock of blond hair. Sander addressed him in German.

Jacques understood his torturer's every word, but he waited for the interpreter to translate. This gave him time to weigh and re-weigh his replies. The interrogation began.

'Do you know this man?'

Poupault did not bat an eyelid. Translation. Jacques turned around. He saw a Russian slumped against the wall. His face was swollen, his clothes spotted with blood. He was a lump of red flesh dumped on the ground, with mad eyes staring out of a face of indescribable suffering.

'No,' replied Jacques. He was not lying. He had never seen him. Sander put the same question to the Russian. The Russian interpreter translated.

'No,' replied the victim, as laconically as Poupault.

Sander insisted. He turned back to Jacques:

'You have never seen him, nor met him, either in the *Revier* or in the camp?'

'No.'

'You are accused of grouping the French with a view to preparing a revolt, of having organized the sabotage in the tunnel and of listening to British radio broadcasts.'

Translation. Jacques recited what he had already said to D at the time of their conversation in Barrack 15.

'The French talk about me, that's not unusual. I look after them, operate on them the best I can. I try to help them.' He added, in order to make his reply more plausible: 'The news I spread around is from the German newspapers. I try to read the headlines, odd phrases that I can understand in the articles.... At least my friends know where the fighting is, on what front, in what town.... They feel less isolated.... I have access to these newspapers, because sometimes Doctor Karr and Sergeant Lorenz leave them lying about.... As for the tunnel, I have never set foot inside it.'

'It's useless to lie! We have proof,' said Sander. 'We must have the names of your accomplices. We know, and your denials are pointless, that you have organized sabotage and that you possess a radio set. Doctor Karr has admitted that he obtained one for you.'

Poupault was relieved. The Gestapo knew nothing. Georges Croizat was truly a champion! He had been peacefully listening to the ss chief dentist's radio for months, every single day, and nobody suspected a thing! The Gestapo were clutching at straws. Now here was Sander implicating Karr. Ridiculous! As for the sabotage in the tunnel, Poupault was clearly not involved.

He felt calm again, despite his critical position in the midst of these gangsters and, after the interpreter had translated, he replied:

'Karr gave me nothing. Our relationship is very cool. We only talk to each other during surgical operations. We have no conversation except about professional problems. As for sabotage, I did not even know there had been any.'

'Your accomplices!' shouted Sander.

'I have friends, poor buggers I take care of and who are grateful for that. No accomplices. Accomplices for what purpose?'

'If you will not admit it we are going to force you to!' thundered Sander, apoplectic.

Poupault longed to offer him a pill or some drops to calm him down. Such a show of cynicism would have delighted him.... But the hors-d'œuvres was over.

'Take him away!'

Kapo Naegele grabbed Jacques by the jacket. He dragged him into the next room for the festivities I was not to enjoy when my turn came.

'Undress and take off your shoes,' ordered Naegele. He slapped Poupault with extraordinary violence. Jacques remembered his first arrest a few months earlier. Would he have the courage to overcome the pain and the humiliation this time?

Naegele took a bull-whip from a hook on the wall. Jacques was naked. 'On your knees!' said the Gestapo agent. Jacques wondered what went through a torturer's mind at such a moment. He obeyed. Naegele raised the whip and dealt him a terrible blow on the soles of his feet. Jacques fell forwards. Naegele forced him upright again. Jacques twisted and turned to avoid the whip, to catch the blows anywhere but on the soles of his feet!

He screamed. He knew from experience that it was better to howl very, very loudly. The tactic was to show that the suffering was more intolerable than it really was. The Gestapo were more excited by those who resisted than by those who wept, screamed and groaned. And Jacques screamed his head off. He kept trying to protect his feet. The whip lashed his calves, his thighs. The ordeal would have been more violent and, above all, have lasted much longer, if Poupault had not screamed like a stuck pig. Suddenly Sander, who was watching through the door, called out: '*Genug!*' ('Enough'). Naegele's demonstration came to an end.

Sander gave Poupault a funny look. What was he thinking? On the command, Jacques dressed. His legs and feet were on fire. He felt that his lower limbs were burning. Consumed by the flames of a funeral pyre. He was drenched with sweat. When he put on his socks and his shoes, he groaned and wept. His feet were balls of fire, and at the same time, he felt as if he were shod with ice-skates.

When Naegele took him back before the group he was staggering. The interrogation seemed to be under the command of Hazel, the Gestapo commandant; but it was Sander who continued to question him.

'Now are you ready to reply? The names of your accomplices?'

'I have no accomplices. I have done nothing. Do you want me to invent any old thing?'

'Must we send you back in there with the Kapo?'

'I can say nothing. I have nothing to add.'

As he replied, Poupault exaggerated his suffering. He grimaced, panted, staggered, righted himself, showed every sign of exhaustion. His voice was hardly above a murmur and he hesitated between every word.

The ss officer who presided whispered to Sander a word that Jacques did not understand.

'Take him away. We will continue the interrogation later,' concluded Sander.

Naegele pushed Poupault, who lost his balance before taking his place at the wall again, into the room where the rest of us were waiting.

The ss guards wait.... We are still standing, arms in the air, under a rain that soaks us to the skin.... We know, now, that they are not going to shoot us.... Then I see Cespiva arrive. Escorted by the ss, machine-guns trained on him. Where has he been? What has happened to him since we set off in the ambulance for Niedersachswerfen? Where are the others? We can tell from the look of him that Cespiva has been through an ordeal.

We hear the sound of a motor. It is a lorry.

'Lower your arms, turn around, march!' And there we are sitting in the vehicle. It is heaven on earth. Blood rushing back into arms, hands, sets them tingling. We rub them, spread out. God, it's good! The ss climb up behind us. The incorrigible Puppo exclaims: 'Thanks to their bloody fooling around I'm going to catch a cold!' The ss say nothing. Puppo takes advantage of this to say: 'Good grief! They're behaving themselves now. Not such pains in the arse!' He pulls out a dirty old bit of rag and mops his brow. He sneezes and wishes himself good health, prosperity and long life. This man is astonishing. He works on the railway. His first name is Joseph. He is a Corsican, from Miramas. His children have been captured. They belonged to the Maquis. His wife has been arrested, and he displays an admirable courage! I shall have occasion to write more about his sense of camaraderie and solidarity. Puppo remains one of the greatest memories of our ordeal – a credit to the human race.

In a corner, Alfred (Brother Birin) is kneeling. His lips are moving. He must be praying. I think: 'Cespiva and Nicolas Petrenko are here with me. That doesn't look too good!' And always the same question: 'What exactly do the ss and the Gestapo know?'

It is impossible to communicate with Petrenko in the lorry. Our conversations have habitually been in German. I continue to think to myself: 'What is certain is that Nicolas has not mentioned our meeting of last night. The names of Ziller and the other deportees at the *Arbeitsstatistik* did not come up during the interrogation. Nor has Claude Lauth been mentioned. Nor Dejussieu; do they know that he was the leader of the *Armée Secrète*? And Cazin d'Honunc-thin? What do they want with Cogny? What a mess! Naegele was in too much of a hurry to hand us over. He did not have enough information. Croizat is beyond suspicion. . . . Lauth has revealed nothing, despite what he must have had to suffer. I am sure of that. Anyway he doesn't know either Petrenko or Cespiva. But I have seen none of the German Communists arrested. Not Kuntz, nor Beam, nor Preul. . . . Oh yes! Schneider. . . . Perhaps there have been other arrests? Other deportees in another room? What does seem odd to me is the choice of the eight in the ambulance.' (I choke at the thought of the ninth: Naegele. . . .) 'And D? Who exactly is he? . . . If the interrogations give them nothing, Naegele will be for it. Poupault is as brave as a wolf at bay, but he is rash; he is too good, too naïve; he trusts people. Particularly deportees who speak French. . . . Strange that André Boyer was not in the ambulance with us! He knows more than Jacques about our activities. Yet he is so discreet he probably hasn't given the ss any reason to suspect him. He has a knack for making himself instantly forgettable.'

The lorry stops. It is day. Ahead, a wall and a monumental gate.

'Terrific! Prison!' cries Puppo. 'I was here a long time before that filthy tunnel. At least we're going to be able to get some sleep. In prison you don't lift a finger!'

His sun-soaked accent and optimism are music to our ears. We must hold on as long as we can! Every day the end of the war grows nearer! With companions like Puppo, everything is possible!

The soldiers line us up. We go into the prison. A fat German, strapped into his uniform, receives us. He must be a reservist. His voice is stentorian. His name is Müller. He takes us off to the cells. Jacques would have preferred to stay with Puppo. But Müller, see-ing his armband *Arzt* (doctor), signals to Poupault to follow him. He says to him '*Mit dem Kolonel*'. In the cell allocated to him Pou-pault finds Colonel Gentil. The cell is clean. There are three beds, one above the other, attached to the wall. Daylight enters through a window, high up, protected by iron bars. No toilet or washbasin. The two men speak in low voices. Gentil tells him that the deportees had come directly from Dora to the prison. Jacques briefly recounts what has happened to us. Gentil points to the spy-hole in the door. He turns his back to it and whispers: 'Naegele is a Gestapo informer.' Jacques replies: 'I found that out the hard way. He was the one who beat me.' 'They must have arrested me because they often saw me with you,' says Gentil. 'Let's get our stories in order. You were a patient. Prostate,' replies Jacques. 'Anyway, they can do their worst, I won't talk,' declares Gentil.

The door opens. A beaming Müller comes in and, turning to Gentil, asks him: 'How are you, *Herr Kolonel?*' He turns to Jacques: 'And you, *Herr Doktor?*'

'This politeness is a change from Niedersachswerfen,' thinks Poupault. His feet, legs and back are bothering him. The rest of his body is aching and stiff. He smiles at Müller. The German takes them to the washroom tiled in white porcelain, with four washstands along one wall, and to the right and left of them, four doors opening to very clean lavatories. 'Back to civilization,' says Poupault. He is limping. He is in pain. 'Have a good wash,' recommends Müller. 'You have time. Soup in one hour.' He leaves them without shutting the main door.

They are beginning to wash when a ghost appears. It is Claude Lauth! He walks with difficulty; his feet and his hands are shackled. His face bears the marks of beatings: lower lip split, black eyes, smashed cheekbones. He has a few days' growth of beard. His physical state is lamentable. He is accompanied by Müller, who removes the chains. He turns to Jacques with a confused look, saying 'Orders are orders.' Müller leaves the room. Claude raises his eyes and says to Jacques: 'You must think I am responsible for your arrest.' He is very upset. This beaten, victimized man only wants to know what his friends think.

Poupault is overwhelmed. His voice is shaking when he finally manages to reply: 'Don't worry. It was Naegele. He was the one. Anyway, if you had talked or if you hadn't, it wouldn't have been any different. I would have been arrested.' Tears flow down Claude's battered cheeks. 'Thank you,' he whispers.

Müller returns to fetch them. Gentil and Jacques go back to their cell. Poupault is asking himself a few questions. Why has he been put into a cell with Colonel Gentil? And why have they had that reunion with Lauth? Jacques does not set much store by co-incidence in a Gestapo lair.... Nor does he give much credence to Müller's negligence.... Who is really pulling all the strings here?...

# Chapter Twenty-seven

# NORDHAUSEN PRISON

I am installed in a cell similar to Jacques Poupault's. I am alone. Am I in solitary? Where are all my friends arrested last night at Dora? Through the tiny window I can see a fine rain falling. It has not stopped since the morning. I am soaking. My back aches.

The door opens. I am handed a piece of bread and a slice of sausage. There must be twelve ounces of bread here. My birthday! Since I do not know if the ration is for twenty-four hours, I keep half of it. I gnaw at the sausage. My sense of economy does me a bad turn. The door opens. I am relieved of the rest of the bread and the sausage. There must have been a mistake in distribution. (It seems the same thing happened in Poupault's cell. Jacques wasn't hungry. He was suffering too much from the treatment dealt him during the night. He offered his ration to Colonel Gentil who was starving and ate both. When Müller returned to recoup the food there was none left. Müller refused to believe it. He searched the cell. Finding nothing, he left laughing, exclaiming: 'Good digestion, gentlemen!')

About an hour passes. The door opens. It is Petrenko. I look at him. The Gestapo have really beaten him up! His face is covered with blood. Without a word, he shows me the soles of his feet – completely torn to shreds. Then I see his back covered in red and purplish stripes. That bull-whip has certainly left its mark! What can I say? I feel oceans away from him.... Nicolas says nothing.... Finally, with a smile, he murmurs in German: 'All the same.... We'll get them.'

We speak quietly. We go over the events. He says to me: 'There is a traitor among the French deportees. We know him.' He adds: 'I have been interrogated again, here, in the prison. There is one deportee wearing a French triangle who must be Russian. He's the one who sold us to the Gestapo. He is only accusing Russians.' In the first case he must be referring to Naegele. At least, I suppose so.... Of the enigmatic D, to whom he was doubtless referring in the second instance, I do not know what to think. I do not want to accuse him nor try to exonerate him and I am too tired to enter into an ideological discussion with a White Russian.

I lie down on the middle bed, Nicolas on the lower one. I am exhausted, too worried to sleep. What will tomorrow bring? I watch the rain through the window ...

Meanwhile, in Poupault's cell, Colonel Gentil, replete with what was at the time a plentiful meal, has fallen asleep. Then he wakes up and feels the need to talk. The former military academician explains to Jacques that he was a ballistics expert. A colonel in the Artillery, he had entered one of the most important circuits of the Resistance at the end of 1942. He describes his arrest. Though tortured, he had managed not to talk. Jacques tells him of the extraordinary conversation he had with D. Gentil finds the story fantastic. He is categorical: D is dangerous.

Much later the door of the cell opens. Relaxed, urbane, D comes in.

'Good evening, gentlemen, pleased to see you,' he says, as if he were beginning a normal conversation in quite a different place to a prison. No one replies. There is a heavy silence in the cell. D pretends not to notice. Turning to Jacques, he adds:

'I warned you of the search and the arrests. To tell you the truth, I didn't think you and I would be involved. I thought only the Czechs and the Russians would be arrested. I had dramatized the situation to put you on your guard.'

'How did you know about it?' Gentil asks roughly.

'Have you ever known an informer or a serious resister give away his sources? We're not playing at war here, we're in one, in a war such as the world has never known. The least indiscretion, the least slip, and it's death. We are going to live together. Let's not just sit here staring at each other. Let's collaborate, if I may use that word.... I have spoken freely to the doctor. I am absolutely sincere. There are huge risks, but let's work together: it'll be worth it. Moreover, I authorize Doctor Poupault to repeat every word of our meeting to you, if he has not done so already.'

'I have.'

D looks reproachful.

'Judging by the events of the past night, your warning came too late.... Our situation now is more than critical,' says Jacques.

'It could all change,' replies D. 'The French have lost nothing. I can assure you that not one of you will be executed. I would not say as much to the Russians and the Czechs.... Have you been interrogated?'

'Indeed I have ... the colonel not yet...'

'You owe all this to that imbecile Naegele.... For a bit of glory, to obtain his freedom and the Gestapo's pardon for his embezzlement, he hurried it up. The ss don't understand any of it anymore. He'll end up badly. He denounced both guilty and innocent – the confusion will save us.'

'Guilty of what?' Gentil asks brusquely.

'... in the eyes of the ss,' smiles D. 'Obviously not in mine.'

'Do you think the ss will see the difference? They hate the French.... I've heard you have never experienced their methods,' says Gentil. 'Were you, in fact, interrogated last night?'

'No.'

'Where were you?'

'I was taken to ss HQ. I served as interpreter for the Russians.' Gentil starts. D smiles gently and adds:

'I shall not try to justify myself, even if I must seem in your eyes an odious person, if not a traitor.... Let me tell you, once and for all, my objective is to stay in contact with certain of the ss in order to save the French at Dora.'

'I did not see you at Niedersachswerfen last night.... Were you there?' asks Poupault.

'No ... I was here. There were interrogations in the prison too.'

What kind of man was this D? He continues:

'There is a Frenchman among you who is behaving like a real bastard, if I may use such a trivial expression.... He has all but compromised everyone.'

'Who?' asks Jacques.

'You'll find out soon enough.' Then, as if he were talking to himself, he murmurs: 'I'll have that Naegele's hide! He's here in the prison. I'll topple him whatever the cost.'

'What prison are we in?' asks Jacques.

'Nordhausen.'

The following morning, very early, a guard comes to fetch D. Enigmatic as ever and seeming absolutely confident in his plans, he turns to his two cell mates. 'See you this evening,' he says as he leaves. It is as if he were taking leave of two charming friends relaxing at their house in the country.

'There's no question of trusting him!' says Gentil angrily when alone with Jacques. 'Perhaps we should pretend to play along.... We have nothing to lose. We'll see where this extravagant adventure will lead us.'

'It's funny,' replies Jacques. 'I can't believe that it's a simple matter of a common informer. And I wonder who he was talking about when he mentioned a Frenchman who's behaving like a real bastard?'

Night. I fall asleep. Suddenly, I hear loud German voices. I have always wondered how those people speak to women, or if they are believers, how they say their prayers. The Germans must be the chosen people; they give orders to God. The corridors echo with shouted commands. I cannot understand a word. Doors slam. I hear shouts. Doors open again and then shut. Now I can hear groaning and moaning. It is impossible to sleep: worry for my friends, fear of being dragged in my turn before noxious people, well-equipped with all the paraphernalia of the perfect torturer...

I spend the night dreading the worst and in a fitful sleep, haunted by the faces of Sander, Naegele, Plazza, Busta, Multerer and other filth.

In the morning, the door opens. We jump up from our bunks. Sander comes in. He goes up to Nicolas Petrenko: '*Sprechen wir noch einmal miteinander!*' Nicolas is going to be taken for interrogation again. He does not move. He is sombre. A few minutes pass; they come back for him.

When he returns to the cell, his face is covered in blood. He shows me his feet, his buttocks.... Horrible! Everywhere, the skin is split and torn.... I try to help him. There is no water in the room to wash away the blood, refresh him a little, give him the illusion of well-being. Nicolas tries to sit down. His face is contorted with the pain. Still without a word, he lies down cautiously on his stomach. Not one word of complaint leaves his lips. What a man! What stuff is he made of? I watch him: his physical resistance fascinates me. Russians fascinate me altogether. Never have I seen so much courage and scorn for death as they display.... They did not even begin to weaken. They were always in the ascendant....

I am deep in thought when Petrenko begins to speak.

'I think they are going to take us back to the bunker at Dora. The SS take us for sub-humans. If we get a chance one day, we'll show them what we're made of.'

'Do you think you haven't shown them already?' I am very moved. I find it difficult to speak. I think I might begin to cry.

'They want to hang us all,' continues Petrenko as if I had not interrupted. 'They are looking for the radio transmitter. They interrogated me to find out where it is hidden. I always gave the same answer: "As far as I know, there is no radio." They are also looking for the receivers that give the deportees the news. They do not know that those receivers belong to the SS.... Consequently, they cannot find them and that has enraged them.... I'm not afraid of death, Jean.... But before I go, I want to be able to do to them what they've done to us. I have only one obsession: the fear that I won't have time!'

'Don't worry.... It's November.... The Russians are coming.... The Allies have liberated almost the whole of France. The bastards don't have much time.'

'Yes, yes.... But every hour counts for us now! Can we hold out till the end?'

We alternate between long silences and grim conversations all day. We are taken once to the latrines where, with my hands, without a scrap of cloth or anything, I try to wash Petrenko's wounds.

The following day Sander returns to fetch Nicolas. I never saw him again.

They bring me two other companions. A Pole, whose name is Josef. He comes from Auschwitz. The other is Nicolas Hronstein, who had done so much to make the Soviet authorities allow his mother to leave Russia. Hronstein works at the *Arbeitsstatistik*. He is not a member of the organization. He has been arrested because his first name is the same as Petrenko: Nicolas. As in the case of Puppo and Poupault, this time with forenames, the Germans, for fear of letting a suspect escape, have taken both of them. Always the (illogical) logic of the SS ...

Nicolas Hronstein and I escape into our imaginations. We

talk of Paris. We take the Métro from Porte Maillot to Vincennes. We get out, change lines. He tells me about the Russia he left in 1924....

In the morning, an armed ss guard accompanies the gaoler; the two of them take us to the toilets. We are able to wash. I have always tried to keep up the barest hygiene at Dora despite the filth and muck of the tunnel.... A bare minimum.... Now this is the Roman Baths, the delights of Poppea!...

I see Claude Lauth on the lavatory. A ball of fire grips my chest. He is alive! His wrists are handcuffed, his ankles chained together. His forehead, his eyes, his lips are swollen. He is unshaven. An armed ss guard stands in front of him. I look at Claude. He says to me quietly: 'Beware of Naegele. He's a traitor.' I wink at him, hoping to be comforting. I do not answer him because the ss guard points his machine-gun at me. No talking!

The door of Jacques Poupault's cell opens. A guard has come to fetch him. In a room, Sander, behind a desk, and Naegele, seated on a chair, arms crossed, an ugly expression on his face, are waiting for him. A typist occupies a corner of the office. Her machine is loaded with paper. The trio are ready for the interrogation.

Poupault is nervous. What else can happen? Sander emanates considerable brute force. Is this Act Two of a play entitled *Variations on a Bull-whip*? Then his anxiety begins to melt.... He feels a sense of detachment.... As if he were a spectator of the scene.... He detects no hostility in Sander's face. Only Naegele seems angry. As if he is keener than the others to invent the guilty...

Sander adopts a bantering tone.

'Well, *Herr Doktor*, are you going to be more talkative than last time, or am I going to have to help you?' pointing to Naegele. Poupault waits for the translation.

'I can talk about various things, but not about things I do not know,' he replies.

Sander looks as if he is enjoying himself.... He begins to read with interest the papers which are on the desk. 'I know why you were arrested in France,' he says. Jacques does not flinch. Sander seems disappointed, as if he was expecting a reply.

'You were a surgeon to the Maquis.'

Poupault suppresses a sigh of relief. The Nordhausen Gestapo know nothing. They are groping in the dark. The dossiers have not been sent on. Relieved, he waits for Naegele's translation and then replies:

'You are mistaken. I agreed to be a surgeon in case of battle on French soil. I would have been able to tend Germans as well as French; that's the humanitarian role of a doctor.' Taking courage, he goes on to talk of the equality of men in pain, of the Geneva Convention; a tribune in the court of the ss. As if he were drowning in the torrent of words, Sander signals for silence. Finally, he grows angry:

'No speeches! What I want to know is your actions at Dora and the names of your accomplices.'

Tirelessly, Jacques repeats his story:

'I have only friends, because I care for the deportees as best I can. That's known throughout the camp.'

Furious, Naegele jumps to his feet. He wants to speak, to strike Jacques. Sander, with a gesture, makes him sit down. 'Naegele is definitely in a tight spot. D was right,' thinks Jacques. He draws some comfort from the Kapo's irritation – 'He instigated this whole affair. If the Gestapo don't find anything, he's had it.'

Sander turns to the typist. He dictates a resumé of Poupault's flight of oratory. Jacques pretends he does not understand, but he is astonished by the German's scrupulousness.

Once again, Sander studies his papers:

'You are on bad terms with Cespiva. He claims that you are a poor surgeon, very self-important. Egocentric. Other people do not interest you at all.'

'Sander can find nothing better than this mediocre subterfuge,' thinks Poupault, as Naegele translates. 'Unless Cespiva claimed to detest me to show that there could be no collusion between us.' Jacques decides to enter into the game. He assumes an irritated air:

'It's professional jealousy. He's annoyed because he is only my assistant. He wanted to be chief surgeon.'

Sander is decidedly diverted. This confraternal antagonism delights him. Jacques is reassured. Cespiva's deposition proves his imagination and wisdom. What skill!

The interrogation is taking an excellent turn in Poupault's favour. If it continues, he is going to be able to exonerate himself completely. Suddenly, Sander's attitude changes. He says threateningly: 'To whom do you give your orders for sabotage? Pay attention! You're going to suffer in a minute!'

'I don't know what you're talking about.'

Naegele leaps up.

'We have the evidence of your accomplices. They have confessed. You are the leader.'

'Under torture you can admit many things: that you are black when you are white, that you murdered your own mother, even if she died when you were two months old.'

'You're going to stop playing the fool ... I promise you!' rages Naegele.

'I want to be confronted by those who accuse me. I want to read their depositions.... All I could be blamed for is that I passed on news to my friends when they came for consultation.'

At the word 'news', Sander shows his teeth:

'From whom, from what source did you get news?'

'I have told you ... from the newspapers forgotten by Doctor Karr or Lorenz....'

'That's a lie! You gave out news before it appeared in the German papers.'

'Aha!' thinks Poupault. 'So Sander's admitting that the Germans delay unpleasant news....'

Naegele can contain himself no longer. He throws himself on Poupault.

'*Ruhe, Mensch!*' orders Sander angrily.

The German does not seem satisfied by the doctor's replies. However, he does not persist. He turns to the typist and dictates the rest of the interview. After he has finished he considers for a moment and then says:

'Do you wish for an Allied victory?'

'I wish to recover my liberty,' Jacques replies carefully.

'If the Allies win, are you not afraid that you will all be killed before they arrive?'

'No, the Germans are soldiers. They are not going to become assassins.'

Jacques is quite pleased with this, but at the same time, he wonders if Sander will be deceived by so much hypocrisy. 'My desire to please is too obvious,' he thinks. The German is looking at him in astonishment. He cannot have been fooled. He contents himself with saying: 'You are right.'

Poupault signs the deposition which is presented to him. Naegele is fuming. Scowling, Sander drums on his dossier. 'He must feel closer to me than to Naegele,' thinks Jacques. A sentry accompanies

him back to his cell. To have escaped torture gives him wings. He
sees the full mess-tins on the table. Gentil is waiting for him to eat.

'So?' asks the colonel.

'Not a single blow. No violence. Not the tiniest slap. Sander
recorded my declarations without falsifying the tone of them. I
could tell when he dictated them to the typist. I feel euphoric!'

'But you're trembling!'

'The tension, the relief, a reaction....'

Jacques is sleeping when D returns to the cell.

'What's new?' he asks.

Poupault comes to. He orders his thoughts: 'I was interrogated
this morning.... It all went well.'

'That does not surprise me.'

'How can D be so sure of himself? Nothing upsets him,' thinks
Jacques.

'Do you know who Naegele is? A Gestapo agent. He infiltrated
the Resistance and had the whole local circuit captured. His own
lot arrested him because he was out for "individual reward". He
had made a profit of four million francs. I must get him chased out
of Nordhausen. I must! Then I would have a free hand. God! I
must get rid of him!'

'Where does D get his information?' thinks Jacques. He says:
'What about the Russians?'

'I have the impression that most of the Russians who were
arrested are strangers to the camp organization. When beaten, they
name names and the arrests are multiplied. The prison is full of
Russians. The poor buggers don't understand why they are here.
In my opinion, except for a few, the ones who are really responsible
for the Russian movement at Dora are not known. They've got
together to cover their tracks. They let the innocents be arrested,
those whom they consider of no use in the struggle; those who are
fighting go to ground, throw up smoke screens, plot and work
underground. The more people there are implicated in the affair,
the less clearly can the Germans see; that is their strategy. This
behaviour is so beyond the Germans' comprehension that their
enquiries have been brought to a halt. The war will be over by the
time they've understood.'

'Doesn't it sicken you to be present at the interrogations and
tortures?'

'There must be a Russian interpreter and a Ukranian interpreter. I think I am one of the rare people at Dora who could take this role. I try to make the declarations seem truthful. As for the Communists, they must know that there are far more camps in the Soviet Union and that torture is practised there on a far greater scale. What is worse, there, is that it is so-called Communists who imprison, torture and inflict forced labour on real Communists. The greatest murderers of the Russians are Russians. Here, they are still the victims of their enemies, they are fighting the ss – the situation is clear. There, it's as if your father, your mother, your brothers and sisters, your wife suddenly, inexplicably, began to persecute you for the pleasure of terror and the look of incomprehension in the victim's eyes.... I repeat, you obstinately refuse to believe it, but it is very important that I remain in contact with certain ss leaders. That is my aim. The only means by which my plan will succeed....'

In the middle of the night there is a great deal of noise. Men rush up and down the prison corridors. They seem to be dragging something. Then it becomes quiet again. The door to Poupault's cell opens. Müller comes in: '*Herr Doktor, kommen Sie mit mir.*' Jacques dresses quickly. Müller explains: 'They've just brought me a Russian. He tried to escape when he was arrested. He was recaptured and beaten up. His head is bleeding. He looks in a hopeless condition.'

Jacques follows Müller. The wounded man is lying on the lower berth of the bunks in a cell. His pulse is regular. The doctor examines him. The Russian's clothes are soaked. Jacques tries to undress him. He is a big fellow, difficult to move.

'Can you call Doctor Cespiva?' Jacques asks Müller. After a few minutes, Cespiva arrives. Müller watches the scene from the doorway.

'Speak French,' says Jacques. 'When were you interrogated?'

'Just before you this morning. I think things are going to be all right for the French ... but for us and the Russians the situation is more serious. They have Nicolas Petrenko's declarations. He is flat out in my cell. He has admitted to me that he said too much. They completely demolished him.'

As they talk, the Czech and the Frenchman attend to the wounded man. 'I've had it,' adds Cespiva. 'I'm going to crack.'

Poupault tries to raise his morale. The Russian is now naked. He has widespread bruising on his body, a deep wound in his scalp. His reflexes are normal.

'There's nothing seriously wrong with him. I think he's faking,' says Cespiva.

'We're not going to be the ones to stop him,' says Jacques, and turning towards Müller: 'Concussion and even perhaps cerebral contusion. He must be kept under close observation. Quiet, rest . . . trepanation might be necessary.' Jacques speaks in French. Cespiva translates.

Müller goes away. The door is left open. There is no longer a guard. The two doctors have a sensation of freedom. Cespiva says: 'The Gestapo are looking for the radio transmitter. . . . For a long time, parts stolen in the tunnel had aroused the ss' suspicion. . . . I'm afraid I'll be tortured in the next interrogations . . .'

Jacques is convinced that the Russian can hear perfectly well, but that he does not understand French.

'It's done me good to have seen you. This wounded man was providential,' adds Cespiva.

'Don't worry. . . . You must surely believe that after this hullaba-loo your friends will have destroyed the radio. . . . Have you any news of André Boyer?'

'I think he is in a cell on the same corridor as this one. There are six or seven to a cell. . . .'

The following morning, Sander is surprised to find Cespiva and Poupault at the Russian's bedside. They both have a professional bearing, without familiarity. Sander looks at the Russian, who has not moved a muscle all night.

'Can he talk?'

'No. It's very serious. . . . Concussion. . . . I have already told you,' replies Jacques.

'It is vital that he recovers. . . . You will answer for it with your life! And it is not necessary for you to be together. . . . You will take turns.'

Poupault pretends not to understand. Cespiva translates. . . . Are they afraid that the man might be murdered to prevent him from talking? . . . Jacques says to Sander: 'I can do nothing. I need cardio-tonics, serum, a probe, bandages.' Cespiva continues to play his role as interpreter. 'Make a list, you will have all that from this morning,' replies the ss officer. 'There must also be a German doctor to con-firm our diagnosis,' insists Poupault.

Sander leaves the cell. Cespiva is amazed at his companion's last request.

'A German doctor is going to make things complicated for us. He will be able to see that our Russian is not in a coma.'

'It's the only way to prove our good faith,' says Jacques. 'Don't be afraid, we'll handle it.... Since you speak Russian as well, tell the Russian that we are not taken in.... He must take some nourishment, explain to him.' But the wounded man remains motionless. In that pitiless place, he would not have trusted his own mother.

Müller comes to fetch Cespiva, doubtless respecting Sander's order. He returns him to his cell. Jacques profits by this to take a few steps in the corridor. He advances with caution. He calls Boyer's name. At the third door, Boyer answers. He is all right. He has not been interrogated.

Poupault strolls along the corridor with a detached air. The corridor is lit by large barred windows. They give onto an expanse of green. A playing field? The doctor passes on. The corridor is at least twenty yards long; there are eight cells. One end is closed off by a wall. The other turns sharp right into a perpendicular corridor. The prison seems to be constructed in the shape of a horseshoe on a single level. Jacques' cell is at one end of the horseshoe.

Poupault makes a complete inspection of the property. He is full of optimism. If he can walk every day, freely within the prison, he will be able to help his friends, as he had at the Dora *Revier*.

Two women with mops and pails are washing the floor. 'All the same, it's a funny sort of prison!' says Poupault to himself. One of the two women, who must be about twenty-five, quite pretty, gives him a bold look.

'Are you prisoners?' asks Jacques in German, pretending to search for words.

'Of course,' replies the younger, laughing. 'What do you think?'

Poupault is puzzled. He returns to the wounded man's bedside. Time passes. He begins to miss the company of the colonel and the surprising D.

Did he fall asleep? Was he lost in his thoughts? He is suddenly surprised to see Müller and Doctor Karr standing before him. He gets up. Karr bends over the Russian, lifts the covers, and asks casually:

'Why is he naked?'

'His clothes were soaking wet because he had fallen into a river,' replies Jacques in halting German.

Karr does not seem surprised.

'Ah yes, that's true. He escaped from the lorry that was bringing him from the camp. He was recaptured when he tried to cross the river. Is his life in danger?'

'I don't know.'

'When will he be able to be interrogated?'

'In a week, perhaps sooner.'

Karr examines the Russian.

'Good,' he says, non-committal.

He takes out a packet of cigarettes and offers it to Jacques. 'I suppose you have no tobacco. . . .' An inveterate smoker, Poupault takes the cigarettes without having to be asked twice. Karr moves towards the door, glances out along the corridor, sees that Müller has gone, turns and says: 'Thank you.' He leaves the cell, haughty as ever, without another word.

'What did he thank me for?' Jacques asks himself. 'For not having wrongly accused him? For not having talked about Fritz Preul's radio?' Suddenly, the thought comes to him that Karr knew of the existence of the radio. Perhaps he had obtained it for Fritz? . . . 'No, I'm fantasizing. . . .'

Time for soup. Müller dishes out two mess-tins. He is not to know that one of the occupants of the cell is comatose. 'On this diet, I shall gain weight,' says Poupault to himself, eating with relish.

Soon afterwards, a guard brings Cespiva. It is his turn to watch over the Russian.

'Karr was here. He has confirmed our diagnosis.'

Jacques has no time to say more. The guard takes him back to his cell.

When, returning to his watch over the Russian, he replaces Cespiva, Poupault finds in the cell all the medicines he has requested from Sander. Never did he have such riches at the *Revier*. The Gestapo are really determined that this boy shall live! Jacques takes the syringe, a needle, a probe. He knocks on the door of Müller's office: 'May I boil these instruments?' The head guard leads him along the corridor. He takes him to a room in the basement. A kitchen. Poupault boils his instruments.

On his return to the cell, he breaks an ampoule of cardiazol, but is careful not to inject it. He sounds the sick man, who lets himself be attended to without moving. His bladder is full. The Russian must be in agony. He does not give himself away. Jacques takes a glass of water to make the faker drink.

Faithful to his tactics, the wounded man does nothing to help him. The water runs down his chin onto his neck. He must surely die of thirst after two days, motionless on the bunk. 'What a man!' Jacques says to himself. 'What strength of will, what perseverance. But he must admit that I am his friend.' In a gibberish, three-quarters German and the rest made up of Czech and Russian words, Jacques makes a new attempt. The man opens one eye. He says something in Russian that Jacques cannot understand. He drinks greedily. No smile of complicity, only that determination that, once again, is evidence of the unknown resources of Man....

Returning to his cell after Cespiva has taken his place in the sick-room, Poupault finds D awake. Gentil is asleep.

'The ss think that the wounded man you are caring for is the leader of the Russian organization at Dora.'

'Is there a Russian organization?' asks Poupault innocently, not admitting that the Russian is pretending.

'Yes,' replies D, not taken in.... 'As there is a French, a Czech and one of German Communists. The ss are cracking down hardest on the Russians, for they fear them the most. If they do not liquidate them at once, there will be a massacre.

'Don't they have a plan to exterminate all Dora deportees?'

'Indeed they do.... But perhaps there will be those who will fail to carry out the plan.... Wasn't Paris going to be destroyed? ... Some of the ss are thinking of the day when they will fall into the hands of the Allies; that makes them reconsider, for, except for a few fanatics, they know they are beaten. My role, I repeat, is to persuade them to come to an agreement with us.'

Early in the morning, D leaves the cell. Jacques wants to tell Gentil about his conversation with the enigmatic White Russian.

'I heard it all. I cannot sleep.... His arguments are valid. But let us continue to be wary of him.'

Colonel Gentil is exhausted and plagued by scabies. Jacques examines him. He has a high fever. His body is covered with lesions. Gentil scratches too much. He cannot help it. On his right leg is a deep sore which looks ulcerous. It is surrounded by inflamed flesh.

Alarmed, Poupault bangs on the door. He asks for Müller. He arrives. 'The colonel is ill. Will you allow me to take medicaments from the Russian's cell?' He does not forget to speak German hesitantly. Müller agrees. Jacques takes sulphonamides and bandages.

For several days, he attends to Gentil. Müller is very understanding. But the sores are suppurating, the fever does not fall. In the end, the sores spread more and more. Gentil feels close to death. Poupault asks Müller that he should be taken to hospital. He does not have much faith in the power of the chief guard, but the latter's efforts result in Gentil being taken to the Dora *Revier*.

'I hope he gets better,' says Müller. 'I really like that man.'

The colonel's deterioration is irreversible. It is D, much moved, who tells Poupault of Gentil's death, from septicaemia, several weeks later.

The Russian knows that he cannot keep up the pretence for ever. Cespiva has explained this to him. One morning Jacques sees a civilian arrive in the sick man's cell. 'He's a top specialist,' says Müller. The specialist is tall, thin and old. He wears round gold spectacles. He is sure of himself, distant. Poupault begins to relate the case history of the wounded man. The other cuts him short. He examines the Russian. He turns to Jacques.

'This man has nothing wrong with him,' he says severely. 'I shall make my report. I shall indicate that your diagnosis was correct [stressing the 'was'], that the patient has come out of his coma and that he can be interrogated in three days' time.'

Brief and to the point. Incontestable. He leaves the room. 'He was cold, but still he treated me as a fellow doctor. He could have finished me . . . ,' thinks Jacques. He cannot tear himself away from studying the Russian's face. 'What are they going to do to him?' He is seized with the anguish of a man who is impotent in the face of misfortune. . . . An anguish familiar to those who were in the camps.

Jacques talks more and more frequently to Boyer. Müller now leaves Jacques' cell door open during the day. D continues to leave in the morning, not to return until the evening.

Sander and six armed ss men come to fetch the wounded Russian. It is during Cespiva's watch. He has warned the Russian that the three days fixed by the specialist have expired. When Sander arrives, the Russian get up, puts on his clothes, seems dizzy, clutches at the wall and goes out staggering. Cespiva is convinced that the Russian is exaggerating his weakness to show the Gestapo that the doctors' diagnosis was correct. Cespiva and Poupault have given him food and water. For his needs, they gave him a jam jar which they went to empty, praying they would not meet either a guard or Naegele on the way.

Müller asks Poupault to see to the health of the detainees. Escorted by a guard, he visits one cell after another. He is only authorized to attend to civilian prisoners. One part of the prison is reserved for women. They are crammed in six or seven to a cell. There are Germans, Russians, Czechs and even a few French women – prostitutes, thieves or civilian workers who have deserted their work. Many of the detainees are affected by scabies. Müller provides several pints of *mitigal*. Jacques organizes treatment sessions. The rudimentary bedding is disinfected. Amongst the civilians, scabies disappears. Müller sings the praises of the Herr Doktor whose influence is growing.

Jacques takes a liking to the young German woman prisoner whom he had seen washing the floor. She was arrested for stealing food when she was working in a community restaurant. She has been at Nordhausen for six months. Not yet tried, she fears a severe penalty. She also prepares the guards' meals. She often gives Poupault cigarettes or a piece of fruit. She tells him that Naegele is alone in a cell at the far end of the prison. He is the lover of a young French detainee. She joins him at night through the complicity of a guard. All the women know about it. 'Here's a precious piece of information,' thinks Poupault. 'Naegele is breaking prison rules.'

Jacques arranges to meet the French girl and to talk to her. An ex-voluntary worker in Germany, she was arrested for prostitution. 'I had to eat! The fools arrested me just when I was beginning to make some money!' Seeing that Poupault is dressed in striped pyjamas like Naegele, she confides in Jacques: 'If you want a letter got to the outside, give it to Maurice (Naegele). . . . For a few marks he'll get it taken out and posted.'

That evening Poupault repeats this conversation to D. 'I've got the bastard this time! I'll make him suffer and take his place! Tell the French I'm doing this for them. They must trust me!' In his excitement, D calls Jacques *tu*.

The prison 'guests' often change their cells. One day, André Boyer and a Pole join me. Nicolas Hronstein and the other Pole go to another corner of the prison. These exchanges enable us to hear news of each other. I am happy to meet Boyer again. 'I have not been interrogated,' he says. 'I have the impression that the Germans are arresting more and more civilians. We shall be squashed in like sardines.'

Often we hear screams. Interrogations followed by torture. Claude Lauth, one of the most victimized, Debaumarché, one of the PTT leaders, and Pierre Caruana – who had received, in one single session, three hundred blows of the baton from Naegele – found themselves together.

A German *Vorarbeiter* called Weber, whom I know from Dora and who has been arrested, brings us our soup. He is very cordial. It is from him that I learn that the French deportees are all incarcerated at Nordhausen while many foreigners are being held in the Dora bunker. Weber intrigues me and arouses my mistrust.

I know what sort of condition Claude Lauth is in, mentally and physically. It depresses me terribly.... Lauth is thinking of his parents, of Liliane. Until he was brought to Nordhausen he had been able to keep, in spite of the searches, a photograph of the woman he loves. The Gestapo confiscated his treasure, mocking his fidelity: 'You are going to die.... Better for her if she forgets you....' Claude gets no rest. His body is so damaged that he can no longer find any position in which he can sleep.

Pierre Caruana, his fellow-sufferer, is a native Algerian. French, of Maltese origin, the cunning and kindness in his sun-tanned face have been erased by an expression of pain. In his rare moments of respite he swears he will have Naegele's skin, if he comes out alive....

Jacques Poupault, the privileged man at Nordhausen, pays us a visit. It is Müller himself who opens the door for him and closes it behind him. Jacques tells us of the conversations he has had with D and this incredible man's plans.

'It's a crazy story, but it must be said, it's our story, and we're right in the middle of the action!' he says. 'At first, D only saw the possibility of saving the French detainees. Certain members of the General Staff in Berlin, some of the SS and engineers at Dora would protect them from the SS fanatics trying to follow Himmler's orders of extermination to the letter.... For that to happen, it would

only need the major Resistance leaders, imprisoned at Dora, to contact de Gaulle, and through him, the Anglo-Americans.... But now
I think that the Germans with whom he is negotiating see much
farther ahead than that. The Berlin General Staff wants to conclude
a separate peace ... at least those who secretly oppose Hitler want
that.... Once the war was over in the West, the Germans would
then be able to turn against the Russians with the Allied armies
at their side.'

'It's mad. That's an incredible story! D may be sincere, but he
has read too many books, seen too many films,' says Boyer, after
having heard Jacques out.

As we listen to these grand designs, we are prosaically munching
on a piece of bread that Jacques has brought us.

Poupault knocks on the door. Müller comes to fetch him. Boyer,
the Pole and I are left....

'I'm sure it's true that some Germans want to negotiate. They
clearly do fear the Russians. But how on earth could D be in contact
with the high officials of the General Staff? Through the tunnel
engineers? Through some ss officers who feel that all is lost and
want to redeem themselves? Is that the reason that the interrogations of the French have become less frequent?' I put these questions to Boyer without waiting for his reply.... I add: 'André, we
must not rely on D. We must only rely on ourselves. Let us plan
our escape. Let's only think of that....'

'But how?'

'The prison rules are typed on a piece of card. On the back there
is a map showing the region of Feldkirch, on the Swiss border.'

'Can you ski?'

'No.'

'The pass to Switzerland is situated at an altitude of about 1,500
yards. At this time of year, there is snow. How would we get
through?'

'If we could get as far as the pass, I wouldn't need skis. I'd fly.'

'We must find planks. They'd do for snow-shoes,' says Boyer,
with a smile.

'I know that there is only one guard at night. I will ask to go
to the toilet and I'll put him out of action. We'll take the keys to
the cells. There'll be such a commotion we'll be able to escape.
Those who want to will come with us.'

Boyer is not convinced.

'Your plan is too sketchy,' he says.

'I know that. Have we any choice?'

'Wait ... I agree with you; let us try to escape. But let us wait for the right moment.'

For a long time we are silent, each dreaming of France, of Paris liberated and us, thin and exhausted, joyously milling with the crowd who will never know the likes of Dora....

A few days later, a visit from Poupault, excited by his conversations with D.

'May I tell him how important you were in the Resistance?' he asks Boyer.

Boyer considers this carefully.

'We do not have a great deal to lose,' he says finally. 'It's a little as if we were putting all our money into a lottery on one number.... Do what you think best. And since we are agreeing to leap into the dark, let us give ourselves more importance and greater influence with the French government....'

Poupault tells us that Jacques Bordier (Bordier-Brunschwig) has been arrested too and transferred to Nordhausen. (Bordier was one of our companions at Dora. Bald, with an intelligent, caustic expression and laughing eyes, he had been a member of the Consultative Assembly in Algiers.)

'Should I let him in on D's plans?'

'Certainly,' replies André Boyer.

As he leaves the cell, Poupault seems intoxicated by his activity and his conversations with D. The latter is becoming more and more involved with the Gestapo and the interrogations of the Russians and the Ukranians.

Trapped in my cell, I only see the D saga through Poupault's eyes. Nevertheless, Boyer and I are terribly impatient. Either Jacques is an excellent story-teller, or a deportee's imagination needs very little stimulus to take flight....

# Chapter Twenty-eight

# KAMMLER, HIMMLER AND CO.

Once again, I feel that I must temporarily interrupt my story. This whole affair of a deportee, in one of the very last antechambers of hell – the gaols of the Gestapo in a Nazi concentration camp – acting as an intermediary between common *Stücke* and the ss warlords, must seem so fantastic that I want to try to give it some substance, if only a little, through the information I possess today.

Despite all our efforts, my comrades from Dora and I have never been able to clarify the dealings of which D was the pivot and for which our lives were a very derisory stake. The same curtain, which after the war fell to separate the hard facts of Dora from the missile research, came down on the negotiations between the Allies and the Germans who held the secret of the wonder weapons. The stake was certainly high enough. The Russians and the Americans were both counting on the missiles to establish their own domination of the world.

Faithful to the format I have kept to throughout, I shall continue to relate what we lived through, hour after hour, day after day, with our false hopes, our innocent dreams, all the errors of interpretation that we could have committed at that time. But thirty years later, I have reached certain conclusions about the shady dealings of the Third Reich, thanks to the odd snippets of information which have come to light here and there, and for the reader to appreciate various repercussions I have decided to record these conclusions.

In November 1944, at the moment of our arrest, Heinrich Himmler found himself at the height of his power. The attempt on Hitler's life of 20 July had enabled him to break the haughty Wehrmacht. His old dream of the ss Empire was now within his grasp: on the

8 August, his right arm, Hans Kammler, promoted to the rank of *Obergruppenführer* SS, was named Special Commissioner for the secret weapons. Seconded, under pressure from von Braun, by General Dornberger, Heydrich's blond counterpart thus became absolute master of the entire missile programme, from the research centre at Peenemünde to the tunnel at Dora and to the artillery units ordered to crush London under an onslaught of v weapons.

The moment was crucial. Certainly, the Allied advance had enabled the Anglo-Americans to seize all the VI launching pads in France, and the last flying bomb fired from the Somme had fallen on the English capital on 1 September. But on 8 September, at 6.43 p.m., 'a clap like thunder heralded the arrival of the first A4 in London'.[1] Kammler's special units had fired the first of the weapons of reprisal number 2 from Holland.

At the end of August 1944, Dornberger and von Braun had in effect managed to eliminate the problem of their missiles exploding in the air with such disturbing regularity. Still continuing the manufacture of the VIS (the flying bombs were from this time on fired at London from aeroplanes or catapults based in Holland until they were required to attack Brussels and Anvers), Dora's production of the V2s was stepped up – 628 came out of the tunnel in September and October against 86 and 324 in July and August.

So one can understand the rage of the SS when our sabotage units were discovered. Less understandable on the other hand was that, having at last uncovered the reasons why the missiles still seemed defective, the idea of negotiating with the saboteurs could have germinated in the minds of the Gestapo.

The Third Reich collapsed in shame. Even the suicide of its leaders seemed as pure sacrifices compared to the torrent of betrayals, selfish skin-saving and sordid haggling which made of the fall of Nazi Germany not the 'Twilight of the Gods' desired by Hitler but one of the most nauseating cesspits of history.

In November 1944, Hitler's Germany was caught in a pincer between the Red Army and the Anglo-American forces. A wind of panic began to blow over the thousand-year Reich; all the rats could not hope to leave the ship. For it was indeed a question of rats.

The heads of the concentration camps and their guards, loaded down by their past as torturers, locked in an inhuman discipline, inflamed by the propaganda about the miracle weapons, could not

have negotiated with D. They were thirstier for atrocity than ever.
Thanks to them, Dora, which had become an autonomous camp
on 1 November 1944, was daily being transformed into an ever more
appalling hell. Perhaps the torturers did fear for their lives, but their
only chance of safety lay in a flight forward in atrocity, until the
pitiful disguises of the final hour that would enable many of them
to escape justice.

Scientists, technicians and engineers had more of a chance. They
had less blood on their hands. It was the aristocracy of evil. They
used the miracle potential to pay for their lives – their research on
the revolutionary weapons. To each his own eucharist.

On 4 April 1945, Dieter Huzel, head of Wernher von Braun's
general staff, was to load fourteen tons of plans and archives into
three lorries and flee along the roads of the Harz to bury his life
insurance in abandoned mines. Less well off, the most junior
engineers hid their meagre loot in improvised caches dug out in the
barns around Nordhausen – one man a blue-print, another an essential component for the manufacture of the missiles.[2]

In November 1944, this had not yet come to pass. Wernher von
Braun and Walter Dornberger were still at Peenemünde; they paid
regular visits to Dora, but their records were still on the Baltic coast.
All the documents were indispensable to the mass-production of
the missiles.

And, besides, scientists and technicians did not hold the major
trump cards necessary for a seat at the negotiating table worked out
by D – full power over the Gestapo.

The administrative staff of the *Mittelwerke* carried even less
weight. The ability to run a factory is not a tradeable secret; it is
within the power of any minor executive. Was not Georg Richney,
general manager of the *Mittelwerke-GmbH* Company, to be seen on
the same defendants' bench in 1947 as Kapo Kilian or the last
camp commandant, Hans Moeser?

One man alone held both the sufficient authority over the Gestapo
killers and a marketable technical knowledge: *Obergruppenführer* SS
Hans Kammler.

Overall head of the secret-weapon programme, absolute monarch
of the concentration-camp missile empire, Hans Kammler knew all
the secrets concerning the conception and the manufacture of the
VIs and the V2s. As Special Commissioner, he was as much the

supreme chief of the scientists and the engineers as of the ss guards or the Gestapo.

Let us not forget Speer's judgement: Kammler, in the image of his master Heydrich, was 'a cold ruthless schemer', a 'fanatic in the pursuit of a goal, and as carefully calculating as he was unscrupulous'. He had proved it in the past by seizing absolute power over the missiles. He was to confirm it later, in April 1945, at the moment when the American armoured divisions were fighting at the gates of Nordhausen. The blond ss leader was then to play an amazing hand of poker; disregarding the 'scorched earth' orders of Adolf Hitler, he was not to destroy the *Mittelwerke* factories which were to fall intact, with their machines, their design rooms, their half-completed v2s, into the hands of the American army. He was to arrange, at the time, to hide five hundred scientists from Peenemünde in the safety of the Bavarian mountains. All the élite of space research, led by von Braun, Dornberger and Steinhoff, were thus to become the fabulous human treasure of the ss.

Thirty years have passed. Sometimes I lie awake for whole nights at a time, so obsessed am I with my memories of Dora and of the prison at Nordhausen. At each dawn after these long, sleepless nights, I always come to the same conclusion: *Obergruppenführer* ss Hans Kammler was the only man who had sufficient power to urge the Gestapo to propose the strange deal to D. He was the only man who could, in November 1944, have sent word to the Allies: 'I can negotiate with you about the future of the secret weapons.'

There was but one, essential, condition – *Reichsführer* Heinrich Himmler must of necessity have been kept informed about the progress of these aberrant negotiations. In that police state which was the Third Reich, the (relative) gentleness of a local Gestapo chief, the promises made to a deportee, the violation of the absolute rule that any attempt at revolt against the Nazi order resulted inevitably in torture and death, could not have escaped the supreme chief of the police and the ss.

As Himmler's slave, I myself have long believed, despite certain allusions made by D, that this condition was impossible.

And yet ...

Heinrich Himmler was one of those monsters that history only throws up from time to time, a curious mixture of a visionary and a twisted realist.

If, in the end, the v2 was to permit man to go to the moon and to instigate a nuclear balance of terror, this futuristic programme did not grant Nazi Germany the possibility of winning the war, despite what certain of those involved believed. On the contrary. The obsession with rockets contributed decisively in the precipitation of the irreversible fall of the Third Reich. The historian David Irving stresses that one single rocket, in its state of development in 1944, could only carry one ton of explosives. Three thousand tons of explosives were thus launched by the Germans in eight months, while the American Flying Fortresses dropped three thousand tons of bombs *a day*. Now the v2 programme swallowed up colossal resources, essential raw materials, the intellectual capital of research – not to mention, of course, the concentration camp labour force which we provided at practically no cost and which was, alas, inexhaustible. All these could have been used for the construction of tanks, fighter-planes, submarines, or in the perfection of anti-aircraft missiles capable of paralysing the Allied bombers. From the point of view of immediate efficacy for the great dream of Nazi hegemony, our sacrifices were thus useless. The Russians and the Americans were to profit by them later, when, with the hell of the Harz forgotten, the rockets left Baikonour and Cape Kennedy and flew to the stars.

The scientific dreams of Wernher von Braun, Dornberger's military obstinacy, Speer's technocratic blindness, Hitler's intuition and Himmler's lust for power gave birth to a project 'conceived not out of military necessity but to quench the innate German thirst for romanticism'.[3] 'Thirst for romanticism'! It appears in every one of Himmler's undertakings. The ss Reichsführer's pathological faith in the necessity of an 'anti-Bolshevik crusade' was so strong that he never understood that others – notably the Anglo-Americans – could not share his faith. Even if they did share it, their faith would admit a priority. And for the moment, that priority was the struggle against Nazism. So powerful was the master of death's contempt for life that he always believed that nothing – not even the gas chambers – would prevent him becoming the privileged interlocuter of the west.

The ss leader's terrifying proposals with a view to a separate peace in the West to order to better combat the USSR did not date from the collapse of the Reich and his contacts with Count Bernadotte in January and April 1945. Several witnesses – notably the diplomat, von Hassel – and historians such as Wheeler-Bennett and Gerald Reitlinger, have shown that the Reichsführer's oblique manœuvres began as early as 1942. At that time, even before the defeat of Stalingrad, Himmler was trying to enter into contact with the West through the German Resistance, all the while concealing it from Hitler. 'The mild-mannered, bloodthirsty ss Führer, the master policeman of the Third Reich, began to take a personal and not altogether unfavourable interest in the Resistance, with which he had more than one friendly contact,' writes William Shirer.[4] As for Gilles Perrault, he adds: 'Himmler counted ... on the Resistance to make contact with the West and open negotiations.'[5]

Himmler's suicide before he could be interrogated, and the understandable silence of the Allied Secret Services, have prevented any light being shed on these Machiavellian combinations. But the obsessional desire for contact with the West, the wish to manipulate the Resistance, the sadistic double game of ss cat with deportee mouse, indeed constitute the characteristic traits of the shady negotiations instigated by Hans Kammler.

The Dora *pourparlers* – of which, I repeat, I knew only the most elementary details – were only, if I am not mistaken, a complementary off-shoot of the major dealings concerning the missiles. They also constitute a new piece of evidence to add to the dossier on the mysterious Heinrich Himmler.

One appalling fact still further reinforces this conviction, reached after years of reflection. We owe our lives to D. But if today I am in a position to tell this story, my admirable Russian comrades are dead. The Russian deportees and the German Communists paid the highest price for the crimes of which we were all accused. To the crazed mind of Himmler – that executioner who fainted at the sight of blood – the West could survive. But the East must die.

But let us return to my story.

# Chapter Twenty-nine

## FREEDOM OR THE ROPE?

Poupault's optimism is infectious. Jacques, often accompanied by Müller who opens the door of our cell for him and leaves him alone with us, says that our adventure reminds him of that of the French officer in the novel *Tendre Allemagne* (*Kavalier Schanorst*) by Des Valières.

'As at the end of the 1914–18 war, Germany is falling apart,' says Poupault. 'The guards have lost their morale. They are well aware that everything is crumbling around them. This is an extraordinary prison. We are having the most unique adventure! To think that our small group could be so decisive in the ending of the conflict!'

We catch some of his enthusiasm.

'If only D could get them to send us to Switzerland! We'd negotiate better there than from our cells here at Nordhausen.'

Even as I say these unusually inconscient words, I am crushing fleas with my fingernails. Boyer and I spend hours in a pursuit as useless as pouring water into the Danaides' well. The fleas may have proliferated at Compiègne – at Nordhausen they invade the cells in their thousands. Sitting on our bunks, we pick them out of the seams of our jackets and ceaselessly crush them with our nails. . . . The action is so routine that we are no longer aware of how degrading it is. . . .

The prison is full to bursting. There have never been so many arrests: civilians, deportees. Food is scarce. The rations are reduced more and more.

Müller opens the cells three at a time. We have more time to wash. The washroom is crowded. There I see Puppo again, Count Paul

Chandon (of Moët and Chandon champagne), Pierre Caruana and his cousin André, Brother Birin, Jacques Bordier, a hairdresser called Barry who sometimes helps to distribute the soup.

André Boyer and I have endless discussions. I tell him of my passion for books and the cinema. He talks about painting, sculpture and poetry. He is writing a poem about our lives as deportees. With a pencil stump and some wrapping paper brought by Poupault, André creates a little masterpiece. I do not remember the lines. Nor does Jacques. Only a certain musical quality ...

In painting, he is fascinated by skies. 'I think they reveal the painter's state of mind,' he says. And he speaks of Malraux with admiration.

'In each of his books there are twenty subjects for a novel. Just one of his ideas, which he deals with in ten lines, would serve Pierre Benoit, for example, for a whole book.'

'What if someone were to make a film of Dora?'

'Too difficult,' he replies. 'Where would you find actors sufficiently undernourished to play the parts convincingly? Only the Americans could film such an epic. But do you think the concentration camps will interest them? It's an aspect of the war that hasn't affected their own people at all.'

In Nordhausen, not knowing if we would survive this adventure, nearer to the death sentence than to liberation, we talked about Fritz Lang and Malraux, of the Impressionists and Great Masters of the past. Who will ever understand the human being?

December 1944. In the corridors, the ss are behaving more arrogantly. They joke among themselves and laugh loudly. What is going on? We no longer have Georges Croizat's radio to inform us. We are eager for news. From snatches of conversation, then from receiving a visit from Poupault who had read a German newspaper on Müller's desk, we learn of the von Rundstedt offensive.

'D is worried too,' says Jacques. 'They no longer have meetings with him. He can no longer leave the prison. His contacts have abandoned him. He does not know whether they have been arrested or changed their minds because they have renewed hopes, or are being watched too closely.'

Poupault tells us what D has said to him: 'Show me the symptoms of angina. Could they tell that one was pretending?' 'I assured him,' says Jacques, 'that once the attack has passed, there is nothing to show that the patient has had a heart attack. I wonder what D is up to. For one usually so confident, he seems very tense.'

We have come down to earth. Jacques' optimism has vanished. We wonder if the Germans still have the resources to repulse the Allies. And I was thinking that they would have capitulated before the enemy even reached the frontier! We are overcome by a fatigue brought on by so many days of anxious waiting. And our anxiety has so much influence on time.... How it drags.

It is through Poupault that we are kept informed of what is taking place beyond our four walls. D was present at the interrogation of the Russian who had simulated the coma. 'He was a flight lieutenant. A prisoner of war, after several escape attempts he had been condemned to be hung. What the ss put him through was beyond belief,' Jacques tells us. 'D gave me an account of it. Despite his suffering the Russian did not talk. Was he involved in the Russian Organization in the camp? No one will ever know. "I am sickened by what I see," D told me, "but I am risking my neck in this terrible business. My neck and all the other French necks too.... I am sickened, but I must not crack...."'

Naegele has been caught out. One afternoon, D took Sander to Müller's office. They summoned Naegele and the French woman prisoner. The Kapo admitted that he was sleeping with the girl, that he was receiving money for passing on letters but that he had never sent them. He beseeched Sander not to send him back to the camp. 'The French deportees will kill me.' He wept. He fell to his knees. He was repugnant. Sander seemed offended by so much grovelling. He sent Naegele to the prison at Dora.

'Believe me,' says Poupault, 'in spite of his isolation, D is still at work. He told me why Bordier was arrested in the camp. He was passing on information from the BBC to someone he took to be a resister. Hardly interrogated by the ss, before anyone even laid a finger on him, the self-proclaimed hero gave Bordier's name. When he was confronted Bordier ridiculed the fellow, but the ss brought him to Nordhausen all the same.'

I ask: 'But isn't D afraid that, whatever he does, our friends will consider him to be a traitor?'

'I said as much to him,' replies Poupault. 'Do you know what he said? "If I save them from hanging what will they think? What I want to do is to regroup the French in the same cells. I don't know if I can do it. For the moment, I am going to try to put the Russians into various cells with prisoners of other nationalities, for if they are put together, they will kill each other." '

We are happy that Poupault, thanks to the obliging Müller, comes so often to visit us. D's name crops up again in our conversations.

'He seems to have regained his confidence,' Jacques tells us. 'What I think is that one of the SS with whom he is involved is none other than Sander. I've seen them shake hands. Though my first interrogation was "severe", the second was almost a polite conversation. You, André, have not been interrogated at all. Gentil was allowed to go back to hospital and I am sure that D had something to do with that arrangement.... So? We can deduce that he is on good terms with Sander?'

News of Nicolas Petrenko! In that heavy atmosphere, so troubled by the German offensive in the Ardennes, it is a joy. He is in the cell with Jacques and D. What interpretation could be put on D's behaviour? Why has he asked for Petrenko to be with him, and why has his request been granted? He must know that the Russian hates him, and yet the two have long conversations. What can they have found to talk about? Jacques asks Nicolas in German. 'He only talks to me of Russia. He is a naturalized Frenchman but he is really a Russian.'

D now leaves the prison every day. He dresses in 'civvies'. One evening, he arrives with a fine overcoat. 'I'm going on a journey,' he says casually. 'But don't worry, I shall be back,' he adds, for Poupault's benefit.

Ernst Schneider, the German Kapo, is also sharing Jacques' cell. He is full of gloom.

'I have known the Gestapo for eleven years. We've had it,' he says whenever he rouses himself from his prostration on his bunk.

Petrenko has recovered. His vitality is unbelievable. Jacques discusses things with him, in the hope of understanding the Soviet Union a little better and of making comparisons with the Western way of life. The discussions come to a swift end. The Bolsheviks have invented everything! Petrenko talks about the Métro in Moscow. Jacques, naturally, without thinking what his companion's reaction might be, describes the Paris Métro in his turn. Petrenko bursts out laughing. 'The Paris Métro? There isn't one!...' Poupault soon understands that Nicolas believes that there is only a Métro in

Moscow. 'But look,' he explains gently, 'the Paris Métro is longer, older. And there is one in Berlin, and in London.' It is impossible to convince Petrenko. He laughs his fine, clear, healthy, spontaneous laugh and says, 'Oh, you French! Everyone knows you are awful liars....'

Like me, Poupault is fond of Petrenko. He still tries to discuss things with him. He talks to him about the press in France, about the different political parties, the opposing points of view, or religion. He tells him about the *chansonniers* who make fun of judges, ministers and the President of the Republic. Nicolas listens, then he smiles and says: 'I am no longer surprised that the Germans beat you. You are mad! If everyone can protest, say what he thinks, strike, how can you be a strong nation?...' But what astonishes Poupault the most is the day that, hearing Petrenko whistling *Tout va très bien, madame la marquise*, he asks him:

'Do you know that French song?'

And Nicolas retorts: 'French song? It's a Russian song!' Adamant ...

I often see Claude Lauth in the washroom. Wonder of wonders! He has a toothbrush. He lends it to me.... All at once, to brush one's teeth, an ordinary daily act, takes on the dimension of a major event.

A rumour is going around: we are about to be hung. More and more of the French take D for a Gestapo agent.

Christian Beam, the German Communist Kapo, is also at Nordhausen. He was arrested the night of 3 November, as we had been.

André Boyer is detailed for the cleaning of the corridors.

'Do you think that D is behind the Russian arrests?' he asks Poupault.

'No!' Jacques replies. 'His role is that of interpreter, that's all. I have even spoken to Petrenko about it. He told me that D had no contact with them at all before they came to Nordhausen. He knows nothing about the Russians' Organization. What Nicolas cannot accept is that he collaborates with the ss. In their code of honour, the Russians do not allow one of their own kind to be an interpreter. There must be absolutely no rapport with the camp authorities.'

The German Communist Kapo Ernst Schneider undergoes a

long interrogation. He returns to the prison a broken man. He does not look as if he has been beaten. Poupault asks him:

'What did Sander ask you?'

'It's not important,' replies Schneider. 'To survive the camps for eleven years, to be hard, pitiless and cruel to others because through having to endure beatings and humiliation either you are destroyed or you become hard, pitiless and cruel, and then to hear yourself be condemned to be hung – *that* is important. We are going to be hung. That is all I can remember of my interrogation.'

And Schneider sinks into a silence that he is rarely to break.

Cespiva is interrogated in his turn. He is away a long time. Poupault can bear the waiting no longer. He goes to Müller's office, where Cespiva has been taken, to try to hear a few fragments of conversation. Impossible to make out what is being said. When Cespiva is brought back to his cell, Jacques watches for Sander to leave.

'What news?' he asks through the door.

The Czech sounds distressed.

'Go to the washroom this evening. I'll ask them to take me there. I cannot talk here.'

That evening, Cespiva looks worried. He is so anxious that his voice is barely audible.

'The ss are convinced that the radio was put together in the camp. They no longer know if it's a transmitter or a receiver, but they are on the trail of the Czech comrade who made it. If they arrest him and he talks, I've had it!'

'In the past, a man like Cespiva would not have spoken in this way,' says Jacques to himself. 'He is physically exhausted by years of the camps!... And instead of giving him tonics, injections and fresh air all I can give him are words of encouragement!' Poupault is angry. But he does his best for the Czech. Cespiva just looks at him. In his eyes a helpless despair ...

One afternoon in December, Poupault is summoned to Sander's office. He has not seen D for forty-eight hours. What is going to happen now? Sander occupies the same office as at the previous interrogation, but this time he is alone.

'We are going to try to talk without an interpreter,' he says.

Jacques waits. His hesitation is obvious.

'That will be difficult for me,' he replies, searching for the words.

'Listen, stop playing the fool. I know that you speak German. Perfectly.'

Jacques knows that he is trapped. Sander's tone is peremptory. It means he has proof. If he wants to, the ss man could quickly confound him. All he has to do is send for Karr, or make enquiries in the prison or at Dora. To one simple question: 'Does the French doctor speak German?' there would be many who could answer yes.

'If the interrogation is not reported to a hearing, I will answer you in German.... But you must understand, when you are interrogated as I have been, you prefer to express yourself in your own language – you don't want to make any mistakes; the least false interpretation could cost dear in such circumstances.'

'Granted. So. What do you know of the radio transmitter built inside the camp?'

Poupault feigns astonishment.

'A radio transmitter for what purpose?' he asks. He pretends to be weary of this persistency.

'Exactly! That is just what I am asking you!' Sander raises his voice. He is losing his temper. There is no longer any sign of sympathy from him. He is a man whose patience has worn thin. Perhaps he himself is being harassed by his superiors because the enquiry has been fruitless. Is he afraid because in such totalitarian régimes, thought to be monolithic, it is not banana skins that litter the corridors as in democracies, but wolf traps?

'A radio receiver, now that I could understand . . .' says Poupault, suppressing these thoughts.

Sander interrupts him. He jumps up from his chair.

'Aha! You admit it! It was a radio receiver . . .'

'I admit nothing.... I know nothing about this story.... I wonder if it isn't more substantial than this famous fictitious radio. All I was going to say was that the deportees, deprived of any news, cut off from the world, could have wanted to build a radio receiver.... They are obsessed with getting news. But a transmitter! With whom could they have made contact without being picked up at once? It would be a suicidal operation, a useless suicide at that. Anyway, I still think that in a concentration camp detainees would not have the means to build a wireless. The whole story is an invention!'

'Did you often visit Fritz Preul?'

Poupault feels himself turning pale. He tries to hide his discomfiture. Hoping that his voice will not betray him, he says:

'Yes ... I enjoyed discussing the *Revier* with him. I saw him two or three times. ...'

'Preul committed suicide. We were about to arrest him. He had taken poison.'

Jacques feels weak. His knees are trembling.

'You seem very moved by that,' declares Sander, nastily.

'It's understandable,' replies Jacques. The news pains him so much that it increases his revulsion towards those who had provoked the German Kapo's death. 'I was very friendly with him. When a human being dies it upsets me. I chose to be a doctor to struggle against death, not to speed it for a man not yet thirty who only wanted to live.'

'I thought that you did not like the Communists. D has told me that you are a fierce anti-Communist.'

'It is true that I would not take to living under a Communist régime. I am not made to support a yoke. But unlike those who adhere to totalitarianism I do not believe that phrase of Alain's: "There is no friendship but political friendship." I don't care what a man's opinions are, as long as he does not try to impose on me his way of thinking or his way of life. The rare times that I spoke with Preul, he did not try to convert me. ...'

'You know that if his party had ordered him to execute you he would have done it.'

Jacques is tempted to reply that Nazis and Bolsheviks are united in this blind obedience, that the police of the two countries are interchangeable. But it already seems so astonishing that he is arguing like this with an ss officer, in a German prison, in the middle of a war, wearing the detainee's striped pyjamas, that he merely says:

'It is possible.'

And here the conversation ends. In the corridor, Poupault again thinks that Sander must be the ss officer with whom D is in contact. Moreover, an allusion was made to D during the conversation. It would have been unthinkable, otherwise, that he could have spoken so openly. ...

Poupault relates his conversation with Sander to Boyer. He talks to him about the Russians, and about his scruples, which André shares.

'What can we do?' asks André. 'If we were to confess everything we still would not save the Russians. We must hope that the Allies arrive before Himmler's orders are carried out.... And those extermination orders concern all of us.'

In the evening, D enters the cell. Despite von Rundstedt's attack, his optimism has risen to the fore again. He tells them nothing, but he must have renewed his contacts with the camp engineers and the ss. On the subject of his absences and his civilian clothes, he offers no explanation. He seems to know about Sander's conversation with Poupault. That evening, his knowledge astonishes Jacques. D smokes one cigarette after another and hands them round. Where does he get hold of this rarest of luxuries – tobacco? He talks about himself as he never has before and as he never will again. There is no 'theatricality' in his bearing. He knows Latin as well as the seven or eight living languages that he speaks. Stretched out on his bunk, he discusses literature, esotericism. He has a surprising knowledge of authors of the 'second or third rank'. He talks of the Middle Ages, speaks with irony of the Renaissance. He says: 'When heretics triumph, they are even more merciless than the possessors of dogma whom they supplant. For the subversives are in full flood, while those who have been superseded are on the decline. That is why martyrs are rarely completely innocent.'

Poupault listens to him avidly. The man is fascinating and his misanthropy becomes more evident with every passing minute.

'You thought me an optimist,' he says to Jacques ... 'You were wrong: I am an out-and-out pessimist.... But when you expect nothing from life or from mankind, you can begin to work seriously.... It is illusions that demoralize and delay us, for they can only be the cause of deception. The pessimist knows what to go by. He makes progress. He travels at such a low level, that he can never fall from a great height....'

'If you were as much a pessimist as you say you are, you would never accept life at all, even less in a place like this. Even you have illusions.'

D also confesses to being married. He worships his wife. 'I have a sixteen-year-old son.... As things are, I cannot watch him growing up.... My wife is a saint. I don't deserve her.'

Jacques interrupts him: 'A true pessimist does not give life to another human being. He does not wish to bring a child into the world to become a man in our absurd existence.'

D does not challenge Poupault's words. He explains that he had a good job in a bank. He describes the time when he was a prisoner of war. 'I escaped as early as 1941; I was not a member of the Resistance. I accepted an honorary post on a prisoners' committee. I facilitated escapes and protected fugitives. I tried to find them work. I was arrested, detained for three months at the Santé prison, then deported.'

Boyer too is increasingly being won over by D's personality. Despite the authorization that he gave Poupault to tell D that he was in the Resistance, Jacques has still not revealed anything.

'I have decided,' he says. 'I am going to tell D everything about my activities.'

'Be careful.'

'I don't care. If the Gestapo arrest me, I shall say that I was boasting to test D. Before the Gestapo see through it, the war will be over. In any case, I shall not get anyone else into trouble. I shall only talk about myself.'

So André Boyer tells the whole story of his role in the Resistance. He talks about his liaisons with London, of his two journeys to England, of his parachute drops. D listens, and asks pertinent questions. Poupault is present at the conversation.

'You see,' he says to Jacques – he now sometimes calls him *vous*, sometimes *tu* – 'I knew that there were important members of the Resistance at Dora.... For the time being I only know your friend Boyer.... But I am sure that there are others.... I promise you both that I shall say nothing. Thank you for trusting me. It will help me. If my plan succeeds, you will have an important part to play,' he concludes, looking André straight in the eye.

Later, Boyer says to Poupault:

'You were right. I cannot believe that he is an informer. He has a far finer quality. I am beginning to think that his strategy is oddly subtle and that he really has got round the SS and the engineers. He's walking a tight-rope.'

17 December 1944. Commotion throughout the prison. Later, Jacques Poupault tells us of the departure of Nicolas Petrenko whom I have not seen since the morning he left my cell for yet another interrogation. 'All the Russians have been moved out.... Brother Birin too. I asked Müller. He didn't know anything, except that they have been transferred to the bunker at Dora.'

It is from D that we have more information. He comes back to Nordhausen stunned. 'All the Russians were assembled on the parade-ground at Dora. Petrenko passed along the ranks and picked out Russians belonging to the camp Organization. More than a hundred of them were arrested. I served as interpreter. I am convinced that Nicolas selected poor buggers who were not even as much as members of the Bolshevik party. It was terrible! But Petrenko was completely calm. I am sure he thinks he was doing the right thing. He did his duty: the innocents bound for the gallows, the guilty spared; in this way the latter can continue their sabotage. The Russian Organization is safe. Petrenko will be hanged with the others, but he has enabled the Russians to continue the struggle. You should have seen the faces of the wrongly accused! If they deny it and manage to convince the ss by giving the names of the real resisters, they'll be killed in the tunnel. If they do nothing they'll be hung. Even Shakespeare did not conceive of the like. Atrocious, but effective....'

At the *Revier*, ss doctor Karr has left for an unknown destination. Lorenz is no longer there. A Polish doctor has replaced Poupault.

Schneider and Cespiva were also transferred to the bunker at Dora. D is less often at Nordhausen. The interrogations of the arrested Russians occupy his days and many hours of his nights. Some of the ss saw through Petrenko's tactics, but the Dora commandant, haunted by the idea of a revolt, is still demanding new arrests.

One evening, D returns to the cell exhausted.

'You cannot continue this work as interpreter,' Poupault says to him. 'You are making yourself the murderers' accomplice.'

'I won't give it up! There must be an interpreter. If I give up they'll find someone else. I do the job better than just anyone. I work wonders at rearranging the replies of those poor, lost Russians who do not understand what a trap they have fallen into.... And I can keep in contact with the ss I need without arousing suspicion.

'I have two friends in the camp,' he continues, 'One is a young lawyer, the other a Parisian street arab. Both know what I am doing. I have asked Sander to have them arrested under some pretext or other. They could be useful. They are brave men.'

Thus D admitted – voluntarily, for Jacques could not believe that he would commit any verbal imprudence – that Sander is one of the SS with whom he is in contact. Forty-eight hours pass. Three men are brought to the cell. One is called Jacques Ruskon, he is barely twenty years old. The other is a lawyer, Charles Donnier. The third is a street arab called Denais....

Donnier confirms to Poupault the relationship that D has with some of the tunnel engineers and some of the SS. He is sure that D was neither lying nor bluffing. 'But to negotiate, to have the trump cards, he must be able to speak for sufficiently important personalities in the Resistance. Without that safeguard, the SS will laugh in his face. And he will be risking his life!'

Charles Donnier tells Poupault of D's plan, which he has known for several months, for D has been thinking about it for a long time:

1    To save the lives of the deportees of Dora.
2    To establish immediately a contact with the Allied authorities.
3    To set up a programme of transmission of precise information concerning the fabrication of the VIS and V2S and the other secret weapons being made in the tunnel.
4    To recruit Germans whatever their political situation (SS or not) in order to be able to begin the action at once.

Certain of the SS are demanding an understanding with the Allies to reverse the situation and attack the Russians together. That was a Utopian idea. A less Utopian idea was to prevent the invasion of Germany by the Russians and see the greater part of the country occupied by the Allies.

They all demand a guarantee of safety for themselves and their families and, in the event of the plan's succeeding, a position of their choice in industry or the future administration. That seems plausible. One question remains: at what level are D's contacts with the Germans?

According to Donnier, D has mostly talked with the engineer Bergfeld,[1] who holds an important post in the manufacture of the secret weapons in the tunnel. A realist, Bergfeld knows that Nazism is in its death throes. In contact with the general officers of Hitler's General Staff, officers who are no longer blinded by Hitler's propaganda, he has been able to convince them of the logic of D's proposals.

D's gift of persuasion surprises Poupault once more. He can even exercise his influence at a distance, through an emissary.

'And he has combined all that without being sure of finding

important members of the Resistance!' exclaims Jacques. It's without a doubt the most unlikely story ever dreamed up in a concentration camp!'

'But in the history of the camps,' replies Donnier, 'has anyone ever been seen to dress in civilian clothes, go out alone into the streets, leave with the SS, return, find cigarettes, change around the occupants of the cells? Where is it all leading us? To the rope?... or to freedom?'

# Chapter Thirty

# CHRISTMAS AWAITING DEATH

If you want to take your chance,
forget all your books;
They teach you only how to live
and you must learn to die.

*Anonymous poem*

Christmas Eve 1944. My second Christmas as a deportee. The Liberation of Paris, the rapidity of the Allies' advance had made us hope for freedom by October.... December, cold, hunger, snow, fear, worry, Poupault's euphoria, sudden attacks of fever, the craziest stories we latch onto: we are still here in our striped pyjamas, exhausted and fairly certain that we will be condemned to death.

When I ask one of Müller's team of guards what there will be to eat for the Christmas feast, he repeats his favourite joke: '*Was es heute zu essen gibt? Gansbraten!*' ('What is there to eat? Roast goose!') All the same, there is some improvement – three cooked potatoes as well as the soup! What a banquet!

As soon as I have eaten I lie down on the bunk with Boyer. We are side by side. I look up to the skylight. The prison is heated. Outside it must be cold; fine Christmas weather, the sky studded with stars. We can see them shining through the skylight. This Christmas seems worse to me than the one before. What has become of my wife? My daughter? Will she have a Christmas this year? Seven years old. Seven years and thirty-one days. Shall I ever see them both again? I am gripped with anguish. I feel as if I can no longer breathe. Underneath my skin, some creature is clutching my throat, my chest, my stomach. How on earth can I go on taking an interest in D's ramblings, in little bits of gossip blown up out of all proportion, when I am in prison and I was arrested in a concentration camp. There is only one way to go now – to the gallows. But Jean Michel, arrested for resistance and sabotage, does not want to think about that! His optimism blows a smoke-screen over the sinister truth! Well, that night, the sinister truth was clear to me, and every sound of Nordhausen was part of it. Hanging lies at the end of the ordeal. Doubtless the camp authorities are waiting for the results of the inquiry or the verdict from Berlin to carry out the sentence.

I don't think I have tears in my eyes as I turn to André Boyer. He too is lost in his thoughts.

'Fucking Christmas!' he says.

And suddenly Life comes back into its own. We discuss the sky, the stars, the infinitely small – man – and the path he follows, his cruelty but also his greatness, the other worlds like ours which must exist, the billions of cells like the solar system that our bodies contain, moral courage, physical courage, all those subjects so often on the lips of human beings and, above all, those vast, immense questions which will mostly remain unanswered.

I feel better. My courage has returned, and I feel that my companion too has warmed his heart with the comforting warmth of words.

Suddenly shouts, booted feet on the flagstones; people are being bustled along the corridor. Tensely, we listen. Silence. Then all at once, screams. Someone is being beaten. We hear the cries of pain for a long time. There must be several men at that flogging session, one after the other. The ss do not celebrate Christmas. They carry out their filthy work even on that holy night. No respite for the Gestapo. That is their way of celebrating the Nativity.

In the morning, we learn from Poupault that the Germans brought Russian free workers to the prison. They were found to have false ration cards. We are relieved: it is not new deportees who have been arrested and beaten. That selfishness is also a part of camp life. . . .

And today, Christmas Day, Poupault says to Boyer:

'I have managed to persuade Müller. You are coming back to my cell.'

I am losing my companion. Jacques has his Resistance chief back at his side. André can see that this move is painful for me.

'Don't worry, I shall be next door.'

That was my Christmas of 1944.

# Chapter Thirty-one

# 'REST CAMP', SS STYLE

'Why do you need a hospital? Why not
simply hang everyone who gets ill?'

*The commandant of Ellrich
speaking to the camp doctor*

January 1945. At last the French are regrouped in the cells. D
has achieved his end. I find myself with Paul Chandon, André
and Pierre Caruana, a man called Pernod – a butcher from near
Dijon, picked up at Dora because his name was like Gaston Pernot's –, Joseph Puppo, Roger Latry, Jacques Bordier-Brunschwig, Claude Lauth and Debaumarché. Pernod is only with us
for a few days. They put him into a neighbouring cell.

Roger Latry imitates jazz musicians. Sometimes he does Louis
Armstrong's trumpet, sometimes Django Reinhardt's guitar. His
father is head chef at the Savoy in London. He owns the *Relais
de la Poste* at Saulieu. A resister, he and his fiancée, Kiki, were
arrested in Dijon. Roger suffers bouts of severe depression. He
has no news of his fiancée. (He is to learn at the Liberation that
she too was deported. They later married.)

Paul Chandon gives us lectures on the making of champagne.
Joseph Puppo, funny as ever, talks about Corsica and his job as
a train driver. When Latry imitates a sax, trombone or clarinet,
Puppo laughs and says: 'Not a patch on Tino Rossi or Ali-
bert....' He tells us stories he seems to make up as he goes
along. His accent, his sense of observation, his natural taste for
the absurd and for caricature, his unshakeable good sense:
astonishing. Nothing gets Puppo down.

The two Caruanas describe their life in Algeria. Lauth talks about poetry. Jacques Bordier, highly intelligent, graduate of the *École Polytechnique*, amuses us with his repartee and dry humour. I have a great deal of respect for Bordier. An inspector in the Ministry of the Interior, he resigned at the Armistice. As head of the 'Liberation' movement, he was very influential. His two brothers rejoined the FFL. One was killed in combat; he has no news of the other. He travelled to England and then to Algiers where he was a member of the advisory assembly. He asked to be parachuted into France just before the invasion.

What else have I been doing since the Cherche-Midi but trying to combat this despair? Once it caught hold it would quickly destroy. We had not chosen to live in this fierce, pitiless place. We are ill-prepared for this earnest hide and seek with death; we are constantly watchful, ever on our guard, for one false step will be one too many.

At Dora, I understood that he who 'gives' has a greater chance of survival than he who has decided only to 'take', thinking only of his own misfortune. What did I give?... Not much: I was as constrained by hunger, terror and violence as the rest. What on earth was there for me to give? Bowls of soup, passes for consultation when I was a dentist and, above all, my interest....

There were many deportees much younger than I. Sometimes I could even have been their father, for several were not even twenty. To them I offered confidence and hope. I showed them nothing of my sadness. We would meet and talk, after roll-call, in the dental surgery.... They must have thought: 'If this man of nearly forty can be so sure he will survive all this, why shouldn't we survive it too?' And off they would go, a little better armed against their fear. It swelled me with pride to see it....

When I felt myself beginning to go under, when my dreams failed to inspire me, when it seemed impossible to deny the irrefutable truth of our situation, everything in me rebelled. Then plans of escape filled my mind and became a hope that saved many of my comrades from drowning in despair.

Did I really believe that escape was a possibility? I did....

Though it was completely illogical, I always believed it.... The irrational lives on in man in both his suicidal impulse and his passion for living.

Was I the only one to restore flagging spirits, renew courage, hold despair at bay? It would be ridiculous to say so. But, in the eyes of my friends, I only weakened once, in the first days at Dora, giving in to despair when I should only have clung to the will to attain even the inaccessible. Hope.... Desperate, obstinate hope.... This attitude deserves no praise. It is innate. I know it helped others as it helped me when I saw a man, prostrate with grief only the evening before, come to our meetings and make some small contribution to our joint enterprise to prevent our destruction and put a spanner in the works of Himmler's robots....

These thoughts that I am trying to express here on paper were the ones that occupied my mind in that cell where Roger Latry was a one-man jazz band, and where Bordier and Puppo competed to see who could raise the most laughs....

Images of Nordhausen fill my mind and memories of conversations...

The first quarter of 1945 saw an influx of SS officers and soldiers. They came from Auschwitz in Poland, or from Grossrosen in Silesia. They were fleeing from the Russian advance. The Germans always boasted about their courage but when the Reich began to crumble around them and they no longer felt quite so invincible they fled as the French had done in 1940. These bastards were assembled at Nordhausen to build a new camp there. The Gestapo thought of organizing a so-called rest camp for the inmates of Dora, Ellrich and Harzungen. This camp was to extend to a part of the *Boelke-Kaserne* where we were being held. Through the window we could see a crowd of prisoners. The SS were swearing at them, beating them. What do you do when you see a bug? Crush it. And to SS men from Auschwitz or Grossrosen, what was a deportee but a bug?...

This camp under construction was divided into two sections. In one were the deportees capable of working by SS standards, in the other all the sick were crammed into a *Revier* without medical staff, running water or medicines. Every day, the 'fit' deportees had to go to work in Nordhausen, in the town or at the railway station. As for those in the infirmary, as there was no gas chamber or mass execution, they were dying of their diseases like flies sprayed with insecticide.

From the Nordhausen camp, 1,963 bodies were sent to the Dora crematorium between 20 January and 3 April 1945.

# Chapter Thirty-two

# THE RUSSIANS SACRIFICED

We live for news; but none of it is good. Bordier, like Boyer, Poupault, Donnier, Denais and Ruskon, tries to believe in D's mad plan. 'It's so extraordinary, it must be true.'

11 March 1945. D returns to Nordhausen. He is in despair. A tragedy has taken place at the Dora bunker.

Already, many of the Russians have been hung. Those who are still being held in the bunker decide not to wait for death without trying anything. They want to escape.

At about seven o'clock on 9 March, the ss go to have their supper. One is left on guard. The Russians have managed to take down the wooden bunk that was fixed to the walls of each cell. This bunk is of no use in the bunker. Cells built for one man are occupied by twenty.

The Russians bang on the cell door as if something very serious has happened. The ss guard opens up. He is dealt a blow to the head with the bunk. The blow is not hard enough to kill him. The Russians take his keys. They free their comrades. Then they flee. The ss guard comes to. He fires his revolver. The other ss men, alerted, give chase and recapture the fugitives. They fire without warning at any suspicious shadow. Some of the Russians who get outside the bunker hide under barracks or among other Russian deportees. In under twenty-four hours, the ss have them all, with the exception of one. (We do not know what became of him.)

The ss torture the fugitives. Atrocities succeed atrocities. When the deportees are reduced to masses of broken bones and torn flesh, they are hanged. In reprisal, the ss also take deportees from neighbouring cells. These are Russians who were unable to escape. A wooden garotte is put into their mouths. It prevents them from speaking while they are being hung. (At an earlier execution, a Russian insulted the SS before the knot reduced him to silence. He promised them everlasting damnation. The murderers were shocked!)

Among the detainees brought out of the cells is Brother Birin, lost among the Russians. Fearing that he is about to die, he cries out in German that he is French. The SS hear him. They put him to one side. Reluctant to lose a victim, they crush his testicles with their Gummis and rifle butts. Before he passes out Birin hears someone say: 'You're a priest, you don't need them.'

It is Jacques Poupault, who continues to roam freely about the prison, who tells us of these horrors. He says that D has returned very disturbed. He no longer has any contact with the SS or the engineers. He is wondering if the *pourparlers* have broken down. Jacques adds: 'I think he is going to fake angina. He hopes to force them to show their hand.'

13 March 1945. Morning. In the cell the atmosphere is heavy. André Boyer is with me again. There are ten of us. André is playing with cards which we have made. Pierre Caruana asks me to read his palm. It is a science or method of divination I believe in. Reading the lines and mounds of my own hands, I saw that I would be in danger of death in about the thirty-sixth year of my life. I saw that I would escape. My wife never doubted it. My friends have always smiled at my alarms and my certainty that I would escape death. This 13 March I am reduced, a shadow of my former self, but for the moment, I am safe.

When I finish with Caruana, the eight other occupants of the cell want to know their destiny too. Superstition? A desire to pass the time? To mock the 'charlatan'? To escape their worries? I borrow the pack of cards from Boyer. Palms, cards: I sound out the future. I announce that we are all going to leave the prison in forty-eight hours with the exception of Boyer and Bordier, as far as our cell is concerned. I also say: 'In one month our nightmare will be over. We shall be free. We shall return to our families.' I do not see Boyer returning. Despite the amused scepticism that such circumstances usually produce, I do not want to alarm André. I inform some of them of my prediction; but I say nothing to the man who, for me, is going to die. (It was all to come true. I do not know what to make of it. Perhaps I was clairvoyant because of the enforced fasting.)

13 March. That afternoon, D enters Müller's office as he often does. Before exchanging even a word of greeting he collapses and writhes with pain on the floor. Müller leaps to his feet. Frightened, he calls for Poupault, who hurries to the scene. He diagnoses angina pectoris. In dying tones, D asks Müller to secretly inform *Hauptsturmführer* Sander. Poupault whispers to Müller that D is in a critical state, if the attack passes, it could recur.

One hour later, Sander arrives. He is accompanied by Hazel. The two signal to Müller and Poupault to leave the room. As he is leaving, the doctor is stopped by Sander who asks him if D's condition is serious. Jacques replies: 'It is difficult to say. A heart specialist must see him. I am a surgeon.' Time passes. A civilian doctor, very courteous, appears. He hears Poupault out attentively, asks him what symptoms he has observed, then examines the sick man. After a detailed examination he says, still addressing himself to Jacques: 'I can detect no lesion. It is true that that is common in this sort of complaint. An electro-cardiogram will be necessary.' He hands over two ampoules of morphine and a tube of tinitrine. 'Advise your patient to always keep these on him,' he concludes as he leaves.

Later D tells Jacques the rest of the story.

'Nothing has been broken off. Hazel and Sander are still in agreement. It was difficult for Hazel to come to see me or send for me. In the Gestapo, everyone watches everyone else. As Sander was away I had no contact with anyone. While he was away, Sander spoke to someone in Hitler's General Staff who has been interested in my plan from the beginning. He is going to take me with him so that I can meet an ss leader.'

D is so excited that Poupault has to try to calm him down.

'Be careful! If Müller comes in he will know you were faking.'

D smiles.

'On the other hand,' he adds, 'all the French at Nordhausen must return to the bunker at Dora. It is impossible to do otherwise, I can only keep Boyer and the occupants of our cell: you, Donnier, Ruskon and Denais. They'll allow me one more. Whom do you suggest?'

'Bordier.'

'See if he agrees.'

Jacques brings us the news. I am unhappy about returning to

Dora, and at the same time, pleased to have D's hopes to cling to again, like a drowning man clutching at straws. Poupault asks Bordier if he agrees to stay at Nordhausen.

'It's such a ridiculous story that it would be a shame not to take part in it and see how it turns out at first hand.'

'Beware,' replies Jacques, 'we are walking a tight-rope. We have no guarantee that it will not serve to hang us, after all.'

'Let's be fatalistic about it. Play along.'

The decision does not please all the French. Debaumarché storms against D. He does not believe in his plan. He is very abusive. Debaumarché and Bordier have a violent argument. But how can we cancel out a decision taken by the SS and the Gestapo? The atmosphere is strained.

I wonder if my friends remember my predictions, now that they are beginning to come true. I think only of Boyer, and hope that I was mistaken as far as he was concerned.

15 March 1945. We are to return to the bunker at Dora. Boyer and Bordier, as Poupault said, are to stay at Nordhausen.

D comes to visit us. 'Do not worry. You will stay at Dora for a few days and then you will be transferred to another camp.' Debaumarché is in a rage. The others are worried but keep silent.

We were leaving for Dora! A decision full of menace. I did not foresee the plunge into the realms of horror that awaited us.... I thought I had already known the ultimate depths of fear....

# Chapter Thirty-three

# THE BUNKER

The journey is made on foot. Nearly all those arrested at Dora on the night of 3 November are there. The march is arduous. We are on our last legs. The prison food has been too meagre. We drag our feet. Yet no one stops to get his breath and strength back. The ss see to that. I am chained to Claude Lauth. The column is silent. Each man lost in his own thoughts, eyes on the road ahead. What else can possibly happen to us?

Dora. The few comrades who see us arrive – chained together, emaciated, gaunt – think we must be ghosts. They thought us dead. Now they imagine us at the end of the rope.

The bunker. They make us undress. Barry, who sometimes used to serve out the soup at Nordhausen, has put on the pullover that Cespiva had left in the prison. Did he think the Czech doctor was dead? Cespiva, doubtless at breaking point, leaps at the Frenchman to retrieve his pullover, and strikes him violently. Barry does not defend himself. He has an enormous anthrax on his shoulder. The blows aggravate his pain. Some days later, Cespiva will add to his vengeance. He will operate on Barry without anaesthetic, cutting his anthrax, carving it up, digging into Barry's shoulder. A blood-bath. Auschwitz, Dora; despair has made of Cespiva a man both vulnerable and pitiless.

Apart from the ss guards, we once again meet up with two Kapos who will always head the league table of the scum of the earth: Kilian and Willy. Kilian is the hangman.

The ss had ordered this filthy work to be done by the former Reichstag Deputy, Kuntz, the German Communist Kapo. On the parade-ground, before all the deportees, Kuntz had refused: 'I have hung pigs, I will never hang a man.' This refusal cost him several terrible days of reprisals. You do not mock the ss.

Kilian was immediately offered the job. Since the hangings no longer took place in secret at the Holzhof, but publicly on the parade-ground, Kilian could hardly contain his joy. He was promoted to star status. From 4 November to now, more than three hundred deportees, mostly Russians, had passed through his hands. He had a flair for the finer points of the spectacle. Willy was delighted to assist him and to replace him whenever necessary.

Kilian and Willy deal out Gummi blows, talk to us of the gallows with relish and describe our approaching end in great detail. As I undress, I hang my belt on a nail, as usual. After the search, I reach for it mechanically. An ss man springs at me and beats me. That belt, recovered at Buchenwald, which passed through every inspection, in which I hid a five-thousand franc note always thinking of the moment when I would escape, I lost in the bunker at Dora – it vanished for ever.

We are crammed into a cell, sixteen of us. The cell is six feet wide and eight feet long. The floor is cement. In a corner stands an empty tin. It is to serve as our toilet. How can you breathe, stretch your legs or lift an arm, crushed together like that? There are sufferings that do not require the presence of the torturer. No need for him to waste his energy.

We decide to organize ourselves in this much-reduced space. Five of us lie down on the floor, against the wall, facing the door. They arrange themselves so as not to waste a single inch of space. The others sit down cross-legged in what room there is left. When the five have had a little rest, five others will take their place and so on, all taking turns. A powerful effort of will is required not to move a foot which has never wanted to move as much, or shift an arm full of pins and needles. We are so thin that it is difficult for us to stay cross-legged for long. We feel as if our coccyxes are boring into the cement.

This effort at organizing rest fails. We are as uncomfortable sitting as standing. The sound of those bodies moving in the silence is distressing. We are forbidden to speak. In a low voice, however, I exchange a few words with Claude Lauth. But what is the point? What is to become of us? When are we to be executed? Despite

D's promises, we realize that things are much worse than we thought. . . .

The day is so long; the minutes are hours, the hours days in themselves. In the evening, they open the door. We are brought some limpid soup. The distribution is ultra-rapid. Bad luck for the man who is too slow or unable to push forward for his turn; even that clear water will be denied him. The door will be closed before he is served.

Pushing and elbowing my way through, I get beside Lauth in the middle of the cell. We try to lie down for a few minutes. We arrange ourselves head to foot, with much shuffling of knees and elbows. Finally we find a position which lets us lie down on our side, curled up in the foetal position. Sometimes, in unison, we change sides.

We spend the night sometimes standing, sometimes sitting, sometimes curled up on the cement floor. In the morning the tin is full of urine and excrement. We are suffocating.

At the time fixed for reveille, an ss man opens the door. We are ordered to stand up and wait. First man out has to empty the tin. We follow him out one by one and head for the latrines. We have to wash very quickly but we are forbidden to drink from the tap. Thirst is a torment much prized by Nazis.

The cell empties at top-speed. The guard brings his Gummi thudding down on our heads like a robot. We try to get past him between blows. As we are all trying the same thing, there is much pushing. A few feet separate the cell from the latrines. To heighten the agonies of this journey, the bastards post dogs along the way. Their job is to bite our legs.

In the latrines, there are two taps. We are so dehydrated that no one can resist; despite the blows falling like hailstones, the deportees drink, those behind push their way through for their turn to drink and be beaten. These bestial scenes last for five minutes. No more. Then we run back to the cell. The door slams to behind us again. Our hearts are thumping. The least effort winds us, exhausts us. For twenty-four hours, we are safe.

Now I know the nature of silence. A heavy, crushing, damp silence. The smallest sound makes us jump with fright. May I never have to relive the hell we endured in that cell! Even groans of pain are smothered for fear of attracting the attention of the ss; one squeak and they burst in with flailing cudgels. As the hours pass, we age quickly.

Suddenly, a great noise. The ss are closing the shutters to the cell skylights. Afraid that we might see what is about to happen? Deep down inside, we know what it is. The poor buggers are going to be shackled, pieces of wood forced into their mouths and tied firmly behind their heads, and Kilian will officiate.

Every day, this grim ritual is repeated. One day as many as sixty Russians are hanged....

But we soon forget the victims. The closing of the shutters deprives the cell of oxygen. Asphyxia soon begins to do its worst, causing fainting and hallucinations. Debaumarché is one of its first victims. He becomes delirious. Bodies collapse in a heap. ... When the shutters are opened we gradually recover and try once again to find a position which might afford us a little rest.

In addition to the clear soup, we are allowed three ounces of bread. The fast causes hallucinations and sharpens our sense of hearing. Debaumarché can tell from the food carriers' tread if the soup is thick or thin.

The dreaded voice calls the numbers of Lauth, Latry, the two Caruanas, Chandon, Debaumarché, Puppo and myself. The door opens. Is this it? Until now the voices answering *Hier* in German have had Russian accents. Today, French. We are ordered to go out into the corridor. The other occupants of the cell remain inside. What are they going to do with us? We are afraid. Silent. Is this the overture to a tragedy?

The ss simply want to move us to another cell. Do they want to bring us nearer to the antechamber of death? We are aware of only one fact: the size of the cell is exactly the same, but instead of sixteen, there are eight of us. Extraordinary! We have room to move! Stretch our legs! Lie down! The cell looks out over the camp. We can see the gate to the bunker and a fragment of Dora.

We can think better in this cell. Our minds are not wholly occupied with the position of our bodies. It is certainly not comfortable, but we can at least rest. We feel that the end of the war is near and wonder if we shall be executed before it comes. D's name crops up. He assured us that everything would be all right.... We, the pawns in the game, are made to suffer conditions that stir up our resentment rather than inspire our forgiveness....

Many days and nights pass. We go over and over the same un-answerable questions. Who will ever be able to describe the life the ss made for us? If we have to wait much longer Kilian will be cheated of his beloved rope. The food is so meagre that we shall die swollen with malnutrition, or reduced to skeletons before time has had a chance to eat away our flesh.

We arrived at Dora on 15 March. We have been here for over two weeks. Ears pressed to the ground, we can hear the rumbling of tanks passing in the night. One morning, there is an occasion for such joy we forget our desperate situation. Through the narrow window, we see a plane pass over the camp, hedge-hopping, and fire at the ss barracks. On 3 April we hear the sound of a bombardment. The next day, it begins again. We try to work out where the bombs are falling. There is the sound of tank movements and above all the thunder of the bombs. The Allied air force is striking not far from Dora but we are incapable of pinpointing where.

On the evening of 4 April we hear the putt-putt of motorbikes. Carefully, we look out at the little entrance gate to the bunker, just across from our window. We see Sander go in followed by D in civilian clothes. Liberation at last? Have the *pourparlers* been successful? There is complete silence in the cell. We are all holding our breath, trying to keep absolutely still. What is being decided in the bunker? Death? Freedom?

Suddenly, the voice of an ss man breaks the silence: he is calling out numbers in German. Terror empties our minds of all but one thought. Please not my number! Please not my number!... The list is completed. Bare feet in the corridor, a door opens into the yard. We cannot see. The shutters have been closed. We wait, it is as if we can see it all through the pores of our skin. Seven shots tear into the silence. We hear bodies fall, then the sound of wheels, the thud of bodies being loaded onto a cart then the sound of the wheels again and the steps of the two deportees who bear the sinister burden.

There has been no hanging. They have just killed seven men, there, almost under our noses. Seven men! God, are we dreaming? Who did they execute?

We are silent. We curl up as if we wanted to disappear, so that the ss would never find us, so that even destiny would forget us. Is our turn to come? Will our numbers be next? Always the silence. We begin to talk in lowered voices. 'That couldn't have been Sander's work.' 'He came into the bunker before the execution.' 'What's D's part in all this?' The bunker gate opens and closes again. The motor-bike starts up and we listen as the sound of its engine grows fainter. Silence again.

The following day, we learn that it was the seven German Communist Kapos who have been murdered. Sander executed them with a bullet in the back of the head. They had all been inmates of concentration camps for more than ten years. On the night of 3 November 1944, they were arrested with us. Except for Christian Beam and Ernst Schneider, for a time imprisoned at Nordhausen, the others stayed in the bunker at Dora. The victims' names were: Joseph Gamish, Christian Beam, Georg Thomas, Ernst Schneider, Ludwig Czimcak, Paul Lutzius, Otto Runke. In the camp these men occupied the following positions: Kapo *Lagerältester eins*, Kapo *Lagerältester zwei*, Kapo *Kammer*, Kapo *Revier*, Kapo *Arbeitsstatistik*, Kapo *Geldverwaltung*, Kapo *Lagerschutz*.

The other Kapo, Kuntz, was tortured to death by the Gestapo in February 1945. His battered, bleeding, broken body was finished off in the bunker.

The ss did not want the German Communists to stay alive. They were all political leaders. They would be dangerous in the future.... A future that was coming nearer all the time....

# Chapter Thirty-four

# THE BOMBING OF
# NORDHAUSEN

What was happening at Nordhausen? ... With the exception of Poupault, Boyer, Bordier, Donnier, Ruskon, Denais and D, the prison was empty of deportees.

Towards the end of March, D disappears for a whole week. He returns in a state of euphoria and over-excitement which is understandable when he tells his story. He, a deportee, his striped pyjamas exchanged for civilian clothes thanks to Hazel and Sander, has been taken to the outskirts of Berlin. There, he had two interviews with a high-ranking ss officer.

'I was under the impression that it was General Kaltenbruner,'[1] says D. 'I had confirmation that the *pourparlers* engaged by the intermediary of neutral powers have failed. The ss want a guarantee that their lives will be spared. In exchange, they undertake to hand over the secrets of the new weapons and to oppose the Soviet Union with the entire fighting power in their command, in order to permit the Allies to invade the greater part of German territory.... They hope to discuss these proposals with the French Resistance.... In fact, they have only one obsession: to save their own skins.... I replied that I would pass on the information. In the meantime, I asked them to show favour to the French deportees.'

Should Poupault and the others believe him? They are so concerned for their friends in the bunker that they clutch at the most slender of hopes. The omnipresence of tragedy is such that anything that cannot aggravate their wounds is welcomed with credulity.

D goes on to say: 'If we can only make ourselves heard by the Allies, thousands of deportees will be saved.'

So they discuss it. Finally, it is decided that they will not attempt the contact themselves, but will supply the ss General Staff with

certain co-ordinates which will enable them to make contact with
the French services. By these co-ordinates, the French services
would recognize detainees like Boyer, Bordier or Poupault. If so
desired, discussions could then begin.

D considers this information to be sufficient. Poupault and his
friends are now at the mercy of the ss. But they have only implicated
themselves. They have not revealed the identities of the other important resisters detained at Dora, like, for example, Dejussieu.

D is eager to allay their suspicions. He has brought three thick
notebooks back from his journey into devastated Germany.

'On the way to Berlin we made a detour. I collected these manu-
scripts from the camp where I was a prisoner of war. Before my
escape, I had entrusted them to a German civilian.'

Neither Donnier, nor Denais, nor Ruskon knew anything about
these notebooks. These notes cannot possibly have been written
during an absence of one week. They make fascinating reading. It
emerges from them that D has not been lying. He was a prisoner.
He did escape. He is not a traitor. The French are gradually convinced that he is indeed negotiating.

The following day, D is missing. He returns defeated, in despair.
Fifty-three Russians have been hanged in the tunnel at Dora. He
says that for the moment Petrenko has been spared.

'What about the French?' asks Poupault. His voice is trembling.

'They are still in the bunker. I am sure they are in no danger.'

'You must stop seeing Sander. He's a murderer. It looks as if
you're allying yourself with him,' says Jacques.

'It was nothing to do with him. It was the camp commandant
who ordered the execution. He's a vampire. Sander managed to save
Nicolas, for the time being.'

'There is nothing to stop the camp commandant from deciding
to execute the French tomorrow.... If Sander asked for a stay of
execution for Nicolas, it's because he needs him for his enquiry.'

'If I drop Sander and he has no more interest in protecting us,
he'll leave us to our fate, and then we'll all hang!'

'We're surrounded by madmen on the loose,' thinks Poupault.
'This is unbelievable. If anyone else were telling me this, I'd never
believe it! Must we continue this scheming with D, or abandon this
charade of entente with the ss and deliberately accept our friends'
execution?'

André Boyer is in an agony of impatience. Inaction is unbearable to him. 'In December, when Jean Michel proposed that we try to escape, I beat around the bush.... Now I've made my mind up, I'll do anything to escape.'

Bordier and Poupault try to dissuade him.

'If you go, the ss will take their revenge on the French left behind, for you are one of the aces in D's hand. At least wait until those in the bunker are safe. Then we'll all try to escape together.'

André finally gives in. ...

As for D, he is worried about the Russians' advance.

'If they get here first, we're for it. The ss, seeing that we will be of no use to them, will wipe us out.'

'I have no intention of putting in a good word for the ss if the Allies are the first to liberate Nordhausen,' says Poupault.

'The point is that they think you will!' says D cynically.

Waves of planes pass over the prison with increasing regularity. Every time, the guards open the cells and rush down into the cellar.

One evening, the sound of explosions seems much nearer. Müller himself opens the Frenchmen's cell and invites them to join him in the cellar.

'There's no point,' says Bordier. 'We'll stay in bed. The British and the Americans know that we are here. The prison is in no danger.'

Not convinced, Müller goes down to the shelter. When the alert is over, he returns to the cell. They all pretend to be in a deep sleep. Müller peers in, then thoughtfully withdraws. 'I think he must be wondering if we were serious,' says Boyer, jokingly.

The Americans cross the Rhine at Remagen. Will they arrive before the slaughter? In the prison, the guards are now all old men. The others have left for the front. There is even a woman, skinny, with a sickly face, uncomfortably clad in an ss *Helferin* uniform. There is also a deathly-pale Walloon, spending his convalescence disguised as a prison guard. He describes his campaign in Russia to the French. 'If only I had known! I let myself be persuaded by that bastard Degrelle. Thank God it's over! But what on earth am I going to say to my father? He didn't want me to join up!'

'The fool thinks all he's going to get is a ticking off from his father!' says Denais.

25 March 1945. Another alert. The explosions are still nearer now. Once again, Müller asks the French to take shelter. Jacques and his friends stand in the corridor. Guards and detainees are running helter-skelter for the cellar. Those who can find no room there crouch down, head in hands, as if reducing their body surface would give them a better chance of escaping the bombs. The thick walls of the prison are shaking.

Poupault, Boyer, Denais, Ruskon, Bordier and Donnier show complete and utter indifference. Their demonstration of cold-bloodedness pleases them. They had been afraid, their heart-beats had doubled, but nothing shows. The female guard returns from the cellar with Müller.

'Well, old girl, getting your knickers in a twist, are you?'

'*Was?*'

'I'll draw you a diagram later if you like.'

'But where were you?' asks Müller.

'We stayed here. We've told you: there's nothing to be afraid of.'

'You don't know that they're American bombers,' growls Müller, stomping off down the corridor.


3 April 1945. Middle of the afternoon. This time, the detainees realize at once that the bombing cannot possibly miss the prison.[2] The explosions are too near. Suddenly, a bomb hits the left wing. Windows and doors shatter. The walls are shaking so much that Poupault and his companions expect to be buried alive. A second bomb follows. All kinds of debris fly into the corridor. Black smoke hides them from each other. The violence of the explosion throws them to the ground. They call out, trying to see in the murk. Boyer has a slight wound on his forehead. His right shoulder is painful. Poupault examines his friends quickly. No one is seriously hurt. The smoke gradually thins. Müller emerges from the cellar. He sees them in the corridor. '*Völlig verrückt*; the prison is in no danger, you said? Soon there won't be a prison left!'

They inspect the damage. A huge breach has been opened in the left wing. Gutted houses appear opposite. The detainees wander around the prison. It is impossible to go back to the cells, all the doors have been blasted from their hinges. Some, more decisive than the others, walk calmly away. The bombing has returned them their freedom. Müller watches them go without a word.

Poupault and his friends spread out through the prison, searching for civilian clothes. Boyer, not able to find any trousers without holes, takes two pairs and wears them one over the other, hoping the holes are not in the same places. Forgetting the danger, they amuse themselves trying on the clothes they have found. Bordier, always deadpan, wants a hat. 'Your hair has grown back,' he explains, 'but I have hardly more than after it was shaved off. If I leave without a hat I'll be picked up at once.' Unbelievably, he finds one.

'Take blankets. We'll escape through the cell where I spent Christmas with Jean Michel,' says Boyer. 'There's nothing left of it and it was on the outside wall. It'll be easy. It's nothing but rubble. It's a good thing Jean Michel is in the bunker. He'd probably be dead if they'd all stayed here.'

Müller sees them go from his office. He makes no sign.

And so, there they are, heading for freedom with Boyer in the lead, but hardly have they clambered through the breach but he sees a Bren gun manned by three of the ss.

'Back. The ss are on guard. Wait until nightfall.'

In the cell, D advises them to hide the civilian clothes and put their pyjamas back on. 'I would not be surprised if Sander, if he is still alive, came to see what had happened to us.'

They obey. Müller is the first to pay them a visit. Did he see them turn back? The head guard has managed to bring them some soup and bread. Strangely, the electricity is still working.

D's prediction proves correct. Sander and Hazel arrive. D takes them straight out into the corridor. After a few minutes' discussion, the two Germans go away.

'They are happy to see that we have not tried to escape. This proves our good faith. They will be back tomorrow in order to make a decision about us.'

'We'll have gone,' says Boyer impatiently.

'You perhaps, but not I. I shall not abandon the French in the bunker. If we leave, they will be hanged. I am sure of it, for Sander and Hazel would be extremely angry.'

All this time an ss man is posted at the end of the corridor. He sits on a chair with a machine-gun on his knee. Boyer is beside himself:

'We can't just meekly let ourselves be taken back to the camp!'

'Be patient,' replies Poupault. 'When the time is right, we'll escape.'

At dawn, the sentry is still there. Poupault, Bordier and Boyer decide to attack him. D does not try to stop them.

Hardly have they set foot in the corridor to put their plan into action when the alarm sounds. D says he will go to find Sander. Jacques Ruskon, little Jacques, goes with him. The others see them talking with the sentry, then head for Müller's office. Müller comes out with them, talks to the guard. D and Ruskon disappear.

The explosions sound closer. Müller and the guard go down into the cellar. Poupault and his companions seize their chance, put on their civilian clothes and leave the prison, Jacques in the lead. Boyer is two yards behind.

They climb through the wall. They are outside. Thick smoke blankets everything. Now the explosions are over Nordhausen, the prison, themselves. An inferno. They try to go forward. They cannot see. Burning shells burst all around them. The noise is deafening. It is no longer possible to move at all.

Poupault lies down, his face in the dust. Between two explosions he hears Boyer calling his name. He turns, tries to see: nothing but smoke. Suddenly, he feels himself lifted from the ground. He loses consciousness.

How long does he lie there? A violent pain in the back wakes him. The noise is still as intense, but the explosions are farther off. He looks around him. The dust is settling. His back hurts terribly. He touches it with his hand: there is no blood. He climbs painfully to his feet. He is alone in the middle of a road in front of the ruins of the prison. Not far from the spot where he was lying is a shell crater five or six yards wide. Legs trembling, he staggers towards the rubble of the prison. Bordier, Donnier and Denais are sitting against a wall which has been mostly destroyed. They are dazed.

'Where is André?' asks Jacques.

'He was in front with you. When you went down, we came back to take shelter, by the wall.'

'We must find Boyer!'

They go out into the street.

'The last time I saw him you were there', says Bordier. He has understood. The crater tells him all he needs to know. 'I wonder how you escaped,' he says t' Jacques.

'I don't know. I felt myself blown away. When I came round, I was ten yards away.'

'Come on, let's go. The ss will come back.'

'I can't leave without Boyer.'

Jacques does not realize what has happened.

'Come on,' orders Bordier, taking him roughly by the arm. He is like a blind man. He totters with every step. His eyes are blank.

'Head for the west,' says Bordier.

Bare, tree-less country lies before them. It is the plain they saw from the windows of the prison corridors. Behind them, the town of Nordhausen disappears in a cloud of smoke.

# Chapter Thirty-five

# FROM NORDHAUSEN TO PARIS

The sun is high in the sky. It is a beautiful day.

'How long did the bombing last?' asks Poupault.

'I don't know. But there were several waves of planes,' replies Bordier.

'We must go back to find Boyer. He can't be dead.'

Bordier tries to calm him: 'We'll go back to Nordhausen later.'

They walk on. They find a woman, covered with blood, lying in the grass. Her ankle is broken. 'We can't leave her,' says Donnier. They lie her in one of the blankets they have brought with them; one at each corner, they advance slowly. The woman is heavy. She groans with pain. Suddenly, shadows seem to emerge from the ground. 'Müller used to say that a sunken river ran under the town. People must have taken refuge along its banks,' thinks Bordier.

The sound of aircraft can be heard once more. Black specks dive at them from a great height. 'Fighters!' cries Donnier. One after the other, the planes begin to fire. Machine-gun fire rips up the river bed. More shadowy figures appear and begin to run in every direction. More planes open fire and shower the fleeing men with bullets. At every sweep of the planes, figures scatter like ninepins; then most of them jump up and take off again.

A plane fires on them and they throw themselves to the ground. Denais remains standing, calmly watching the approaching plane.

'Lie down!' shouts Bordier.

The aircraft passes very low, just above their heads. The guns blaze. Denais does not move.

'If the Yanks think I'm going to buy a Ford from them after a stunt like that, they're very much mistaken!'

Bordier laughs. 'Idiot! Why can't you lie down like everyone else?'

'Well, lying down or standing up it's all the same to me,' replies Denais, joking about his small stature. 'The Bosch tried it in 1940. They always missed me. Don't tell me the Americans are worse than they are.'

The fighters disappear to the north. It is peaceful again. They are still carrying the wounded woman. Arriving at a clump of trees, they see about twenty people, men and women, grouped under the budding branches. They abandon their burden. The pain in Jacques' back is getting worse. He asks Bordier to look at it. 'You've got quite a bad burn, but, funnily enough, your trousers aren't even torn.' They press on. Dark shapes litter the plain; the dead, the wounded; a man lying in the grass calls to them as they pass. They continue on their way without stopping. A little farther on, they see a group of deportees. What are they doing? They draw closer. A dead horse, partly carved up, lies in the middle of the group. The men, with bloody hands, are tearing great handfuls of flesh from it which they are eating. What camp are they from?

Crossing a railway line, Jacques and his friends come to a wood cabin. Two deportees are sitting on the doorstep. Jacques speaks to them. He learns that a camp for the sick – tuberculosis cases probably – had been set up not long before in a large semi-ruin. The very one we could see the roof of from the prison. The bombardment has destroyed most of it. Many are dead. Most of the survivors have escaped.

'We're going to stay here,' say the occupants of the cabin, 'the Americans are only a few miles away.'

'I'll stay with them for a bit, then I'm going back to Nordhausen to find Boyer and see what has happened to D and little Jacques.'

'You're mad. You'll get yourself arrested. André must have taken the full force of the bomb. He must be dead.'

They settle into the cabin. The occupants welcome them as brothers. The stove is lit. Potatoes are boiling in a pot.

'We stole them.'

After eating and having a short rest, Poupault and Bordier set off for Nordhausen.

'What you're up to is idiotic, but I don't want to lose you. You're as stubborn as a mule!' Turning to Donnier and Denais, Bordier adds: 'You stay here. There's no point in us all being caught. If we haven't come back in three hours, forget about us.'

Nordhausen is a heap of smoking rubble. Everything seems dead. The west wing of the prison, where their cell used to be, is intact. The east, where they escaped, is completely gutted. They climb down into the bomb crater. They turn over rocks and earth; no trace of Boyer's body, not a scrap of cloth, nothing. Figures appear in the distance. A soldier with a dog begins to move in their direction.

'Let's go!' commands Bordier. Jacques obeys mechanically. He cannot believe that he will never see André Boyer again. Dead on the last day! So near to freedom! And killed by an Allied bomb! Poupault feels responsible for his death.

'If only I had escaped when he wanted to, this wouldn't have happened,' he says to Bordier.

'You're mad. You had no chance. You would both have been hung. Come on, hurry up. We have no right to search any more for him or D or Ruskon. André would be the first to tell you that. Let's find the Americans and get back to the war!'

There is a good smell of cooking in the cabin when they arrive.

'Jugged hare!' announces Denais. He explains that he had extricated a hare from a window where it was caught by its paw.

They have not had such a meal for years. It does not, however, make them relax too soon. They decide to leave that very night. It is a difficult walk. They follow a river in the hope of finding a bridge. A star guides them westwards. They spot a farm, then a hamlet. They make a detour in order to avoid any dangerous meeting. To fail so close to the end would be terrible.

Dawn. It is cold. They are exhausted. They cross a tarmac road. On a signpost they read: Nordhausen seven miles. They reckon that they had set off one mile from the town. So in seven hours they have only covered six miles! They have been walking in circles. They stop at an isolated house on the river bank.

'Let's rest awhile,' says Bordier. 'After all, we are in civilian clothes. We look like tramps, but we could be workers whose factory has been bombed and who have been ordered to get to Weimar under their own steam. When we set off again we'll follow the road. We'll never get there across the fields.'

Three hours later, they start again. A fine rain is falling. Once again, they cross a railway line. They follow a path which winds up a wooded hill. The rain stops. They are walking at a good pace, though the going is steep.

After having travelled south for a few miles, they come to a cross-roads. An unmarked road leads west, heading up the valley. When they reach the top, they see another plain like the first. These plains succeed each other in waves, like an angry sea. They are forced to climb several crests to keep to their course. Since leaving the abandoned riverside house, they have kept up a good pace. It must now be about five o'clock in the afternoon, and they reckon they have covered twenty-five miles. No one complains of hunger. Several months in the camp, five months in a cell, a night with hardly a wink of sleep, and not one of them shows any sign of fatigue. They are happy. So far, no one has tried to stop them. They would have strangled the first man who did try, without a moment's hesitation. Denais picked up a branch in the woods which he is using as a cane. 'It might come in useful.'

A village appears at the end of the valley. They head straight for it. They go through the village without drawing attention to themselves. They see a group of men, no better dressed than they – French workmen from a region near the Rhine. One of the workmen says that they are going to make a stop for the night at a camp where food is waiting for them. It is growing dark and the idea of something to eat entices Poupault and his friends to join them. 'We're going to Weimar,' says Bordier. 'Really? I thought Weimar had been shelled too.' 'We don't care, they told us to go to Weimar and we're going!' 'Well,' says the other, 'you have to do what you're told.' And they are accepted without further question.

The camp has been set up in a large room at the town hall. Fresh straw is strewn along the walls. It is the banqueting hall. On the far wall, there is the clear outline of a picture that has been removed. It was probably the classic portrait of Hitler which the mayor had prudently taken down. A huge demon of a man, who seems to be the head of the detachment, begins to dish out the food. 'We have no mess-tins.' Donnier vanishes and is back almost at once with two mess-tins in his hand. He hands one to Bordier and the other to Poupault. 'If I don't find any others we'll have ours after you've finished.' They have not yet been served, when Donnier returns

with two more tins. 'You've found the factory?' 'No, the kitchen.'
Out of his loose jacket he takes a sausage and a whole loaf of bread.
'We appoint you senior commissariat officer, with the rank of cap-
tain,' says Bordier sententiously.

After the meal, everyone settles down for the night. No one takes
any interest in them. They are all together in a corner. They decide
to rest rather than set off on the road again.

Poupault is the first to wake. Day is breaking. He shakes his companions who are all in a deep sleep. 'We'd better leave before the
others wake up. There's no point in them seeing that we're not going
the right way for Weimar.'

The follow the path of a river. The road still heads west. Around
a bend in the river they come to a bridge. There is a man who seems
to be guarding it. Bordier advances resolutely. The man leaning on
the parapet makes no move. Jacques waves to him. He waves back.
He has a *Volkssturm*'s armband and a short rifle. A hundred yards
on, Bordier turns and looks back. The man has still not moved. 'He
must have been put there to stop the tanks. All by himself!' It's
all so easy. . . . After months of despair, they feel cheerful. It's such
an unfamiliar sensation!

As on the day before, they cross the valley only to climb to another
crest which gives onto another valley. From time to time, they meet
a peasant or a cart on the road, but not one soldier, not one car.

'I wonder if we are near the Front,' says Donnier. 'It all seems
very quiet.' They look down on the plain. Two windmills gently
turning crown two little hills. The calm is broken by the sound of
an aeroplane engine. It passes low overhead. Three more follow.
The leading plane climbs sharply, the others do the same. The first
swings round, then the others.

This air ballet is danced over the heads of Poupault and his
friends. They hear machine-gun fire, then a continuous rumbling
as if all the planes are firing at once. Suddenly, black smoke floods
out of the leading plane and it drops like a stone. The three planes
circle for a moment above the burning wreckage. A burst of
machine-gun fire rings out, like a victory cry. The three planes skim
the crest and swoop over the trees. A white star shines out from
their fuselage.

'There's a man burning to death in that plane, but I can't help
rejoicing,' says Bordier, with great sadness in his eyes.

Poupault's back is no longer painful. Despite their wooden shoes, his comrades are keeping up a good pace. There is no sound of war, except the occasional throbbing of aircraft.

At dusk, Poupault proposes that they stop at an isolated farm and ask for a little food and a place to sleep. They agree and approach a large farmyard. All is quiet. There are electricity cables, but they can see no telephone wires. Poupault is the one who speaks the best German.

'Wait close by. I'll go in alone and come back for you if it's all right.'

The yard is huge, surrounded by buildings. A man appears, pushing a wheelbarrow. Jacques goes up to him. The man stops.

'Will you let us sleep in a corner?' The man replies in very bad German. He must be Polish. 'I'm not the boss.' With his head, he indicates a low-built house. Jacques makes his way towards it. A man comes out of the house and stands at the top of the steps, watching him. He is a giant. He wears a green velvet waistcoat over a white shirt; a thick gold chain is draped across his stomach.

'I am with three other French labourers, and our factory at Kassel was bombed,' says Jacques. 'We are going to Weimar. May we spend the night in one of the farm buildings?'

The man looks at him closely. He calls to the Pole:

'Bring four bales of straw into the shed.'

Poupault thanks him and goes to fetch the others. The man comes down the steps and waits for them in the middle of the yard. He must be in his sixties. He takes them to the shed himself. It is really a stable: three horses are tied up in stalls. The bales of straw have been put into the corner. The floor is cement and the horses' bedding is very clean.

As he turns to go, the man says to Jacques:

'You must be hungry.'

They are sitting on the scattered straw when the man returns. He is carrying a coffee pot and a large round loaf, a *kougloff*. The Pole follows, carrying four bowls and four spoons.

'Here,' says the farmer, 'it's *café au lait*, but there is no sugar.' His manner is rough; he stays to watch them eat. When Poupault has finished, he asks him to come outside.

'You are no labourer, you are an escaped prisoner of war and you are trying to find the Americans.' It is not a question. It is a

statement of fact. Shrewdly, Jacques says neither yes or no. He
keeps quiet and looks sheepish.

'You may stay,' the farmer continues. 'I was a prisoner too, once,
back in 1917. But you must leave very early tomorrow. You never
know ....'

Poupault repeats this conversation to his friends.

'Let's stay until dawn,' says Bordier. 'The farm is very isolated
and there is no telephone; if he wanted to give us away, he wouldn't
go on foot, he'd take a horse, and we'd hear him.'

The straw is thick and Jacques sleeps soundly until he feels a
touch on his shoulder. He wakes with a start. The man is standing
beside him. It is daybreak. The coffee pot, the bowls filled with
bread, are laid before him on the floor.

'Eat and go.'

They devour half the bread and keep the rest for later. Their host
accompanies them as far as the main gate to the yard.

'The Americans can't be far off, I heard their guns in the night.'
He points. 'Cross those hills over there. It wouldn't surprise me if
you were to find them in the valley.' They are about to leave when
the German calls them back. 'Tell them when you see them that
all Germans aren't bad.'

'He's no Nazi,' says Donnier.

'Nobody will have been a Nazi, and yet there were thirty million
of them,' replies Bordier.

Three hours' march brings them to the broad summit of the hill
overlooking the valley. They cross this plateau. Suddenly, Donnier,
who is walking a few yards in front, stops and points out fresh tank
tracks. The tracks disappear into a little wood behind them, to their
left.

'Don't stop,' warns Bordier, 'a tank might be hidden in that wood
and it could mow us down like rabbits if we are seen.'

With thumping hearts, they quicken their step. Now the plateau
runs down a gentle slope towards another, more enclosed valley,
dotted with windmills. In the distance lies a sprawling country
town. It is unusually quiet. Too quiet. Not a cloud in the sky. Birds
pierce the silence. Everything is marvellously serene. A hare darts
up at their feet. They follow the road, making swift progress towards
the town. The surrounding fields seem to have been abandoned.
Not a single peasant or piece of farm machinery to be seen anywhere.

The town too seems deserted. They walk along the main street. Still not a living soul. What if a soldier were to leap out with a machine-gun at the ready? How could they explain what they are doing there?

'We must be getting closer,' says Poupault. 'Let's get out of this town quickly. We don't want to be caught now.'

They are standing in the square facing the church when a voice hails them in French. The voice comes from a long building, which looks like the town hall or banquet hall. Three or four heads appear at a window.

'What the hell are you doing there?' continues the voice; 'Come up here.'

'Everyone can see from fifty yards that we're French,' mutters Donnier. A man runs down the iron staircase on the side of the building.

'Come up, come up, don't stay on the street,' he says. He leads them into a large room: a barrack room with stacks of beds occupying one of the walls. A table and chairs furnish the centre of the room. A dozen men are gathered here. They look kindly at Poupault and his friends.

'What on earth are you doing here? You can talk to us, we are French prisoners.'

'So are we. We are prisoners of war,' says Bordier.

'Are you trying to reach the Americans? You missed them; they were here yesterday evening, but they have gone.'

The prisoners are amused at their astonishment. Then they explain. The day before, during the afternoon, some soldiers and two German light armoured cars passed through the village, heading south-east. The rest of the morning and the early afternoon were quiet. People were lying low at home, white sheets had appeared at the windows. In the evening, an American light tank followed by two jeeps arrived. In the square, the prisoners spoke to the occupants of the vehicles who gave them cigarettes. Then the little detachment went on its way. Very early in the morning, the two German light armoured cars reappeared. The white sheets were whisked indoors. The cars followed the same road as the Americans. They did not come back. Not one single burst of gunfire had been heard.

'But where is the line of battle and the German army?' asks Jacques. 'Where is the fighting?'

'There is no front line and there is no German army, at

least not here. For the last ten days, we have seen little groups of
soldiers who look more as if they're trying to hide than fight. It
seems, from what we've heard on the radio, that Patton's army
has launched a spearhead into the region. Stay with us, we have
provisions, in two or three days the whole region will be taken
over.'

So their adventure is over. Blindly marching, without map or
compass, they have chanced upon this little village where, since the
day before, the Germans and Americans have been playing hide-
and-seek. They thought they still had obstacles to overcome to avoid
recapture, and they have arrived in the no-man's-land, without even
realizing it. Now they have only to wait quietly and the Americans
will arrive and say: 'How nice of you to welcome us. It's all over
now, you can all go home.'

It would be absurd to say that they are disappointed. But they
feel cheated out of their adventure. An escape that never really was.
And how they had dreamed of escape, when they had not even dared
to meet their tormentors' eyes. Though they are all weak and ill,
they are not even troubled by fatigue. The pain in Poupault's back
has actually eased with the constant walking. Does he realize that
he came so near to death that his entire future is like a reprieve?
He feels well, full of a sort of calm euphoria, savouring every second
of freedom. But Poupault knows why this joy is weighted down by
sadness. His happiness is tainted with a profound sorrow, a revolt
against injustice. André, his friend, is dead. He died on the last day
of their ordeal. From the moment that the blind bomb fell, everything has been so easy! Did there have to be a final sacrifice for
fate to be well-disposed towards them? Why Boyer, who had the
finest mind, the greatest intelligence of them all?

Bordier can see how unhappy Jacques is.

'Come on,' he says. 'There's no point in waiting. It'd be better
to go on and get to the American lines as quickly as possible.'

Why do they now deliberately run unnecessary risks? Is it to involve
Poupault in action, to stop him thinking? They cannot return to
Nordhausen until the town is in Allied hands. They have to reject
the easy solution. They owe it to themselves, to their friends, both
living and dead. Gently, wisely, the prisoners try to dissuade them,
yet when they insist, they give them some provisions and a rough
guide to the lay of the land. They agree to head approximately west-

north-west. A little-used road crosses the valley, climbs back up towards the hills and descends into a valley parallel to the one they are in.

Donnier and Denais refuse to abandon Poupault and Bordier. And so all four set off together.

It is eleven a.m. The village still seems uninhabited. The checkered green and brown plain stretches before them for a mile or two, before climbing the hill. There are more and more windmills. At right angles to their road they see another tarred road. It leads to a large town situated several miles away to the left. Suddenly Denais, who is in the lead, stops short. 'I can hear an engine over there.' He points to the right.

They hide quickly in the ditch along the roadside. Up to their eyes in the long grass, they hear the noise getting nearer. There is definitely more than one vehicle. A convoy? Friend or foe? Now the cars are passing them. They hear the sound of their tyres on the tarmac. The sound dies away to the left. Denais, who is in front, slips out of the ditch.

'That was two German light armoured cars, probably the ones the prisoners told us about. They've gone. The coast is clear.'

They get cautiously to their feet and watch the cars driving slowly away in the distance. They seem to stop as they reach the town, under a hangar. Poupault and the others continue on their way, heading for the hills. When they reach the summit they discover, about three hundred yards away, a windmill, which has been hidden from sight.

Again Denais gives an order:

'Get down!' He throws himself to the ground. He crawls back to his friends. 'There's a man who I think is wearing a cap. He's sitting on the steps of the windmill.'

The others look, peering through the grass.

'He's an American. I recognize the cap,' says Bordier.

Cutting across the fields in great excitement, they hurry towards the soldier. He sees them. He does not move. He is as motionless as a Western gun-fighter. Can he have any idea of the emotion he causes these men running towards him? Is he surprised to see these emaciated tramps? His gun lies across his knees. As soon as they are within earshot, all four shout out:

'We are French! We are French!' They run up to him. His skin is brown, coffee-coloured, with prominent cheekbones. Poupault

thinks he looks Mexican. He is chewing his gum with an unperturb-
able calm.

'We want to see one of your officers,' says Bordier in English.

'Follow the wire,' says the soldier, pointing to the field telephone
beside him.

So it is all over. Simply: 'Follow the wire.' At Dora, at Nordhausen, the tiniest morsel of bread, the shortest moment's rest, a
day without one of them being beaten was a major event. Where
are the SS, the days and nights haunted by fear, D's efforts to save
them? All they have had to do is walk for four hours from the prisoners' village, and arrive at the exact spot where an American from
New Mexico seems to be waiting for them. 'Things are always less
beautiful than the dreams we have of them,' quotes Poupault.
'Proust. I don't know if they are less beautiful, but from experience
I would say that they are different. Who would have thought our
escape would be just a stroll through the country!'

They learn that they have found the reconnaissance group of the
Sixth Armoured Division of Patton's army. Out of the whole American army, this division has penetrated the deepest into Germany.
They reckon they have covered seventy-five miles since Nordhausen, and not once were they really worried.

The telephone line is laid along the ground. It leads down into the
valley. They follow it for about 1,500 yards. They arrive at a village.
Ten light tanks are drawn up, surrounded by a fleet of jeeps. Armed
soldiers are milling around the machines. They go up to an officer.
'We want to see the head of the detachment.' Poupault explains who
they are, where they come from. The officer shows no surprise. He
signals to them to follow him into a large house on the square.
Several officers are in one of the rooms which is littered with tele-
phones and radios. A captain listens attentively to a brief outline
of their story. He is most interested in the two light armoured cars
they saw on the road. He asks them to point out the exact position
of the village on a map. 'It must be about three or four miles from
here,' says Poupault. The captain sends out an uncoded radio
message about the two armoured cars. Then he turns his attention
to them. 'I'm going to send you to the divisional HQ. You'll have
to wait till tomorrow because we haven't cleared up the rear.' Does
he change his mind when he sees the disappointment on their faces?
The fact is that he adds: 'Well, I can send you right now in a jeep,

I don't think there's any danger.' He gives the orders and a few minutes later a jeep draws up outside the house. It has a huge machine-gun installed in front of the passenger seat. There is a driver and a gunner aboard. The officer signals to them to get in, and the four of them squash into the back seat. Suddenly, five or six planes swoop overhead. Almost immediately, they hear explosions. 'There you are, we tell them about two miserable buggers that one of their tanks could easily have dealt with and they mobilize an entire squadron!' Not three-quarters of an hour have passed between the radio message and the bombing of the village.

From Nordhausen to the meeting with the Americans, they have been in no danger, but their last hour seems to have come as soon as they set foot in that jeep. They cover about twenty miles. The driver does not try to conceal his ill humour. He drives flat out. He probably thinks that the faster he goes, the less risk he runs of falling into an ambush or coming under fire. The four of them cling on for dear life. They arrive aching all over, black and blue, their barely-covered bodies having little protection from the buffeting of the journey. An intelligence officer is waiting for them, accompanied by a French liaison officer. They present themselves and at once tell everything they know about the v1s and v2s. The American takes copious notes. In conclusion, all four express the desire to stay with the American army. Their aim: to get to Nordhausen and Dora as quickly as possible.

'I can't promise anything,' says the American. 'You are French officers and I must refer you to your superiors. First thing tomorrow morning, I'll put in a report to Paris.'

The French officer takes them to a hotel, where two rooms have been requisitioned for them. The manager views their arrival with displeasure. He is not accustomed to a clientèle of tramps.

Bordier and Poupault take one room. The two beds seem the height of luxury. The officer leaves them, promising to return with food, soap and towels and, if possible, some presentable clothes. He offers them numerous packets of cigarettes. They are lying on the beds smoking, when Bordier says:

'Now I can tell you something we have kept from you for the past month. D had obtained the assurance that no Frenchman would be executed, except one – you.'

Jacques has been close to death many times since June 1941, but never has he felt as much fear as now in this hotel room, far from danger. The danger was past, but he experiences it retrospectively as if he were living it all again.

'The camp commandant insisted on your execution. In his eyes you were the very heart and soul of the Resistance at Dora. D insisted that he be told well in advance of your transfer. We decided to say nothing to you and try to help you escape in time. If it was not possible for all of us, it might be possible for one on his own.'

Can Bordier have any idea how Poupault feels? Was André Boyer so insistent that they try to escape to save him, Jacques? Did André make that sacrifice because he thought the camp commandant was coming for him, even though the ss were finished?

The officer returns. He has brought not just four rations, but several cases of food. On his own initiative, he has added a dozen bottles of schnapps. There is also soap, razors and clothes that are almost their size, also requisitioned.

Washed and dressed in their new clothes, they go down to the hotel restaurant. The small number of Germans cast longing eyes at the cases of rations they have brought down to their table. After months on a 'strict diet', they discover the quality and variety of the GIS' menu. This food impresses them far more than the fabulous abundance they have discovered since arriving in the little town.

In the morning, they report to the lieutenant. He has already had a telephone call from Paris. The BCRA has ordered that they be repatriated at once.

They were hoping to be part of the liberation of Dora without having to return to France. For them only Dora matters: the bunker, the plight of their friends, the arrest of the ss criminals – a redundant expression. Seeing the disappointment on their faces, the lieutenant assures them that they will be back from Paris before he will have reached Nordhausen.

For two days, they wait for their departure. They eat, drink, smoke and sleep. The food does not upset them. 'I must send a report to the Academy of Medicine,' jokes Poupault. 'I think our organisms are resistant thanks to the quantity of alcohol they have absorbed, contrary to what the dieticians say.'

At last, the passes are signed. A car is put at their disposal. The lieutenant accompanies them in a second car to speed their passage at each control point. They cross the Rhine at Sarrebruck. There, the lieutenant must desert them and return to his post.

On 11 April 1945, they drive into Paris. For them, the horror is over. But we are still in danger of death in the bunker at Dora....

# Chapter Thirty-six

# EVACUATION
# TO BERGEN-BELSEN

Forget the smile.
Alas! When hope returns
A happier evening
is followed by a day of disaster.

*Anonymous poem*

4 April. Morning. An ss man opens the door of the cell. He hands
us each a tin, unopened and with no means of opening it, a piece
of bread and a blanket.

He orders us out, delivering a few random Gummi blows for
his personal enjoyment. The dogs are straining at the leash.

For several days, I have had dysentery. I could not eat. The last
survivors of the bunker are all standing in the corridor. The ss surround us, machine-guns at the ready, as if they had something to
fear from ghosts, for we are a legion of ghosts that leaves the bunker
that cold, sunny morning.

We are still together: Lauth, Latry, the two Caruanas, Chandon,
Debaumarché, Puppo and I. Camp comrades see us go by. They
are wondering if we are about to be liquidated. I catch sight of a
deportee with whom I often used to chat after roll-call in the dental
surgery. His name? Graff. I call out to him. He does not answer.
A few steps farther on, I hear him say: 'Shit! It's Jean Michel!'
He did not recognize me although I passed right by him. Have I
changed so much?

We march towards an unfamiliar railway station. It stands at the
far end of the camp. Deportees are already crammed into the
wagons. Several thousand detainees are waiting to be loaded in their

turn. The ss hurry us along with their boots and gun butts to a wooden wagon. It is empty. Others are already full.

The eighty men from the bunker – Russians, Poles, Czechs, French – are bundled inside. There is hardly any space at all. Our little group is crushed in a corner. Physically, I can go no further. This dysentery is driving me mad. I resist it with all the strength I have left. The ss settle into the wagon in front. That reassures us. They are not going to kill us right away. Let this not be one of those infamous transports from which no one ever returns. The Heaven Kommandos.

Some have ingeniously managed to open their tins, using a spoon as a tin opener. The tins contain pork, full of fat. Impossible to eat a single mouthful. I offer mine to my friends, overcome with nausea.

The wagons continue to fill up. The sky is clouding over. Towards evening, the convoy finally gets under way. The ss are watching our every move. Word spreads that we are heading for Czechoslovakia. We stop, start, reverse, set off again: the train is insane. But all is insanity. When we left Dora the hysteria and dementia already seemed greater than usual.

In our open wagon, the night is made terrible by the cold. We huddle together. Claude Lauth and I will not leave each other's side. We are also on our guard against the Russians, who want our blankets. They have tried to steal them three times since we left.

Even heaven has no pity! An icy rain pelts down relentlessly. We spread several blankets over us as a cover, but the water soon soaks through them. Dysentery, cold: am I to die just a few days before the Liberation? I am convinced the ss will not kill us. We shall find a way to stop them.

The convoy continues on its hesitant way, but mostly making progress southwards. During the second night, we pass through a burning station. Two trains are on fire. Our train slows down to a walking pace. The heat of the fire warms us. The flames create a fantastic sight. We are transfixed by it, but at the same time we are afraid there will be an explosion.... Taking us with it!

In the morning, another prolonged halt in open country. On the roads bordering the railway, long columns of civilians are walking, running, laden with baggage, in every direction. The people are terrified; women, children, old people – few men. It is the same panic and chaos as the French knew in 1940. We can hear gunfire. The front is close at hand.

At night, we see the lights of combat. Time is on our side; the SS have only a few days left. We just have to hold on. And this damned dysentery is draining every scrap of my strength!

After hours of indecision, our convoy begins to head north. The following day, we witness a surprising sight. In the sky, missiles change direction as if they were guided. It is a new American weapon. We have never seen anything like it.

The train stops. We wait and wait. Then the SS make us get out. They post themselves all down the train. I have still not eaten. My stomach refuses food. Claude and I decide to make soup. The SS guard watches us scoop up some water from a ditch with an empty tin. I pull up some grass. I slip a bit of sodden wood between two stones. While Claude tries to make a fire with a few matches found I don't know where, I place the tin on top. The train starts again when the water is barely tepid. I swallow it. But my grass soup does me no good. My dysentery worsens and I suffer terribly. Hang on! Hang on! I repeat this to myself like a litany.

Never have I had so strong a feeling of my insignificance or clung so much to life. Hang on! Hang on! I must hang on! Victory is coming ... Man can withstand anything since from the moment of his birth he knows that one day he will die. It is the evidence of his own mortality that prepares him for life's ordeals.... A training in the postponement of his inevitable fate....

Finally we discover why the convoy is stopping so often in open country. The train drivers have no intention of being captured by the Allies while driving a trainload of deportees. On various pretexts – no coal, breakdown – they detach the engine and go to the nearest station. There, they abandon it and run away. The SS are obliged to go to the town on foot, find new drivers and requisition them.

'Are they aware of the horrors they have concealed with their patriotism and their silence, or do they only discover them when their own lives are at risk?' asks Claude Lauth. 'It's extraordinary how the ideas of fanatics can seduce men from every level of society, and when things go wrong, they all decamp.'

The countryside changes. We are in a wood. Through the bare trees we can see sand dunes. Word goes round that we are going to Hamburg. Two Russians beyond hope have died in our wagon. They make a seat for the other Russians. The deportees are so thin that any cushion is welcome. We feel as if our buttocks are boring holes in the floor.

The convoy stops.

'If only these were stops for food!' I say to Lauth to keep our spirits up.

The ss stand in front of each wagon and ask:

'How many dead?' In our wagon the Russians do not want to give up their seat and reply: 'None.'

Soon several corpses are laid out along the tracks. The ss supervise the digging of holes in the forest to bury the bodies. When this has been done, the train moves off again.

After a few more miles, they change their minds. The train stops, reverses along the line. The ss order the corpses to be dug up and put back into their respective wagons. Doubtless they want to have the full number of deportees when they arrive. Always following orders!

On the morning of 11 April (the day that Poupault and his friends arrived in Paris, but I did not know it then), the train stops in the middle of a wood. The railway tracks go no further. Other convoys are there already. I see shadowy figures filing out. They are being herded God knows where. I pity those poor men, not realizing that my companions and I are in the same state. We climb down from our wagons and follow the procession of derelicts. A phantom worn out with dreams, I refuse to give up, but have no strength left. I have not eaten for eleven days.

Supported by Claude Lauth, I discover the camp of Bergen. There is an infirmary. I go to it. And suddenly, I am in luck! The luck to find myself face to face with Doctor Jacques Déprez! Jacques Déprez! It was thanks to him that I became a dentist! Thanks to him that I finally escaped that tunnel where death wreaked greater havoc than anywhere else in the world. He looks at my poor carcass. He arrived on a convoy too, one evacuated from Harzungen. He has been here forty-eight hours. Our meeting is emotional. Déprez acts first. Is he alarmed by my physical delapidation? As official doctor to the Harzungen deportees, he takes me into the Bergen infirmary, gives me a dentist's armband and what sulphur drugs he can find.

That evening, we talk. We have so much to tell each other....

'It took a week to get from Harzungen to Bergen, average time for a journey from Moscow to Vladivostock on the Trans-Siberian Express,' says Déprez. 'I had got permission to set up an infirmary in a wagon. All the equipment you see here comes from Harzungen. If I had not managed to convince *Osscha*[1] Reinschmidt, there wouldn't even be this embryonic infirmary at Bergen. The ghost train wandered south-north, north-south.... The sick were in their hundreds. Those unfit for work filled the wagons, while *Stabsarzt* Reiherr accompanied those in good health, or presumed to be, along the road. Air-raid alerts were incessant. The sky was invaded with Mosquitoes. In the moments of respite between raids, we cared for the sick and removed the dead....

'The day after our departure, at dawn, the convoy came to a halt in a little station. On the track parallel to ours was a goods train.... Between the wagons, gun platforms, capped gun-crews at the ready. I thought: "This time we've had it ... it's a munitions train ... we'll all go up." I didn't want to alarm the poor buggers with me. What was the point of creating panic and giving the Germans a pretext for shooting them. I said nothing about the munitions train.... You should have seen what happened next! The Mosquitoes dived us, shelling and machine-gunning. "This is too bad, we're going to die just as our ordeal is almost over," I thought. The whole war passed before my eyes, Belgium, Dunkirk, my pal Marcell killed at my side, all our miserable days at Dora: a broken kaleidoscope, sinister, dirty, without a single moment of happiness for so many years! It took ten minutes.... Ten minutes by the watch of the ss guarding us.... I couldn't believe it.... We seemed to have trembled under that torrent of fire for hours.... And that sentry wasn't any braver than we were!

'We started off again, and stopped again. There was a farm nearby. I asked our guard for permission to go and fetch some water with Martin, one of the orderlies. By some miracle he agreed. We had been in that train with no food or drink for five days and the men were dehydrated, hallucinating or prostrate with hunger. The Germans had provided nothing for us. I wondered what the guard intended to do when we were far away from the wagon. Might he not think our quest for water was an escape attempt and shoot us? We were so thirsty we wanted to run. Then suddenly what did we see? Not only a tap, but a well-filled feeding trough at which a string of piglets were stuffing themselves. Martin and I fell to our knees, shovelled aside the piglets with both hands and fell to stuffing ourselves in our turn. A royal meal. Behind us the guard, whose belly was full, roared with laughter. He signalled to the occupants of our wagon to join us. And all the deportees plunged their heads into the trough. The guard thought this the most extraordinary thing he had ever seen. He had an irresistibly funny story to tell till the end of his days – *Sau-Franzosen* fighting with screaming piglets for their meagre food! Yes, he had seen it, with his own eyes! Let no one call him a liar! In any case, those little pigs saved the lives of many deportees.... Without that water and that food many would not have reached the end of the journey....

'And we reached that journey's end on the seventh day. Shouts of "*Raus, Mensch Los Tempo! Sau-Hunde*" bustled the detainees out of the wagons. If they didn't move fast enough, blows with rifle butts speeded them up.... By chance, on the station platform I met a former Kapo from Harzungen, a fine man, an exception in that pack of hyenas. He told me what was happening. Our medical convoy was to be taken by lorry to Bergen-Belsen. As for the healthy – the ss really have a macabre sense of humour! – they were to go to Bergen on foot.

'Bergen-Belsen ... Bergen ... I knew the first name. I had heard it when the unfit were taken away to a destination unknown or too well-known to the "initiated". When the advance of the Russian army had forced the ss to evacuate the extermination camps of Lublin and Maidenek, that's where the deportees were taken.... Bergen-Belsen was the place where death was certain, but Bergen – who knew? – Perhaps there might be a way out.

'I reported my deductions to the others and made it clear, without further explanation, that it would be preferable to leave by road, on foot. "Don't worry, Bergen is quite nearby," I said, to encourage them, though I had no idea how far we had to go. The majority heard me out and came with me. The only ones who went in the lorry were those who really could not walk another step. In a few hours they would be dead.

'Germany, as every walker knows, is the country in Europe where the signposting is most thorough. There could be no mistaking our route. To the right and left striped shapes pointed the way. They were the corpses of those who could not keep up with columns that had gone before. The ss had slaughtered them on the spot.

'Would the distance be greater than I had estimated? How many of us would make it? I asked myself these questions as we made our way through a chorus of shouting and barking. Who could tell the difference between the ss and their mad dogs? For those who love hunting, a day on the road to Bergen would either have been pure joy or pure horror. The kills followed fast, one on the other. The exhausted quarry lying on the road was a man, or what was left of one after months and months on a concentration camp diet.

'Dirty, pitiable, pathetic, but marching in formation, we arrived at Bergen. I spotted, on his little motorbike, the *Rapportführer* from Dora, Koenig, a sinister red-haired man with asymmetrical features, the cheerful organizer of the *Himmelkommandos*. Like a jackal, he lay in wait for a deportee to collapse so he could send him into the manure pit – *eins, zwei, drei, vier* – the place of no return. (Later, at the trial of war criminals, Doctor Jacques Déprez was able to reveal the truth when Koenig protested his innocence.) In order to prevent Koenig from getting his ration of corpses, I asked all the detainees in the convoy to march slowly and carefully. No one fell. Consciously or not, they all obeyed me. We passed through the gates without mishap. Koenig will have to wait for other convoys....'

I listen to Déprez' story. I am so exhausted that I no longer have the strength even to be indignant at such cruelty. Deportees cut down for peccadilloes, I have known that too – and the charnel houses and the convoys of death and bastards like Koenig. But what did we not know in that senseless world where we fought to keep alive for so many months! I also relate to Déprez some of our adventure since he left Dora for Harzungen (via the disciplinary Kommando for having stolen some potatoes and made chips with motor oil). I tell him all about D, his crazy projects, the hangings, the long wait for death in Nordhausen prison and the Dora bunker. I tell him about my friends Poupault, Boyer, telling him that I do not know what has become of them.... Drunk with fatigue, trembling with fever, so thin I was translucent, I feel such joy to find myself with Déprez that I talk as if my strength has returned to me, or as if, afraid of dying, I want to tell him everything....

Déprez explains to me that Bergen is a former Wehrmacht barracks. He describes to me how he managed to find a place for his hospital as soon as he arrived.

'Perhaps you have had time to notice,' he says, 'that the buildings, arranged in a square, surround a vast area where the grey crowd of deportees are crammed together.... Hardly had we entered the camp than I spotted an empty building. It was guarded. I led my little column there, still marching in strict formation. I asked my men to stop fifty yards from the entrance. "Whatever happens, do not break rank," I told them. I advanced, and at once the sentry aimed his gun at me. He was a sorry sight, as pathetic as we, or very nearly. He was wearing a faded greyish-yellow uniform. (I learnt later that he was a soldier of the Hungarian Legion.) I stopped and showed my Red Cross and doctor's armband. He lowered the machine-gun. I took a few steps. He raised the gun again. I showed him the armband again. Finally, on the third attempt, I was near enough to explain to him in German that, being responsible for a column of sick men, *Oberstabsarzt* Reiherr had appointed me to organize an infirmary. I awarded my *Stabsarzt* the rank of *Sturm-bannführer*, that is to say of General,[2] in order to impress the poor Hungarian. I told him that the *Sturmbannführer* was soon going to come and see how we had got on. The sentry stood to attention and opened the doors of the building for me. And that's how the Bergen hospital came to be,' concluded Déprez, very pleased with himself.

12 April 1945. I discover how much Jacques Déprez has done in such a short time. That man has unknown reserves of energy when it comes to saving people and taking care of the sick, for whose physical and mental well-being he was responsible.

Still using the prestige of the *Sturmbannführer* – 'He is going to make an inspection' – he orders the Hungarian guard to find brooms, mattresses. One of his orderlies, the most resourceful, finds a huge ampoule of morphine in a disused veterinary surgery. Other pharmaceutical products are discovered in the same place, all sorts of invaluable things. The barracks must have housed a cavalry unit. Comparing the weights of a horse and a deportee, Déprez calculates the necessary doses for the best effect.

The same orderly fits up a room and reconnects a rudimentary water-heating system run on wood. The water has not been cut off. An experienced concentration-camp inmate could find wood on the moon. The result: Jacques Déprez takes his first bath in ages, wondering if he will one day be able to change his underwear....

I have my dentist's armband again. The Russians in my convoy attack the vet's surgery that the orderlies have not yet completely emptied. They ransack the place. They swallow every liquid they can find, embrocations, methylated spirit. Someone comes to find me saying: 'Doctor, try to reason with them. They must be told they're poisoning themselves.' I can hardly stand up but I go. I try to explain. '*Scheissegal . . . Scheissegal . . .*' they reply. What they mean is that they do not care. Other Russians attack the pot carriers bringing the soup. You have to fight to eat.

They were many, those who, in deepest despair, still thought of survival. There, at Bergen-Belsen, another's death was sometimes wished for; a corpse was one less mouth to feed, thus a greater possibility of survival for the *Haftlings* who remained. Guided only by instinct, you can help the dying on their way. . . .

# Chapter Thirty-seven

# LIBERATION

The fighting is getting nearer.

In the evening, climbing up to the attic and lifting a skylight, you can see a glowing red line on the horizon. Is the front line being re-formed? One thing worries Déprez: the arrogance of the ss. Are the Allies marking time? Although it is forbidden, a young patient is seen near the kitchens. An ss man puts a bullet into his stomach. The wounded man is brought to the hospital. (The word *Revier*, imposed by the Germans, was banished from the deportees' vocabulary.) Déprez makes every effort to save him. Injections, serum, constant nursing: nothing does any good.... The boy will die in the doctor's arms on 15 April.

Inmates of Dora arrive. I see Dejussieu.

13 April. A great surprise. The ss in green uniform have disappeared. Only the pathetic Hungarian ss are left to guard the detainees and they seem more frightened than we.

The Russians have recognized Follette, a Kapo guilty of several hundred assassinations. Other deportees join the Russians for a punitive operation. Déprez is called by his orderly Martin to try to stop the lynching. On the parade-ground, a crowd hurl insults and accusations in every language. A human figure breaks away, runs towards the electrified fence and climbs it. 'That would be the best way out,' thinks Déprez, 'but the current must have been cut off.'

The Kapo keeps on running. He reaches a Hungarian guard who, fearing for his own life, takes him back into the camp through the main gate. Like an amoeba engulfing and digesting its prey, the crowd swallow up Follette. Disembowelled, one eye torn from its

socket, impaled by mouth and anus, bleeding, gurgling, but not
dead, Follette is taken to the hospital. Déprez gives him a shot of
morphine, this time of horse's dosage.

14 April. In the morgue, on a heap of bodies, I discover the fat
white body of Follette. The flesh has been sliced from his buttocks.
Those two red marks on the white, among the emaciated remains
of nothing but skin and bone, are etched deep into my memory.
No outrageousness, cruelty nor provocation of the surrealist cinema
has ever reached such a degree of madness. And that's the truth.

Two Hungarian guards come for Déprez. The deportees are mas-
sacring another Kapo. The doctor and two orderlies, carrying a
stretcher, push their way through the crowd. The Kapo is not yet
dead. He is laid on the stretcher. The prisoners stand around in
a circle with murder in their eyes. There is total silence. Impossible
to break the circle. An immense Russian steps out of the crowd,
brandishing a hammer. With the precision of a blacksmith, he
smashes the Kapo's skull. It is the morgue they take him to. The
Hungarian ss, petrified, say nothing.
    At the morgue, Déprez can see that other buttocks have been
carved up. All those who had died not, for various reasons, reduced
to the state of skeletons, have no buttock muscles left. 'There'll be
fresh meat tonight in the canteens,' says one orderly to the doctor.
Déprez investigates. The menu varies: grilled meat or brains. He
learns that the brain is removed after the skull is burst open between
two stones. A Kapo's calling certainly has unexpected con-
sequences.... Unless he can sneak away in time....

15 April 1945. One of the orderlies hurries down from his observation post in the attic. He is beside himself. 'I've seen them! They're
here!' he shouts. 'Who?' asks Déprez. 'Them, them of course! The
English! I saw the tanks, great big ones, sort of yellow, not like the
Germans.' Déprez goes up to the attic. On the road he sees a grey
shadow rumbling along. Great things are about to happen. It is
the end of the tunnel! We caper like madmen all over the parade-
ground. How can I describe that moment?

Three p.m. On the parade-ground a strange little square box on
wheels advances. It jolts its way to the middle of the crowd of
detainees and then stops. It is the Liberators' jeep. More of the

British arrive. They are amazed to see such a collection of raga-muffins and tramps, whose fleshless faces seem all eyes. They do not understand that men can be reduced to such a pitiful state. They assume that we are convicts evacuated from German prisons. We have to meet the officers to convince them that we are members of the Resistance. Lauth and Latry become the official interpreters. Along with Bollaert, Dejussieu is put in charge of the French, Déprez officially in charge of the medical service. In every language, the camp public address system tells all the deportees that they are free, that their ordeal is over, but that to prevent an epidemic, measures of hygiene and sanitation have to be taken.

It all happens so quickly. At first the crowd just stands in a dazed silence, then everyone bursts into tears. To see those men, those shadows of men, standing there, arms dangling, tears of joy running down those faces that have known nothing but unspeakable hard-ship for months, for years, is indescribable. Full of emotion, they throw their arms around each other. Every nationality mixes with every other. Some of the British soldiers weep.

15 April, three p.m.: zero hour of freedom.

Dejussieu asks the British to set up a separate kitchen for each nationality, to avoid scuffles with the Russians. The British medical corps visit the hospital Déprez and his orderlies had installed in such haste and congratulate the French on such a successful opera-tion. There is nothing like it at Bergen-Belsen. The British officers ask Déprez to go there to help. They put a jeep and medicines at his disposal.

The British General Staff hear that there have been incidences of cannibalism at Bergen and ask Déprez to make out reports. He writes a dozen of them and could have written more. At the bottom of the last one, he puts these words: *Do not judge, I beg you, do not judge. You cannot know what the deportees have had to suffer....*

On 17 April 1945, a young boy of twenty, who was one of the convoy of the 'Twenty Thousand' and who arrived at Dora two weeks before me, finds an object in the camp yard. It is a grenade. It explodes and kills him. To have endured so much only to die two days after the Liberation seems an overwhelming injustice.

The minute the British liberate us, my nerve gives way. I know that I am saved; I have no resources left.

In the infirmary, in the next bed, is Alfred, Brother Birin. We are both in a lamentable state. I have dysentery, broncho-pneumonia, a temperature of 105 °F. Like an animal aware of coming death, I want to be alone in my corner. But I know that I shall not die, quite simply because I do not want to. I have survived thus far. I have hung on to see the Liberation. Lying in my bed, I withdraw into myself. I rekindle my strength, gather it together again to defeat the threatening dragons inside me. I think of the memorable words of Guillaumet when he crossed the Andes: 'What I have done, no beast would have done.' Well, we too have done what no beast would have done, and we have lived to tell the tale!

I ask Jacques Déprez to give me chloroformed water and sulphonamides. When Claude Lauth comes to see me with another deportee, Castelli, I hear them say: 'Jean Michel is going to die.' I cannot believe it! My whole being rebels at the idea. I cannot even speak to them, but in my semi-conscious I say to myself over and over: 'Keep talking, Claude, I'm resting, I'll surprise you!' That visit from Lauth is my last memory of that day; I slip into a coma which lasts for forty-eight hours. When Jacques Déprez returns from Bergen-Belsen, he finds me on my feet. Not very fit, but on my feet.

'I was very afraid for you,' he confesses to me. 'First of all on the day you arrived at Bergen. I was busy with a wounded man in the hospital. I turned around: there was a long, scrawny spectre in the doorway, eyes blazing with fever, every bone sticking out. You had to say your name, I did not recognize you: "It's me, Jean Michel, from the bunker at Dora ..." you said. Jean Michel! The athlete! The out-and-out optimist who tuned in to Radio-London at Dora! Jean Michel who never believed I had pneumonia, who always restored my morale when I was in despair! I said all this to myself. I was scared and desperately trying not to let it show. I took care of you, but I was resigned to destiny.... Allah is great! And then when I saw you pass out and go into a coma, I really panicked....'

'You know me: my sole quality is that I do not know despair. I must believe in psychosomatic medicine or the Coué method! We've seen too many die of despair not to have learnt from it.'

Jacques Déprez describes to me his visit to Bergen-Belsen.

'An immense caravansarai of a multitude of deportees of all ages, all sexes, all nationalities. They were in such a state of malnutrition that it took my breath away, an old hand like me. . . . How on earth could some of them still be alive? If they had not been gassed it was because there were just too many of them. Detainees were arriving from everywhere. The installations of crematoria and ovens were insufficient. The ss let them die where they were, of hunger, typhus, dysentery. . . . There was no sanitation, no isolation block. It was as if an ill wind, desiccating and putrefying everything in its path, had blown over that cursed place. . . . A sub-Middle-Ages, swept by epidemics and famine, right in the middle of the twentieth century! Castelli, who was with me, had found his wife. Arrested in 1943, she was deported to Ravensbruck, then, having fallen ill, she had been transferred to Bergen-Belsen. Dazed, Castelli stammered: "I have no wife left! It's awful to see what the ss have done to her!" In the blocks, men, women and children, with dysentery and typhus, lay groaning and dying on the floor. There was no help, no food. Up until then I had seen mounds, even heaps of corpses, but never the mountains of tangled bodies that I saw at Bergen-Belsen! Bulldozers were ceaselessly pushing them into enormous communal graves, before the cameras of the Canadian Army Information Service. Throughout the camp, those deportees who were still relatively fit impaled the dead on hooks and dragged them to an area just swept clean by the burying machine. The British driver of our jeep was petrified, rooted to the ground at the sight. Action was needed. I managed to have a block evacuated, disinfected under great clouds of DDT, and I installed a sort of basic infirmary. I set up a team of orderlies, volunteers recruited from the deportees. I left them written, precise instructions, promising to return as soon as possible. . . .'

When will we leave Bergen and return to France? When can we be removed from these slaughter-houses, these cemeteries, this leprosy? I did not then know that Pierre Roumeguère, who had become a medical captain, was looking for me in every camp in Germany. Profiting by mission orders, every morning he took the plane and landed to see if I was among the deportees he was saving. Every other day, he telephoned Suzanne, my wife, to reassure her and tell her that he was still looking. . . .

The British were hesitating. . . . Should they put us into quarantine or let us go, risking that we spread infection and start an epidemic?

Dejussieu and Claude Lauth insisted that the British should capture the ss who had disappeared. They had to be judged as war criminals and not accepted as combatants going home after being demobilized. Their cruelty had depleted any remaining reserves of tolerance. But the British were too busy continuing to fight the war. Nevertheless, Bruno Kramer, the camp commandant, inveterate sadist, was captured. The deportees wanted to lynch him. The British prevented it. Kilian, the willing volunteer executioner, was also apprehended. He too was protected from the anger of the survivors of Dora....

The waiting became more and more unbearable. I wanted to see my wife, my daughter, all the while knowing that she would be afraid when told that that ghost was her father....

The joy of being liberated was immeasurable; but now we wanted more: we wanted to walk on French soil, kiss our loved ones....

27 April 1945. The British finally yield. We can go! They come into our blocks armed with cans of powder and, brandishing giant sprayers, they disinfect us thoroughly from head to foot.

Dejussieu and Bollaert leave for Paris first to pave the way for our return. The lists are ready. Our names are called. Lorries take us away. Farewell Dora! Farewell Bergen! Farewell to the constant degradation, abomination, decay and courage too! Farewell to the bone-yards!

Until that moment, we still feared that we might be only names in the archives of horror. Now we are free. We are going to live. We are coming out of the darkness and into the light.

During the journey, the deportees begin to unwind. They have suffered so much that they need to show their joy. They have come so close to death so often that it is impossible not to snap their fingers now at this Germany that engendered their tormentors.

At Celle, a very warm welcome awaits them from a young second-lieutenant. He is a son of François-Poncet, the ambassador. He has requisitioned a hangar in a field. The men can spend the night there. In search of food, a horde of savages descends on the village. One hour later, the field is bright with the flames of the deportees' fires. We grilled chickens, rabbits, even a pig. It was a scene out of a Bruegel painting; all those ragged figures, greedy eyes blazing out of their gaunt faces as they watched their food roasting under the night sky. There was feverish activity around each fire. Later, with full bellies, we all slept under the stars.

28 April. The lorries make their way to Göttingen. From there we are flown to Brussels. The Belgians give us an unforgettable welcome.

Dressed in a rough greatcoat which had belonged to a Russian, I wander through the streets. I had for a moment abandoned my companions: I wanted to be alone to feel really free. My face was full of fever sores. I was so thin I must have been repugnant. A woman of about forty stops me and asks me questions:

'Which camp were you in? Have you just come out? Will you have something to eat?'

She takes me to the Bon Marché store and there – was she the restaurant manageress? – everyone dances attendance on me, vying with each other to be the most attentive and thoughtful. I was touched by such kindness. But all that my stomach could accept was a sole. I disappointed my hosts, who wanted to stuff me with food.

In the afternoon, having gone back to my friends, I fainted. . . . I missed the reception that evening organized in our honour by the Belgian Senate. . . .

29 April. The last stage of the journey: to Paris. . . . At Lille station, there is chaos. We are given no priority at all; despite the euphoria of that day of our return to France, we are all totally exhausted. I protest. The *Préfet* is there. He listens to my complaints. He questions me. I reply firmly. He authorizes me to telephone my wife, doubtless to pacify me.

The moment I have been waiting for! How many times at Dora, at Nordhausen, wherever I had been, had I imagined what I was going to say, what Suzanne would say to me, 'It's me ... I'm alive. . . .' This imaginary exchange helped me through the worst times, and I could even feel the emotion on the other end of the line. My legs are trembling as I pick up the receiver. At last the moment has come. My wife, who has never given up hope, is about to hear my voice. What a shock it will be for her! And for me! ... I can only manage a few stupid words, purely practical ... 'Come and fetch me by car ... I'll be arriving at the Gare du Nord at about five a.m.'

Suzanne says nothing. When I hung up, so did she.... Why was I so cold when I wanted to say so much? And she said nothing at all! She must have been trembling so much that she could not utter a word....

30 April. Five a.m. Leshci sits near me on the way. Claude Lauth stayed at Bergen to work as interpreter. At Brussels, we were welcomed as heroes. At the Gare du Nord, nothing was prepared for us.

I climb out of the train. I scan the crowds. Suzanne is there, faithful, gentle, shaking with emotion, one of those beings one can always rely on, a blessing in a man's life.... It is still impossible to say all those things I used to say so often all alone. She looks at me and tears come to her eyes. 'Is that skeleton really my husband? What have they done to him? Can it be possible?'

She says: 'I found a car.... It wasn't easy.'

At home, I take a bath. Will it wash everything away? Suzanne leaves the room, so as not to show the pain she feels at the sight of that emaciated body which seems to hang together by some slender miracle. I hear her say to our daughter who has woken up: 'You know, Daddy has changed a lot. Don't say anything and don't show him that he has. In a few days he'll be back to his old self.'

Clean at last, dressed in a pair of pyjamas, plain, I come out of the bathroom. Monique throws her arms around my neck. She kisses me. Her first words? 'Come and collect me from school.... I have to show the other little girls that I have a daddy too, because they say I don't.' We have just lived through unspeakable horror, and age-old, petty cares continue to trouble a child's world.

Despite the bath, the soap, the eau de Cologne, the odour of the camp clings to me. It is not so easy to shake off the domination of that evil place. I am impregnated with all its venom and every sacrifice too, every loss of its every victim. Much later, my wife was to tell me: 'For three months, you smelt of death.'

How do people know I am home? Almost at once, the telephone begins to ring. Deportees' families. Too often, I can only announce the death of a father, a brother, a son. This inventory of death and suffering is painful to me. I can see the lost man's face, hear his voice and feel the sadness on the other end of the line: I have just snuffed out their last glimmer of hope.... Of the 1,070 deportees in the convoy of the 'Twenty-one Thousand', 52 returned alive....

Pierre Roumeguère arrives, dressed in the uniform of medical captain. Not even he knows what to say. He takes me in his arms, gently, as if afraid of breaking me, kisses me and bursts into tears. Temporarily denied physical well-being, I want at least to be told about life's enthusiasms and hopes. Roumeguère explains to me that after our arrest and his release by the Gestapo he rejoined the Maquis in Auvergne. With every blow struck against the Germans he thought of me.

And the telephone continues to ring. Those voices expecting good news from me, which fall silent or groan when I tell them what I know, give me a battering my state of health can ill sustain. They obliterate that will to overcome all obstacles that has never abandoned me.

I must leave Paris. I must renew my bond with Nature. I must learn to live again....

# Chapter Thirty-eight

# THOSE WHO
# CONTINUED TO SUFFER

A storm had broken over us; and tracing the course of this storm
was not just a question of observation.... You had to post yourself
wherever it blew, wherever it forced men to measure its strength.
It was a time when fear eliminated hope, changed faces beyond
recognition and authorized more and still more upheavals against
all reason.

The reader who has had the patience to read this far has seen
that I have tried not to restrict myself to my own experiences and
reflections. The storm that raged relentlessly over Dora played
havoc with those whose stories I have tried to tell. What became
of all those men? Most of them have since become friends whom
I see often; men with whom I share something fundamental – the
impossibility of lying or deceiving each other; for we met at a time
when our frightened faces plainly showed our feelings and had
dropped their masks. Should one of us try to hide something, the
rest of us would know it at once. For if Dora was the tyranny of
villains with all the cruelties of which the *nouveaux riches* in violence
are capable, it was also an unequalled revealer of character....

So how did my companions in misfortune leave the scene of our
tragedy?...

Poupault, Denais, Bordier, Donnier, as we have seen, returned
to Paris on 11 April. Doctor Jacques Déprez entered the capital one
day after I did. His comment: 'I have just got my demob money:
1,200 francs; I've had my hair cut: 750 francs.'

D, the fantastic D, who gave our story the ingredients and quality
of a true spy story, adventure or mystery tale, was liberated by the
Americans with Jacques Ruskon. The Kapo Naegele was arrested
thanks to the efforts of all the deportees. (He had been found several

months after our liberation in an English barracks where he was working as an interpreter. Brought back to Paris by the police, he was tried, condemned to death and shot.) There was not the same unanimity, in our group, for D. Only a few, including Debau-marché, called for his arrest by the military police. They considered him to have been in the pay of the Nazis. They hoped to throw light on his behaviour towards the ss, the German engineers, the Gestapo. D was tried by the French military tribunal at Rastatt. He was acquitted.

My cell companions from Nordhausen – with the sad exception of the marvellous André Boyer – also returned to France: Puppo went back to his locomotives in Miramas, Chandon to his champagne cellars, Latry to his casseroles.... Of the Russian, Nicolas Petrenko and his leader, 'the Asian', I know nothing. I sincerely hope that if they survived Dora they were not swallowed up by the Gulag Archipelago.... Cimek and Cespiva returned to Czechoslovakia, where Cespiva, a Communist, became a national hero....

Georges Croizat, the man who from 23 November 1943 until the end, when the Americans liberated Dora, tuned in to the BBC every day under the noses of the ss, again walked in his beloved Pyrenees with his wife, who had also been deported. René Laval the dentist, Alfred – Brother Birin – were others who survived the nightmare....

Gaston Pernot, who had challenged the impossible in escaping from Dora, owed his safety partly to a case of scarlatina. Arrested, with us, on the night of 3 November, incarcerated at Nordhausen, he was wondering if this arrest had something to do with his escape attempt. It was only when he saw us all up against the wall that he understood that it was not his personal case that had aroused the interest of the ss, but our whole organization. He had been picked up by the Germans in the Dora infirmary. ss Doctor Karr insisted that he be returned. He was contagious, he had scarlatina, he could not be left with the other detainees. In the *Revier*, Gaston was shut up in a room with barred windows. On the door a notice stated that he was to be handed over to the Gestapo as soon as he recovered. A friend among the orderlies, Blasy, found a way to avoid this ominous outcome. With the aid of the other orderlies, he prolonged the period of illness and convalescence as long as possible. When he considered that it was no longer possible to maintain this state of affairs, he simply removed the notice. He then busied himself in getting Pernot into a Kommando, recommending him to lie low for a while. But on 2 April Pernot was back at the infirmary. He had a temperature of 104 °F. 'Erysipelas,' said the doctor. On 5 November the ss evacuated Dora in chaos, only leaving behind those of the ill who were untransportable. Wehrmacht soldiers replaced the ss. They did not have time to destroy the deportees. On 11 April the Americans arrived at Dora. On 21 November, Gaston Pernot breathed the air of Paris. His survival was something of a miracle.

Jean Kopf, arrested with me in the Rue Hamelin, also returned to France.

Of the Compiègne seven – where friendships were tied then strengthened in the nightmare of the travelling coffins during the transportation, in the discovery of Buchenwald and its quarry, in the ordeal of Dora – Max Princet was the first to die.

Pierre Clervoy struggled for six months after the Liberation to regain his health. His spent body finally gave up the fight. When he died he was only twenty-four.

Lauth and Rozan arrived in France, one from Bergen, the other from Dora. Roger Cinel and Louis Murgia had an adventure before reaching Paris.

The following account was given to me by Cinel.

'At the beginning of April, the ss wanted to carry out Himmler's secret order: "On the approach of Allied troops, all deportees in the concentration camps must be liquidated without exception, so that not one falls into the Allies' hands."

'The bastards assembled us in the tunnel for a general roll-call. At the entrance stood a battery of machine-guns. Were they going to assassinate us a few days from liberation? Every face was drawn. We were ready for anything rather than let ourselves be mowed down without lifting a finger in our defence. Suddenly, lorries loaded with civilians arrived. The civilians were fleeing from Nordhausen and the bombing. They were taking shelter in the tunnel. The ss tried to keep us apart. But soon women and children were among the deportees. We were surrounded, our tormentors dared not fire.

'A few hours later, while the civilians watched us nervously, as if we came from another planet, Wehrmacht soldiers appeared. There was a disagreement between the Wehrmacht officer and the one in charge of the ss. Despite the latter's protests, the Wehrmacht took over the guarding of the tunnel. We had escaped the worst. The deportees felt even safer. But the ss did not give up.

'Shortly afterward, they returned to the tunnel. Again they gathered us together. An order was given for us to go to the station to leave for an unknown destination. We instantly thought of the Heaven Kommandos. There was total panic. But it was impossible to lose ourselves among the civilians. Our striped pyjamas stood out too much, faded though they were.

'In rank, we marched about fifteen miles. Those shits gave us their luggage to carry. We were so exhausted that we wondered if we were carrying all the v1s and v2s, the bags seemed so heavy. A box of matches would have been heavy to us in the state we were in. We dragged our feet, bent double under the burden. The slightest show of reluctance was punished by blows with rifle butts. At last we saw the station. We didn't know the direction of our convoy, which after many detours was to arrive at Ravensbruck.

'I was with a friend, Jacques Lehmann. We climbed into a wagon. The ss were in the middle. They had also armed the Kapos. There were about seventy-five of us to a wagon. It was pointless to try to sit down or rest for even a few seconds ...

'As the time passed some deportees went mad. They tried to eat the next man's ear or gouge out his eyes. At night, when a detainee screamed because he had just been attacked, a Kapo, guided by the cries, illuminated the scene with an electric lamp. Where the light fell, instantly, an ss man fired. The bullets penetrated forehead, nose, mouth, an eye. More deportees who had lasted until the month of April 1945 and who would not live the sublime moment of liberation. It was horrible. Blood and brains spurted everywhere. We were dazed and terrified. Terror alters everyting ...

'Close to Lehmann someone cried out in pain. We dared not go to help him. In the morning we were still without food or water. One man went absolutely crazy and started to scream. Others leapt on him and beat him until he was quiet. They were afraid the ss would open fire at random again. That was our only thought. Suddenly Lehmann cried: "That hurts!" I looked: someone was busy chewing at his ear. It was badly torn and bleeding. I elbowed my way through to the madman and made him let go.

'For several days and nights we endured this travelling lunatic asylum. We stopped at Magdebourg. At that precise moment, the Americans were bombing the town. Our convoy stayed in the station. The ss stood outside to prevent escapes. We did not even realize the danger.

'When the bombing was over, the ss came past each wagon with platforms on wheels. They ordered the deportees to throw out the dead onto the platforms. When the inhabitants of Magdebourg realized what a horrible thing was happening, they objected, but the protestors were dispersed. Then the guards ate and drank while we still were given nothing. Nothing to drink. Nothing to eat.

'We arrived at Ravensbruck after ten days of this. We were maggots who got out of those wagons. Most of us were on all fours. They were no longer capable of standing. The ss giggled and hit us. We saw women deportees who were leaving the camp. The ss said: "It's their last journey, we're going to kill them." This seemed to delight them. Red Cross wagons stood in the station. Stoves were set up. We were sent to what the Germans called the "little camp". Some French deportees who were still interned took from their meagre rations to give us a little something to eat. That was what camp life was like: unspeakable horror and then overwhelming generosity.

'Still nothing to eat. Finally a few Red Cross parcels were distributed. There wasn't enough. Famine took its toll. More than a third of the convoy died of dysentery.

It was at Ravensbruck that I found Louis Murgia and another friend, Jean Hubert. They dressed us in civilian clothing bearing the infamous KL motif like at Buchenwald. We were given blankets. A few days later we were evacuated. "The Russians are coming." The word spread quickly. Was it true? Now we were guarded by false ss, the *Volkssturm*. The élite of the Third Reich were running away like rats leaving a sinking ship, now that the time had come for the settling of accounts. Louis Murgia was sure they were going to kill us. But I knew him, his life would cost them dear.

'That evening they crammed us into a barn to sleep. There must have been about seven hundred of us. Murgia, a man called Auger, two Dutchmen in stripes and I climbed up onto the beams. In the morning the Germans emptied the barn and counted the detainees. The count was short. They came back into the barn and fired into the air. Not one of us was hit. We must have looked like parrots on perches. When we decided to get down from this precarious refuge the convoy had disappeared. We set off into the countryside.

We found a dead horse covered with flies. "Don't move, we'll have a feast," announced Auger. He was a butcher before the war. He got to work on the horse, dispersed the flies, and we devoured enormous steaks, neither cooked nor raw, for the fire we tried to make never really caught. . . .

'That night, we again slept in a barn. Murgia, always independent and far more resourceful than most deportees, vanished. He reappeared dressed as a French soldier, right down to the puttees. You'd have thought he was a private from the First World War off to battle. But you can't be surprised at anything with Murgia! I'd not have found it peculiar if he'd turned up in chain mail, as a dragoon or in a dinner jacket. Still secretive, he refused to tell me where he had found his uniform . . .

'The sky was fiery red. The front was not far off. At dawn, I spotted a German civilian who must have slept with us. He got up and slipped away. With the Russians round the corner, that idiot had gone to tell the soldiers about us. I called Murgia and we decided to move on before there was trouble.

'Hardly had we left the barn but we saw the whole gang arrive. There were civilians with us. I didn't hesitate. There was a woman with two babes in arms. I took one child, grasped the woman's arm and in German explained to her that I had to get out of the trap. Murgia followed. I don't know what became of Auger; but the Dutch were taken and I think they were shot, because two ss men with dogs had joined the soldiers. The woman played along perfectly. She did nothing to give me away. On the other hand, the man who had denounced us pointed out to the soldiers that two deportees had disappeared. That informer was a tenacious bastard. I returned the baby to its mother and, arriving at the village square, Murgia and I ran like the devil. It wasn't until we reached a little wood that we stopped to catch our breath. We stayed there for two days.

'One night we heard noise. "Wonderful, here come the Russians!" We went to investigate. It was the French of the ss division Charlemagne taking up position. We hid. In the morning a Russian shell just missed us but did not explode. The soldiers of the Charlemagne division had gone. We made our way towards the Russians. We saw them perched on Berlin taxis, those taxis with black and red checks that I knew so well, having studied for a time in the German capital.

'The Russians were dressed any old how. They had only one thing in common: they all carried a machine-gun.

' "Franzouski! Franzouski!" I shouted excitedly as I ran towards them. Did they take us for French ss in civilian clothes? They greeted us with their fists. Murgia and I were sent flying. The Mongols wanted to kill us on the spot. A taxi containing about thirty men drew up. It was the General Staff. A giant got out. An officer. He had huge gold-braid saucers on his shoulders. High-ranking Russians are festooned as the capitalist military would not dare to be.

' "Franzouski!" I repeated, without too much conviction.

' "Do you speak French?" asked the officer.

' "Yes," I said with new hope. "I was deported. I am with a friend. We have escaped."

' "ss filth!" screamed the officer, hitting me across the face with Herculean force.

'He then made us undress. When he saw no ss tattoos on our bodies he calmed down. Meanwhile, the Mongols had captured the men of the Charlemagne division. Without the semblance of a trial, the Russians shot them. As they died, they cried, "*Vive la France!*" Tears came to my eyes. It was not the bodies that moved me; I have seen so many die that shootings and hangings are like normal, everyday occurrences. It was hearing them cry "*Vive la France!*"

'We carried on our way. En route, we picked up Czech women escapees from Ravensbruck. Farther on, we saw a column of German prisoners, well-dressed, guarded by four bedraggled Russians. The Russians were on horseback. Among the German prisoners, the Czech deportees recognized a girl, a guard at Ravensbruck. They pointed her out to the Russians, explaining to them the base role the guard had played. She was taken out of the column. The deportees wanted to cut off her hair. The Russian did not understand what the Czechs wanted to do with the scissors. He took them himself and put out the girl's eyes. He seemed as satisfied as if he had just done her a service. Other Russians lay the girl on the ground and kicked her between the legs. That night, the unfortunate girl was not quite dead when the dogs devoured her. The starving animals were as mad as the men.... You had to beware of everyone and everything.

'We were in a hurry to leave the Russians and find the Anglo-Americans. Then at least we would feel safe. But our wanderings were not over even then! Our company of deportees swelled in number.

'When we arrived at the River Elbe, we found the first organized Russian troops. A squadron of mounted Cossacks, with their huge pearl-grey coats, astrakhan hats, big horses and sabres. Entire regiments dressed in khaki with puttees.... A medical service.... American tanks with the white star and inscriptions in English....The Russians were massing on the banks of the Elbe. They planned to cross to the other side to hold off the Americans. In all that multitude, I remember a Russian officer, a seven-foot giant, built like a tank, who was looking for old newspaper to roll cigarettes with; and another, who wiped his nose with his hand and then shook the deportees' hands. How much longer would we have to stay here? I had expected to get back to France quickly after leaving Dora, and now here we were, still far from home. This was not the way I had dreamt of our liberation.

'Finally, barges arrived, and without any explanation all the French were allowed to cross to the other side. As I speak English and German, I took charge of our ragged bunch. We headed for an American guard post. A Texan sergeant received us. What a difference between the Americans and the Russians! We were back to civilization! But I was too quick to rejoice. Our welcome here was far from warm. Firstly, the Americans were suspicious because we came from the other side: they wondered how many spies had been slipped in among us. Then, seeing the state we were in, they were afraid of disease.

'The sergeant had us escorted, at a distance, as if we had the plague, to an old abandoned German cavalry barrack. We were installed on the ground floor. We waited all day. Still nothing to eat! I went out, marched to the guard post and shouted at the sentries, which I would not have dared to do with the Russians. "We have no orders about you," one of the soldiers told me. "Before we feed you, a doctor has to see you." Then the sergeant added: "Whatever you do, don't go up to the first floor of the barrack." Murgia and I could actually hear death rattles. With two prisoners of war, we decided to go and investigate. We went upstairs. And what did we see? A whole convoy of deportees dying in a huge room. The Americans were so afraid of germs that they covered their faces and pushed mess-tins containing a little food into the room with long poles. We went in. Those poor men must have had typhus. Was this the Allies, the Liberation? To have suffered so much to come to this?

'In a fury I rushed to the guard post. Murgia was with me. And what did the American officer say? "You went up there? I warned you! Well now I put you in quarantine! Go back and join them!" I thought I would kill him! I screamed at him: "I am a member of the French Resistance. I was deported. I want to see someone from the General Staff at once." My anger did not impress the sergeant. Then I changed tactics and put on a mysterious air. "I was liberated by the Russians. For several days I was able to see what they were planning. They are at this moment collecting landing-craft to cross to this side of the Elbe and attack you. I found out a great deal. I want to make a report to someone in authority."

'I don't know whether the sergeant was an avid reader of spy stories, but his attitude changed. I was disinfected with DDT, and taken by jeep a distance of about six miles. I was received by officers. I talked to them about the deportees. "You cannot just let those men die. You must do something! After what they have been through, aren't you ashamed? To think we waited for you like the Second Coming!"

'The officers replied that they could do nothing because of the risk of contagion. Then, once again, I told my story of the Russians preparing landing-craft and the conversations I had overheard. "They are going to cross the Elbe and attack you." I asked them to permit me to go to fetch the other deportees who were with me. "They will corroborate everything," I said. The Americans agreed. Unanimously, we warned them of the Russian intentions, and the Yanks decided to reinforce their troops.

'Was it in thanks for services rendered? The following day, sanitation cars arrived. I hope that those men promised a certain death could be saved ...

'I was not satisfied with these measures, I considered that much more could be done. The Americans were only concerned with the German girls that they had brought with them. They were plying them with goods and cigarettes while we were weak with hunger. I informed a chaplain. I told him that I was a Protestant. I told him of the tragedy on the first floor. I took him to see for himself. Furious and charitable, he reacted at once. The following morning, seven lorries were put at the deportees' disposal; the prisoners had access to those places left over.

'We made for the British army. The Americans also handed over to us six captured French ss men. In the lorry, deportees and prisoners made life hard for them. When we arrived, the British made them take off their shoes and walk barefoot all day. Personally, I am against such practices. I have more respect for men who have fought, who have known the war on the Russian front, than for those who went freely to work in Germany. The latter sold themselves with the minimum risk.

'Murgia and I stayed with the British for two days. They wanted us to stay longer. They had engaged us to interrogate French prisoners of war. We had to weed out those who had tattoo marks on their arms. They were ss men. They could have slipped in among the prisoners. The Germans marked them in this way to indicate their blood group.[1]

'It is true that we were being of service, but I could not stay away from my family any longer. I was tired of the horrors, of the war, of the endless humiliations, of the terrible and almost identical stories.

'As a favour, we had access to a train which carried French officers. Our status of deportee accorded us this privilege. Thin and in rags, Murgia and I stood in the corridor of the train, while the officers were comfortably installed in the compartments. I had had enough of this sort of indifference. We were physically more dead then alive and those well-fed officers were lolling there with an arrogance that exasperated me. I said to them: "Let us sit down, we are deportees." It was as if I had uttered something like: "Isn't it a lovely day?" Not one of those shits gave up his seat to us. "Perhaps we're in the Soviet Union," said Murgia.

'So it was standing that we watched the French countryside pass by, the villages, the woods, the towns, the stations and then the suburbs and then Paris.... I forgot my anger.... Paris!

'Gare de l'Est, 26 May, a change of scene. The officers' scorn was succeeded by the warmth of a welcoming committee. Had France begun to realize what had gone on in the concentration camps? Boy scouts came forward. They asked the passengers: "Are there any deportees among you?" Murgia and I replied: "Yes, we are." "Is that true!" "Yes." Then the boy scouts seized our bags – Murgia, who always had his wits about him, had collected quite a few things during our prolonged stay in Germany – laid us down on stretchers, took off our shoes and in front of everyone, including those officers from the train, washed our feet ...

'We were taken to the Hotel Lutetia. Our names were put on a list. As the authorities had gone into premature mourning for us and thought that fewer would return from the death camps, there was not enough room. We slept on the floor. Murgia had brought back a carpet from Germany. We used it as a mattress.... For our meals, a restaurant several miles away had been set aside for us. German organization was replaced by French organization: but I prefer the latter.... Every day we were taken to the Gaumont to see films.... In the evening, cars brought us back to the hotel.... My parents knew, by consulting the lists, that I was there the day after I arrived.... I had telephoned home to Angers to tell them but they were in Paris where they were looking for me. It took them a week,' concluded Roger Cinel, 'to find me.... French organization!'

# Chapter Thirty-nine

# THE FINAL SLAUGHTER

Put all the deportees in the tunnels at Dora, block the exits, pump in poison gas and blow the lot up: the SS were unable to carry out this plan. But, a few days before the Americans' arrival, the Germans committed a crime which will figure in the annals of horror as one of the greatest abominations of all the iniquities in history. I speak of the murders of Gardelegen.

Inmates from Dora, Ellrich, Rottleberode and the thirty-one annexed camps arrived at Gardelegen on 11 April 1945. They had left their respective camps on 5 April. Their exodus had lasted six days and nights; six days and nights in which they knew killings on the road when they were on foot, the certainty of being executed in Czechoslovakia as they were told to frighten them still more, air-raids, stifling conditions in the wagons, hunger, thirst, the death of friends, all the calamities suffered by outcasts among outcasts.

After having walked the thirty miles which separate Mieste from Gardelegen, the survivors of this convoy of 2,500 to 3,000 deportees were lodged in the buildings of an old cavalry school. During this time, the American troops were approaching the town.

The commandant of Gardelegen – the *Kreisleiter* – was a fanatical Nazi. He had taken Himmler's orders to heart. He announced to his *Volkssturm* his intention of liquidating all the deportees. The General Staff, to whom he declared his determination, approved.

But how was it to be done? It would appear there were problems of organization. German officers of the army and air force, when consulted, encouraged the *Kreisleiter* and assured him of the co-operation of their units but the stumbling block was the question of effectiveness. The SS convoy commandant vetoed the *Kreisleiter's* suggestion of shooting all the deportees in the very yard of the cavalry school – the school was situated in the middle of the town, the place was hardly suitable. And then, the method would not be swift enough. After a final meeting, a decision was taken to burn the deportees in an isolated barn, at Isenschnibbe. These deliberations had lasted two days.

Friday, 13 April 1945, German deportees were summoned by the SS. They were asked to act as guards for the others. Twenty-five agreed; among them were several Germans of Polish origin. They were dressed in SS uniform, death's head well in evidence on the cap, and armed with rifles.

At the end of the afternoon, all the deportees were assembled. There were just over a thousand of them. In groups of one hundred, they were taken from Gardelegen to the barn at Isenschnibbe, outside the town. Among the hundred guards, there were Luftwaffe soldiers, soldiers from the front, *Volkssturm* and the twenty-five volunteer deportees. People who had watched the preparations said nothing. Twenty young parachutists, stationed at Gardelegen, came to reinforce the number of guards.

At seven p.m., all the deportees were crowded into the barn. The guards ordered them not to move. A parachutist opened fire with his machine-gun. He killed several detainees, wounding others.

The floor was covered in straw. The straw was soaked with petrol. The doors were closed and wedged fast with stone blocks. An SS sergeant half-opened the door and lit the straw with a match. The deportees put out the flame. The SS came back with torches. The detainees put out the little flames with their bare hands. Then the SS opened the door, threw in incendiary grenades and fired into the crowd. SS, parachutists and other guards formed a chain around the building. Dogs patrolled to prevent any escapes.

The flames spread. The cries for mercy and help would have melted the heart of the most hardened criminal. The deportees were being roasted alive. The fire raged for seven hours. Miraculously, there were some survivors. Some had dug holes, others had taken shelter under the piles of cooling then calcifying, stinking bodies.

When the fire died down, the *Kreisleiter* ordered petrol to be put in to burn the bodies completely. During this time, the *Volkssturm* were digging trenches in order to bury the victims and hide the evidence of their crime.

On Sunday, 15 April 1945, at seven a.m., the 101st American

Infantry Division reached Gardelegen and the barn at Isenschnibbe. The assassins had fled. After the Americans' first reaction of horror, a search was made for the bodies; 574 had already been buried, 442 were found in the barn. Out of a total of 1,016 victims, only 4 corpses were identifiable by name, 301 by number; the 711 others could not be identified at all. Among the martyrs there were Belgians, French, Dutch, Hungarians, Poles, Russians, Czechs, some Greeks and Lithuanians, as well as German political deportees.

# Chapter Forty

# 'TO EACH
ACCORDING TO HIS DUE'

As the years passed, death was to prematurely cut down, one by one, those who had escaped hell; their bodies were used up.

2 April 1945 – two days before the convoys of death moved out of Dora to scatter their cargo of living skeletons in other dreadful places – SS *Obergruppenführer* Hans Kammler played his last card.

'"He was on the move day and night," General Dornberger observed. "Conferences were called for at one o'clock in the morning somewhere in the Harz Mountains, or we would meet at midnight somewhere on the autobahn.... We were prey to terrific nervous tension.... Kammler, if he got impatient and wanted to drive on, would wake the slumbering officers of his suite with a burst from his tommy-gun."'[1]

This supercharged young wolf did not spend his demented energies in the execution of Hitler's scorched-earth directive: 'If the war is lost, let the nation perish!' He did not issue instructions for the destruction of the tunnels and laboratories. What he did do was far more constructive. A list of the best scientists was drawn up and, on 2 April, five hundred technicians and engineers, under the protection of one hundred of the SS, embarked on the missile director's own special train: 'a sleek, modern engine, twelve sleeping cars and a dining car. The latter was well stocked with food and fine wines.'[2] Destination: the Alpine retreat where, according to von Braun and Dornberger, the man in Himmler's confidence expected to 'bargain with the Americans or one of the other Allies for his own life in exchange for the leading German rocket specialists'.[3]

Von Braun did not share the luxurious voyage. His arm in plaster after an automobile accident – the Harz mountains presented unforeseen dangers – the young thirty-three-year-old scientist was travelling to Munich in a passenger car. The genius of space research was on his way to join Kammler. But he was careful to arrive empty-handed – his chief of staff, Dieter Huzel, and Bernhard Tessman, chief designer of the test facilities, were scouring the Harz, searching for the ideal place to hide the fourteen tons of personal archives he had entrusted to them....

On 4 April, von Braun arrived in the Bavarian Alps at Oberammergau, a 'quiet village of woodcarvers and old brightly-painted peasants' houses'.[4] A paradise. Except for one particular – the experts from the luxury train were locked up in a military camp guarded by the ss. Installed in the Hotel Jesus, run by Alois Lang, the Nazi hotel-keeper who played the role of Christ in the village passion play, *Obergruppenführer* Hans Kammler did not seem disposed to freeing his ransom.

What did it matter? Von Braun – and this is additional proof of his exceptional importance in the ss empire – demanded an audience. Kammler, with his 'bronzed clear-cut features', was in an excellent mood. He made the scientist sit down, offered him a glass of liqueur, nodded his head with satisfaction when von Braun told him that his team was in a position to recommence its research. Bringing the relaxed conversation to a close, Kammler stood up and announced that he was about to disappear 'for an indefinite length of time'.

No one was ever to see him again.

What followed belongs to vaudeville.

Von Braun explained to Kammler's General Staff that keeping the scientists together in a camp made them vulnerable to attack by American bombers. Probably sensitive to the beauty of nature, the ferocious ss became as idyllic as the scenery; they agreed to the five hundred experts being scattered throughout the neighbouring mountains. Von Braun, who never wasted any time, took advantage of this to have his arm attended to at a hospital in Sonthofen. Let us pass over the surgery that made the dear man suffer and over his fear of being at any moment abducted and murdered by the ss. The reader will have read enough unbearable accounts. On 25 April, it was not the Gestapo that knocked at the door of this martyr to science, but an emissary from his old accomplice Dornberger.

Still as dynamic as ever, von Braun did not need to be pressed. He joined his boss at a winter sports hotel in the Austrian Tyrol, at Oberjoch, where, as if by chance, the other guests were Dieter Huzel and Bernhard Tessman (the two men who knew the hiding-place of the v2 archives), von Braun's own brother, Magnus, respon-sible for the manufacture of gyroscopes at Dora, Dornberger's chief of staff, Axsten, and Hans Lindenberg, specialist in combustion chambers – in effect one of the essential pivots of the v2 project. If the intellectual war treasure was at full strength, it did not escape the watchful eye of the Black Order; thirty of the ss were ordered to execute the scientists rather than let them fall alive into the hands of the enemy.

Feydeau continued to supplant Wagner: those ss were not bad buggers; their co, 'a maudlin, guilt-ridden weakling worried about his own skin'[5] let himself be disarmed by Dornberger. In this whole story, it was only the deportees who had no chance: unlike von Braun, the martyrs of the Gardelegen barn were really unlucky. And it has to be said that they did not have Dornberger's bargain to offer the ss – of offering them impunity in providing them with simple, *feldgrau* Werhmacht uniforms.

Cinel, Lauth, Murgia, Poupault, all of you, who shared with me the tunnel and the convoys of death, I hope you will appreciate the edifying end to the appalling adventures of the scientists whose slaves we were:

'We lay on the terrace of our quarters and let the sun beat down on us,' writes Dornberger. 'We gave ourselves up to our thoughts ... slowly achieved detachment from the march of events. About us towered the snow-covered Allgäu Mountains, their peaks glitter-ing in the sunlight under the clear blue sky. Far below us it was already spring ... it was so infinitely peaceful here! Had the last few years been nothing but a bad dream?'[6]

What style!

2 May 1945. Units of the 44th Infantry Division of the American army were patrolling the valley, followed closely by the First French Army, when a cyclist suddenly appeared in their path; it was Magnus von Braun, descended from his eyrie to negotiate the sur-render of his brother and friends. Taken before the officers of us Intelligence Magnus obtained the necessary safe-conducts imme-diately. The following day, the future conquerors of space exchanged Hitler, Himmler, Kammler and company for their new masters.

'They didn't kick me in the teeth or anything,' said von Braun, relieved, 'they just fried me some eggs.'

Less than five months later, Wernher von Braun arrived at Fort Bliss, near El Paso, Texas, the American missile base. He constituted the advanced guard of the one hundred German scientists Washington had decided to bring to the United States. On 14 March 1946, the first rebuilt V2 made its test flight.

Thus began the American programme of intercontinental and interplanetary missiles. . . .

Even the raw materials benefited from more attention and care than those who survived deportation. Thanks to the intelligent initiative of *Obergruppenführer* Hans Kammler in not destroying the *Mittelwerke*, the envoys of the Pentagon Ordnance Technical Intelligence Service were able to set to work as soon as Patton's troops had finished clearing the region.

*From as early as March 1945* Major Hamill had had an order from his chief, Colonel Toftoy, to take possession of one hundred V2s. Armed with a personal instruction from Eisenhower which authorized him to ship the captured German weapons overseas, Hamill reopened the tunnels and began the completion of the V2s under construction at the time of the American invasion of the Harz.

Miraculously reappearing from their hiding-places, Dora's German engineers retrieved the parts which they had scattered about the countryside. They joined in the work themselves and managed to overcome a deplorable fact – the deportees, complained McGovern, 'in their fury at their German captors and frenzied joy at being freed from them, had destroyed many priceless rocket components and machine tools'.[7]

22 May 1945. 341 goods wagons departed for Belgium, where the missiles were to be embarked on sixteen Liberty ships, despite the fury of the British who would have dearly liked even a small part of these fabulous spoils of war.

Only General Walter Dornberger was a little less fortunate. As a career soldier, he was considered a prisoner of war. Having failed to lay their hands on Kammler, the English had the absurd and inconvenient idea of trying to hang him after Nuremberg. The father of the V2s was not set free until July 1947. Though he handed himself over to the United States, his past as a Wehrmacht general prevented him from again working with von Braun and his team. He had to work directly for American aviation. The door of NASA remained closed to him. He nevertheless became vice-president of the Bell Aircraft Company and of the Bell Aerosystems Company. Skills, it is well known, are always rewarded. Who said that crime does not pay? Probably some romantic novelist – every social class has its 'literature'.

The conditions under which the Allies dropped the plan to make Dornberger stand trial are not widely known. According to the theory Dornberger expressed to McGovern, it was because it would have been all too easy for him to declare in the international court that his v2s had finally caused less damage than the Allied bombing of Germany, not to mention, of course, the atomic bombs of Hiroshima and Nagasaki. One might wonder if the true story was not more complex. The era which began with the liberation of Nordhausen by the Americans was, in fact, marked by some very peculiar dealings; over those dealings lies the shadow of Dora....

On 27 April 1945, the American officers charged with the recovery of the v2s and the scientists learnt an astonishing fact. The zone of Nordhausen, occupied too quickly by Patton's army, had to be handed over to the Soviet authorities on 1 June. The cold war had not yet begun. There was no question of destroying the *Mittelwerke* installations. But the scientists and technicians remaining in the region, the scattered archives and the v2s under construction could not at any price be allowed to fall into Russian hands. While Hamill mobilized the German technicians to mount the missiles, another US major, Staver, set off to search for von Braun's documents. On 31 May he succeeded in persuading Doctor Walter Riedel to reveal the hiding-place of his superior's archives.

Von Braun and Dornberger, who were still under interrogation in Bavaria, in this way lost a major trump card. But they still held other cards strong enough to bring their influence to bear on the race between the Russians and Americans. They produced a series of reports which proved that they alone could master the technique of rocket propulsion;[8] the scientists still in Nordhausen or 'Kammler's hostages' who had gone to find their families in the Harz had complete confidence in them; and then Dornberger had also hidden archives of an inestimable value.

In the end, the Russians did not occupy Nordhausen until 1 July

1945, which gave von Braun and Dornberger plenty of time to organize the departure of the principal missile experts to the American Zone. The general's archives were recovered a few hours before the arrival of the Red Army troops.

A sentimental people, the Americans were unable to forget such priceless services. The Russians, with their thirty thousand deaths caused by the Nazi invasion, had a more expeditious, more realistic attitude. Though their leaders were never much concerned with humanitarian principles even towards their own people; or particularly towards their own people ...

In February 1945, the Yalta Conference had defined the partition of Germany. But the Red Army was not yet in a position to take hold of its due. In an attempt to check the 'Bolshevik unfurling' the Germans fought like fury. The Soviet troops were held up at the Oder. The Americans did not meet the same resistance in the west. The bridge at Remagen, on the Rhine, fell into their hands, and at once the impetuous Patton plunged into the centre of Germany. He penetrated as far as Leipzig, and thus the Russians got wind of the SS empire of secret weapons.[9]

Churchill wanted to take advantage of this heaven-sent situation and wait until the Potsdam Conference to hand over to Stalin what had been promised him. The new US President Truman refused. On 1 July 1945, Soviet troops arrived in the *Mittelwerke* zone, where since 26 May a group of Russian secret service officers had been installed as an advance guard, encouraging the scientists and German engineers of Dora to stay where they were for wonderful rewards.

To their great amazement the Russians did not find a desert. They had known about the existence of the subterranean factory, but they thought the Americans had destroyed everything.

It is true that the best missile specialists had been evacuated to the American Zone, but the tunnels were intact and three thousand technicians had stayed behind. At once the Dora installations began to function again, this time for the Soviets; new V2s were assembled in the tunnel and testing of motors and jet-pipes started up at Bleicherode. Helmut Gröttrup, the guidance director's assistant, the man who had been arrested by the Gestapo with von Braun in March 1944, had stayed in the Russian Zone and agreed to undertake the direction of their missile programme.

Dora continued to function until 22 October 1946. On that day, General Serov's Soviet secret police burst into the homes of the German technicians in the eastern zone. Women, children, relatives – over twenty thousand people – were shipped to the USSR with their bags, their furniture – even their tins of sauerkraut. The Russians' plan was simple: to force the German scientists and engineers to teach everything they knew to their Russian counterparts. They were returned gradually, from 1951 to 1953, when they had completed this mission.

The great brain raid seems to have paid off; on 30 October 1947, a V2 was launched in Kazakhstan. Ten years later, the first Sputnik, made by Russian scientists from knowledge acquired from the Germans, took off into space. The Americans had stolen a march on Russia in 1945 by taking von Braun and the élite of the Peenemünde team, but they lost ten years in not knowing how to make use of them.

Von Braun and Dornberger naturalized Americans, Gröttrup 'borrowed' by the Russians, the small fry employed in French and English laboratories,[10] there is only one name missing – Hans Kammler.

The chief of the SS secret weapon empire, the man in Himmler's confidence, disappeared without trace. Even more disturbing is the fact that the architect of the concentration camps, builder of the gas chambers, executioner of Dora, overall chief of all the SS missiles has sunk into oblivion. There is the Bormann mystery, the Mengele enigma; as far as I know, no one, to this day, has taken much interest in the fate of *Obergruppenführer* SS Hans Kammler.

The only evidence I have found is from General Dornberger – that Kammler must have died in Prague after the German surrender, on 9 May 1945, at the time of the SS' last battle with the Czech Resistance.[11] The *Obergruppenführer* would have ordered his aide-de-camp, SS Major Starck, to kill him rather than let him be captured by the partisans. Starck would have obeyed; machine-gun in his hand and a smile on his lips, Hans Kammler would have rushed out of a besieged bunker. His aide-de-camp would then have shot him in the back. Thus Hans Kammler would have found almost as glorious an end as Adolf Hitler, killed by his own SS men.

This ending is a fine image. Too fine. It raises many questions. That Kammler should have fled to Prague is not too illogical. In the collapse of the Third Reich, Czechoslovakia attracted floods of refugees and the SS. The deputy Sudeten leader of Bohemia and Moravia, Karl Hermann Frank, was of the race of Nazi fanatics, narrow-minded and die-hard. On paper he had forty divisions of Schörner's army at his disposal.

The Germans had only forgotten one thing – the Czech Resistance. On 6 May 1945, it pounced on them like the scourge of God. The ensuing fighting involved such a wealth of atrocities that one can understand Kammler, caught in the trap, not wishing to fall alive into the hands of Czechs wanting to avenge hundreds of Lidices.

Nevertheless, this logic is contrary to everything we know of the personality of Hans Kammler. Over a month passed between his leaving Bavaria and the insurrection of Prague. What had that highly dynamic man, who flew from conference to conference waking his SS lieutenants with machine-gun fire, been doing during such a long delay? And why had the 'cold and brutal calculator' described by Speer, so abruptly discarded the trump cards he had so patiently accumulated?

Kammler had not blown up the secret-weapon factories. He had left, in the tunnels, sufficient parts and machine tools for assembling v2s. He had built up a veritable personal 'treasure' of five hundred scientists. And if von Braun and Dornberger put their archives in a safe place, why should their boss have been less far-sighted? ...

My wakeful nights are filled with new nightmares. Brooding on one's past as a deportee does not often bring an answer to the question why.... But I know that I shall ask it until my dying day....

In Prague, Hans Kammler, missile chief without missiles, had absolutely no ambition to satisfy but only debts to pay. For this born calculator, this unscrupulous SS officer, it would have been more logical to carry out the intention attributed to him by Wernher von Braun: to negotiate with the Americans. That would have been one of his chances of survival.

Alas, there is ample proof that mass murderers speak a common language after shedding the blood of innocent people.... What does the suffering of martyrs matter when one can exchange state secrets with 'technicians'? Allen Dulles, head of the American OSS (Office of Strategic Services) in Switzerland, negotiated the return of German troops in the north of Italy with Karl Wolff, Gestapo and SS

chief in that region. Walter Schellenberg, head of the ss Intelligence
Service (of all Hitler's Germany since February 1944), lived out
his life peacefully in Switzerland after having revealed all his secrets.
ss General von den Back-Zalewski, the butcher of the Warsaw
ghetto, made an unexpected appearance at the Nuremberg trials as
witness for the prosecution. General Gehlen, Chief of Intelligence
on the Eastern Front, lives in Federal Germany after having
directed her Intelligence Service for more than twenty years.
Colonel Reile, who commanded the counter-espionage operation in
Paris which arrested so many members of the Resistance, was for
a long time Gehlen's assistant, charged with the hunt for Soviet
spies. And so many others, less well known, for the list could be
added to indefinitely.

So, why not Kammler? We know that through D he tried to make
contact with the Anglo-Americans. Why would he not have succeeded with the American special services? Bavaria, where he lived
when last heard of, 5 April 1945, is not far from Switzerland, which
was swarming with American agents....

Everything is possible in a mad world. Kammler could have
guided Patton's troops to the missile factories. He could have
revealed the hiding-places of von Braun and his companions in
Bavaria (the scattering of the scientists around Oberammergau
served his purpose in rendering him possessor of a more difficult
secret to crack; it is troubling to record that the American troops
beat the First French Army to von Braun's lair by a short head).
He could have provided the list of technicians who had remained
in the Nordhausen area. He was in a position,[12] thanks to his
archives, to provide the method of v2 assembly. Kammler's past,
the horror of Dora, are sufficient to explain the absolute secrecy
which would have surrounded these eventual transactions. Unless,
though engaged upon, they could not be successfully concluded,
forcing the butcher of Dora at the last minute to go to his death
in Prague.

Thirty years have passed and I still want to know. Did Kammler
die in Prague, leaping out of a bunker, pretending to take on six
hundred partisans? Is he living peacefully in the United States as
James Smith in one of those provincial American cities which have
sprung up like mushrooms around the missile centres of the us Air
Force and NASA? Or did he perish in a Gulag, where the Russians

would not have failed to send him after having extracted all his secrets?... So many questions that obstinately give me no peace....

In these pages, I have done my best to patiently reconstruct the life, the deeds and the feelings of those human moles we became at Dora. Without being a historian, I have consulted archives, books and documents to try to make understood the unspeakable machinations we were caught up in.

The reader will perhaps be surprised that in my epilogue I let myself be seduced by the phantasmagoria of theories. The reason for it is simple. It has become clear to me that the cynicism of the great powers was merciless. While the bodies of Dora's martyrs were still warm, they impassively organized the recovery of the V2s and the Nazi scientists. The curtain lowered on the tragedy of Dora is so opaque that thirty years later I have come to believe that in the icy domain of state reasoning, or in the fever of distorting history to make it palatable for the new slaves of the consumer society, anything – absolutely anything – can happen.

Until the very last, before they decamped in the face of too immediate dangers, the ss defied the most elementary principles of humanity. They tortured, beat, strangled, dispensed slow death or brutally assassinated defenceless people. When I was under their yoke, I dreamed of the day when one of them would fall into my hands. I was sure that I would take revenge for all the blows, the pain, the anguish, the hunger and that I would avenge those of my comrades who, completely exhausted, were unable to hold out to the end. Is it for good or ill? I have never had the occasion to make one of those destroyers and murderers suffer what they made me suffer, what they made us suffer. Not one of those criminals was handed over to me, I could not capture a single one of them myself. Thus circumstances have spared me from being put in my turn into the sinister position of tormentor.

Delivered from the spirit of vengeance, but in a spirit of justice, I participated in two trials.

The first was that of Dachau, which opened on 7 August 1947, presided over by Lieutenant-Colonel William Berman, Chief Prosecutor of Boston and New York. My various depositions were spread over six weeks. Thirty-nine of Dora's torturers were in the dock. They received diverse sentences. Among them, Hans Moeser, the last commandant, who had been determined to carry out Himmler's secret extermination orders. The verdict? Death. In the dock there were also Joseph Kilian, the voluntary murderer; Heinz Detmers, one of the Gestapo who had 'welcomed' me to Nordhausen; and two Kapos from the tunnel, Richard Walenta and Willy Zwiener. How can I explain? I was unable to analyse my feelings at the sight of those assassins in captivity while I was free. I felt as if I were only a cog in the judiciary machine: those men had to be punished but I no longer had any desire to transform the trial into a settling of personal scores.

The second trial took place on 30 January 1968. (Twenty-three years later!) The accused were Sander, Hazel – both of the Nordhausen Gestapo – and Busta of the ss. The sentences were, in my opinion, lenient. Sander, for example, got eight years forced labour. It was the Cologne public prosecutor who officiated. He did not welcome the depositions of former deportees.

I still regret that certain Kapos, some of the ss, certain murderous doctors whom I remember, and those who betrayed me to the Gestapo in France, have not been arrested. And if life in the concentration camps taught me the meaning of time, space and friendship, that period of my life also taught me that we must always be on the alert as soon as a totalitarian régime comes to power in any country. We must do everything in our power to put men and women on their guard to prevent the rot spreading. But the lessons of history are rarely heard. Evil breeds more followers than Good: the slopes are easier to negotiate. Those who choose to rule by injustice and violence can count on legions of courtiers and slaves.

I often think of Dora. I see that *Metropolis* cavern where we suffered so much and where so many of my comrades died. I see that corridor which led us to our bunks when we were beyond exhaustion. I see the insurrection of ghosts on 14 July 1944: when one has decided to die, one can undertake anything. I hear the noise of the picks, the dull thud of falling bodies, the lugubrious ring of the bell that haunted us so, the cries of pain of those who were still clinging to life enough to feel the coming of death. I think of the convoys of one thousand, of those men rigid, eyes staring in the cold, as if the ice had frozen them open.

For me, Dora is a presence. English, French, Americans and Russians have shared the scientists and technicians who were our masters. And I could not watch the Apollo mission without remembering that that triumphant walk was made possible by our initiation to inconceivable horror.

Not long ago, the English came to dig up the skeletons of the Napoleonic battles to turn them into fertilizer; others, among the allies of that time, made bone-black with the corpses of the 1812 Russian campaign. Today it is with the tribute of blood, sweat and tears paid to the Nazi scientists and technicians that our flight out into the Universe was possible. The escape into space had its beginnings in the burial of the living dead of Dora, who used to dream of impossible escapes....

East Germany, where Dora is now, has stopped up the entrances to the tunnel. Pressure and negotiation were necessary to reach this decision; for, it was said, secret weapons were still being made there. Thus the Harz has closed up on the processions of 'Muslims', the legions of spectres.... It keeps hidden within its flanks the secrets of victims sacrificed to the madness of a few, when men lived as moles.

The tunnel is blocked. But the miasma of Dora could still pollute the world. Despite, or perhaps because of, the suffering I endured, every day I discover the joy of living ... and also a frantic, never satisfied desire to KNOW.

# NOTES

## Chapter 2

1 Quoted by David Irving, *The Mare's Nest* (William Kimber).
2 Only twenty-five were launched over a period of ten days and more than a year after the Führer's decision.
3 David Irving, op. cit.
4 The astonishing ways in which the British discovered the existence of Peenemünde are described by David Irving in *The Mare's Nest*.
5 Notably Marie-Madeleine Fourcade's circuit.

## Chapter 4

1 In general, each convoy was made up of one thousand prisoners, which explains why we called them 'convoy Twenty Thousand ... Thirty Thousand ... Seventy-seven Thousand' – the last being the final convoy to leave Compiègne on 17 August 1944.

## Chapter 6

1 Owing to the advance of the Russian armies, the Germans had been forced to evacuate camps in the Ukraine to Buchenwald, the 'distribution' camp. It was the central camp, its registers recorded every deportee's name.

## Chapter 9

1 Albert Speer, *Inside the Third Reich*, pp. 370 and 372 (Weidenfeld).
2 David Irving, op. cit., p. 74.
3 Albert Speer, op. cit., p. 370.
4 Ibid., Mr Speer seems to be ignorant of the fate that was in store for these deportees. He will learn what it was if he will do me the

'honour' of reading on. In particular, the chapter 'Heaven Kommandos'.

5 Unlike the bombing of Peenemünde, the Allies bombed these two factories by mistake; Friedrichshafen because the Zeppelin establishments were thought to manufacture radar, Weiner-Neustadt because the Rex were thought to be aeronautic factories (Irving, op. cit., p. 309). The English had only touched on the secret of Peenemünde, but Hitler could not have guessed this.

6 Albert Speer, op. cit., p. 369.

7 Albert Speer quoted by David Irving, op. cit., p. 122.

8 The factories of Vienne and of Friedrichshafen were to constitute the Southern Works, and the Eastern Works plant was planned for Riga. (David Irving, op. cit., p. 188.)

9 Obviously my friend was referring to the conditions of work. He had not forgotten that Auschwitz was an extermination camp where millions of Jews perished.

## Chapter 10

1 Alben Sawatski was one of Speer's associates.

2 I cannot guarantee the spelling of this word. I write it phonetically as it was pronounced in our deportee slang.

## Chapter 13

1 ss statistics, which should be viewed with some scepticism, mention that there were 18 deaths at Dora in October 1943, 172 in November, 670 in December. The total number of deportees in November was 3,000. The increase in deaths, though recorded by the ss, is revealing.

2 I discovered this name in 1967 in David Irving's book written from German archives: *The Mare's Nest*, p. 204.

## Chapter 14

1 Albert Speer, op. cit., p. 370.

2 Ibid., p. 371 (Jean Michel's italics).

3 *V2* (Hurst and Blackett, London, 1954).

4 Dornberger, *V2*, p. 256.

5 David Irving, op. cit., p. 183.

6 Dornberger, op. cit., p. 224.

7 (Barker, 1967.)

8 Yet, curiously, they have written more about Auschwitz, Ravensbruck, Dachau and Buchenwald.

9   Dornberger, op. cit., p. 256.

10  James McGovern, op. cit., p. 120.

11  Ibid., p. 79.

12  This passage deals with the approach of the Americans; so 'the deterioration of conditions' took place, according to McGovern and his 'witnesses', in February 1945.

13  James McGovern, op. cit., p. 110.

14  Von Braun, without a doubt!... But what about those who laboured in the bowels of the earth, so that his dream of space might come true?

15  *The Dora-Nordhausen War Crimes Trial*, p. 13 (1947).

16  Dornberger, op. cit., p. 250.

17  *Vorhaben zur besonderen Verwendung* (Project for Special Dispositions).

18  James McGovern, op. cit., p. 92.

19  Ibid., p. 93.

20  Ibid., p. 113.

21  An engineer in the armaments industry told me that the placing of every single screw hole on a prototype must be supervised by the engineers. And David Irving found a most revealing figure in the German archives: 'Both von Braun and Dornberger later estimated that by now, as the rocket was finally cleared for mass-production, over *65,000 modifications* had been made to its basic design.' (David Irving, op. cit., p. 282, Jean Michel's italics.)

22  Quoted in the brochure *Dora* (Editions du Comité International de Buchenwald-Dora).

23  This revelation is made by James McGovern, op. cit., p. 134.

24  Michel Bar-Zohar, *The Hunt for German Scientists* (Barker).

25  Dornberger, op. cit., p. 224.


## Chapter 18

1   'Some Kommandos stayed for six months without ever leaving the tunnel.... When the survivors returned to the surface they were dazed, their eyes could no longer distinguish colour, the world had become dull and neutral, without the sun.' (*Memorial des camps de Dora-Ellrich*.)


## Chapter 19

1   In London, Boyer, friend of Gaston Defferre, strengthened the ties between the Socialist Party and General de Gaulle.

2   The 'VIPS' were deportees considered important by the SS.

## Chapter 20

1   Numbers are sometimes more eloquent than words. In the ss records one can see that in mid-winter, in frosts of minus 4 °F, the number of deportees *without clothes* was 868 on 1 December 1944, 1,258 on 2 January 1945, 1,847 on 3 January. This was out of a total of 7,000. Over a period of eleven months, out of '3,500 French sent to Ellrich, 210 returned, that is 1 in 17'. (Complaint of the *Amicale* of Ellrich deportees against the men responsible for the camp.)

2   In fact he was talking about a more revolutionary weapon than the V2: the anti-aircraft rocket *Wasserfall* (Waterfall), which is the forerunner of all modern missiles which destroy moving targets. Experts agree that if the Nazis had directed all their research to the *Wasserfall* instead of the V2, they could have extended the course of the war.

3   Cespiva has described the actions of the Czech group in the pamphlet of the International Committee on Buchenwald-Dora and Kommandos, with a preface by Marcel Paul.

## Chapter 22

1   In fact the Allies, who had very quickly discovered the secret of Peenemünde, did not learn of the existence of Dora until September 1944.

2   The VI launching pads were bombed at enormous risk to the RAF and Free French pilots. Contrary to a commonly-held opinion, these suicide raids were not decisive, for the Germans, with foresight, had built other ramps set further back than the first.

## Chapter 23

1   D as for Destiny. Some consider the part he played to have been beneficial, others harmful, but all are agreed that it was important. Though my life depended on it, I cannot make up my own mind about this controversial figure. I have therefore decided not to reveal his name, more especially as my efforts to find him again have been in vain.

2   General Delestraint, one of the greatest figures of the French Resistance, was executed on the eve of the Liberation in Dachau, on special orders from Himmler.

## Chapter 24

1   *Memorial des Camps de Dora-Ellrich*, which inspired this passage about Claude Lauth.

## Chapter 28

1   David Irving, op. cit., p. 285.
2   James McGovern, op. cit.
3   David Irving, op. cit., p. 304.
4   William Shirer, *The Rise and Fall of the Third Reich*, p. 1017 (Secker and Warburg).
5   Gilles Perrault, *L'Orchestre Rouge*, p. 335 (Fayard).

## Chapter 29

1   I have never found the name of Bergfeld again in all my research. I asked some information officers, comrades from the Resistance; most curiously, the French Secret Service seems to be totally ignorant of the names of the top-ranking scientists and technicians at Dora.

## Chapter 34

1   I write this name as I heard it at the time. We did not know then of the existence of Kammler nor the identity of all the scientists. On reflection, I wonder if we did not confuse Kaltenbruner, a very well-known personality in the Third Reich, with Kammler.
2   When the Allies discovered that the secret weapons were being made at Dora, in February 1945, the Americans proposed saturating each tunnel with an inflammable mixture. If this plan had been adopted, I would not be here now. As for the machines, they would have been spared, for they could resist high temperatures. So as not to sacrifice the deportees, Dora was not bombed. They decided instead to destroy Nordhausen. Was it because of the railway station or part of some incomprehensible decision as often springs from military minds? Many of our comrades perished at Nordhausen. The subterranean factory remained intact.

## Chapter 36

1   Deportees' abbreviation of *Oberscharführer*, ss adjutant.
2   Déprez was wrong. The *Sturmbannführer* was only a major in the ss hierarchy. We knew the ranks of those gentlemen less well than those who today buy their uniforms in the Flea Market, or devour the rubbishy literature published everywhere glorifying them.

## Chapter 38

1   The tattooing thus enabled the wounded to be attended to quickly. This practical measure finally worked against the soldiers of Hitler's élite, since it often permitted their identification after the war. The mark of distinction became a brand.

## Chapter 40

1   James McGovern, op. cit., p. 109.
2   Ibid., p. 112.
3   Ibid., p. 111.
4   Ibid., p. 129.
5   Ibid., p. 139.
6   Dornberger, op. cit., p. 254.
7   James McGovern, op. cit., p. 156.
8   In his report of 16 May, von Braun wrote notably: 'When missile technology has progressed further, it will be possible for us to reach other planets and to go to the moon.'
9   Patton's advance, which would have enabled the Western Allies to march on Berlin or liberate Czechoslovakia, was not stopped by Eisenhower until after the conquest of Nordhausen. Although the combatants of the American Third Army Armoured Division had received information from Intelligence, information that they 'would find something interesting in Nordhausen', there is no way of determining if the *Mittelwerke* were conquered under the thrust of Patton's offensive or according to a precise plan of the American Command aimed at seizing the German rocket factories before the Russians. This halt of the American troops is in my opinion one of the great mysteries of the war, a mystery in which no one – to my knowledge – has taken any interest.
10  A certain M, a former 'Peenemünde scientist', was for a long while an important figure in the French missile research programme. After the creation of the Bundeswehr in Federal Germany, technicians of the same origin directed and still direct German research programmes under the auspices of NATO.
11  James McGovern, op. cit.
12  Kammler's shadow fell over the way in which the Americans recovered Wernher von Braun's fourteen tons of archives. McGovern relates that Staver saw two civilian investigators of *General Eisenhower's office* arrive at Nordhausen. This visit was of some importance. The investigators handed him a note which allowed the scientist who remained to believe that Staver knew their secret. 'According to von Ploetz, the documents relating to the V2 weapons are hidden

in a salt mine at Bleicherode.' This is what the note said. And, knowing that von Ploetz was Kammler's Intelligence Officer, it is not difficult to imagine Kammler, in the wings, pulling all the strings.